# FULLY HUMAN

# FULLY HUMAN

3 Steps to Grow Your
EMOTIONAL FITNESS
in Work, Leadership, and Life

# Susan Packard

TarcherPerigee
an imprint of Penguin Random House
New York

**tarcher**
perigee

An imprint of Penguin Random House LLC
penguinrandomhouse.com

Most TarcherPerigee books are available at special quantity discounts for bulk purchase for sales promotions, premiums, fund-raising, and educational needs. Special books or book excerpts also can be created to fit specific needs. For details, write: SpecialMarkets@penguinrandomhouse.com.

Library of Congress Cataloging-in-Publication Data

Names: Packard, Susan, author.
Title: Fully human : 3 steps to grow your emotional fitness in work,
    leadership, and life / Susan Packard.
Description: New York : TarcherPerigee, 2019.
Identifiers: LCCN 2018049348| ISBN 9780143132745 (hardback) | ISBN
    9780525504658 (ebook)
Subjects: LCSH: Emotional intelligence. | Leadership. | Communication in
    management. | BISAC: BUSINESS & ECONOMICS / Workplace Culture. | BUSINESS
    & ECONOMICS / Leadership.
Classification: LCC BF576 .P33 2019 | DDC 153.9—dc23 LC record available athttps://lccn.loc
.gov/2018049348

Printed in the United States of America
10 9 8 7 6 5 4 3 2 1

Book design by Pauline Neuwirth

To my dad, an early hero of mine, who was the first to show me what emotional fitness looks like.

To Angela and Brenda. In your gentle ways, you taught me the wonder of becoming fully human.

# · CONTENTS ·

*As you set sail for Ithaca,*
*hope that your journey be long,*
*full of adventures, full of awakenings,*
*fear not Cyclopes and Laestrygons,*
*fear not mad Poseidon.*

*You will not meet such monsters on your way,*
*if your thoughts remain noble and high,*
*if your spirit and body are touched by passions.*

*You will not meet such monsters*
*if you do not hear them in your soul,*
*if your soul does not set them before you.*

—FROM "ITHACA" BY CONSTANTINE PETER CAVAFY

*You've learned how to manage your temper, but certain people in your workplace still set you off. And honestly, you don't know why.*

*Sometimes work feels like the loneliest place in the world.*

*You love what you do, but the culture of your company is at odds with your beliefs and values. The job fits great. Not the company.*

Emotions drive workforce happiness, and happiness powers people to succeed. This book is about bringing our strongest emotional selves to work each day, and how best to do that.

It's rather funny, ironic really, that I'm writing a book about how to deeply and authentically express emotions on the job. Before I was thirty years old, three traumas, two work-related, closed the spigot on my emotions—other than fear—and certainly on trusting anyone at work. Then, when I was thirty-nine, I landed a wonderful job at HGTV and began working with a group of guys who taught me I could let down my guard. Bit by bit, they showed me what it meant to build trust and to work together in community. Imagine that, a woman learning about emotions from a group of guys.

I didn't know how to have real interdependent work relationships until then. I was like little eleven-year-old Riley in the Pixar smash hit *Inside Out*, who struggles through a few tough days in her life, as seen through the animated characters Anger, Disgust, Fear, and Sadness. It seems I had a few tough days that lasted three decades. What I learned at HGTV was that open and honest emotions play a vital role in the workplace. I learned how trust is the most powerful emotion that binds us together to do our best work because it keeps us moving toward common goals with speed and focus. It leaves out the messy human dramas that can quietly creep in, wreak havoc, and disrupt your peace of mind.

In my leadership and coaching roles, I've worked with plenty of women and men who carry around small fears and discomforts that inhibit their success, like a fear of standing up in a crowd and speaking. Or the fear of learning a new skill, and the worry you'll fall flat on your face if you try. Maybe it's a feeling of general unease, like you're simmering in a chronic, low-level anxiety you can't define. Maybe you find no purpose in your work except for a paycheck. You might feel emptiness or loneliness, even in a roomful of people. My friend Anne once described that sensation this way: "It's like you have a hole in your soul." The Centers for Disease Control and Prevention reported that suicide rates rose steadily in most states from 1999 to 2015, up by 25 percent nationally, and that the lack of social "connectedness" was among the factors.[1] Certain emotional triggers might keep you trapped in a cycle of addiction or other toxic behaviors.

You don't have to feel this way. *Fully Human* tackles the emotions men and women deal with as we seek happiness and fulfillment at work, and offers a useful paradigm, which I call **EQ Fitness (EQF)**. EQ Fitness is a solutions-based road map of three steps to help you prepare for, master, and grow in emotional intelligence and maturity. When we apply EQF to our whole lives, not just our professional ones, I call that **emotional fitness**. Emotional fitness is bringing our strongest emotional selves to all we do. EQF is how we use it at work.

At its most basic, **emotional intelligence (EI)** is awareness and control of our emotions, and the ability to identify and respond effectively to the emotions of others. In the business world, emotional intelligence is often referred to as "EQ," as an offset to IQ—it's why I call the three-step process "EQ" Fitness. Just like we all have an IQ, we all have some baseline EQ, that ability to manage our emotions and to read others. Whatever your baseline as you begin this book, you can grow it significantly through the steps I lay out here. This will enable you to claim the full spectrum of your humanity, to become fully human, both in work and life.

While emotional intelligence has been studied and applied by various scientific disciplines and industries since it was first labeled in the mid-1960s, it has taken root in business thought leadership since the early 1990s. As a science journalist for the *New York Times*, Daniel Goleman happened upon an article written by two psychologists about how success was not due to just knowledge but also to this concept called emotional intelligence. A psychologist himself, Goleman published the first book on the subject, *Emotional Intelligence*, which is still popular today. A 2009 follow-up, *Emotional Intelligence 2.0*, by Travis Bradberry and Jean Greaves, brought EQ into the new millennium.

Emotional intelligence was one of the most important breakthrough ideas in career building, and it remains so today. In the World Economic Forum's *Future of Jobs Report*, EQ was listed as one of the top ten skills that will make candidates desirable to employers in 2020.[2] Its importance has only grown, even in the face of digital technologies transforming how we work; in fact, they make emotional intelligence *especially* important.

And yet, most workplaces still lack EQ. Much of this falls to a lack of mature leadership. Too many executives operate first from self-serving agendas, where money, power, and prestige are their primary drivers. Consider this: research shows that one out of five CEOs are psychopaths,[3] and the rate of diagnosed psychopathy is three times higher among corporate boards than in the general population.[4] If leaders demonstrate a knowledge of and pay lip service to EQ, it can be clinical and superficial or mask other problems. And the traits often associated with "strong" leadership, like risk-taking, long hours, and financial success, also often overlap with high-functioning substance abuse or dependence. In fact, data shows that the higher your income, the more alcohol you consume.[5] As my story unfolds here, you'll see I came to know that data only too well.

With poor leadership that no one wants to model, and employees not addressing the confusions, fears, and longings they bring to their jobs, these workplaces are emotionally crippled. People lash out in anger, and distrust and paranoia abound. It's like watching a bunch of people with sprained ankles and broken legs trying to run a marathon; without healing before you enter the race, the run will be slow and clumsy at best.

This is how I navigated work relationships for a long time, but increasingly it felt artificial and robotic, and I never trusted anyone. No one knew this but me, which shows you how counterfeit the entry-level behaviors of emotional intelligence can be, or at least how half-measured. I believe my experience reflects a common reality: many of us just don't know *how* to manage our emotions. We stuff down whatever is unsettling us. We may feel anger or fear or some deep ache, but we don't know what to do about it. How, then, can we be expected to effectively deploy this great skill called emotional intelligence? EQ Fitness offers the tools to help us maximize a precious human gift we're given—our emotions—so we can forge healthy, interdependent relationships at work and in life.

As we work the three steps, we can arrive at a place of transcendent growth, which reflects both emotional and spiritual insight. I can already see some eyes rolling. *Spiritual what? At work?* Let me try to help. I'm not referring to organized religion or any given denomination of religion. This idea goes beyond church, mosque, or temple. What I call God you may call by a completely different name. Spiritual insight is really a state of heart. It nudges you away from fanatical self-reliance and toward building community—a network of trust-filled relationships. When you have spiritual insight, you have the quiet confidence that you're not alone. It's a humbling reminder that your success is owed to others too, not just you. To become fully human takes inner work, and if we skip the inner work, our outer work will pay a price. What's really gratifying about spiritual insight is that it makes bringing our strongest emotional selves to work a whole lot easier, and *that* makes being successful a whole lot easier.

Emotional fitness is, in essence, a place of *steadiness*. You can recognize it in people. They're not flash-in-the-pan types. They're willing to pause and listen. They're balanced and accountable, and you can trust them. They are a steady force for good and a model for living life well.

It took me three jobs and a lot of trial and error to put this together. But oh, the rewards! EQF provides a new paradigm for emotional intelligence, which, when practiced in its highest form as emotional fitness, is a transcendent place of mind, heart, and spirit that will, time and again, trump self-centeredness. You might say *Fully Human* is a master class in EQ. By reading it, you can become emotionally fit much quicker than I did.

The tools you need are out there and waiting, and I'll be your guide on the path.

## THE THREE STEPS

*Fully Human* is organized around the three core steps of EQ Fitness, which also function as the three sections of the book:

1. Develop a **willingness** to do some self-discovery to identify, understand, confront, and dispel unproductive emotions.
2. Deploy emotional intelligence to build authentic relationships of **trust**.
3. Use **We Principles** to create as a leader, or as an employee to perpetuate, a collaborative workplace culture.

Each of these is a step up: you need to get yourself right before you can use your EQ knowledge to form trusting relationships and then to create and facilitate a collaborative workplace.

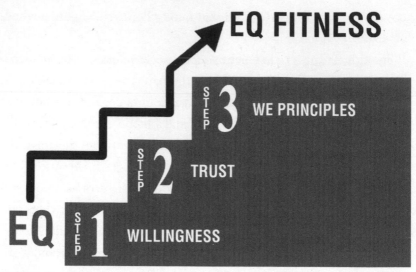

**FIGURE A:** Step Up to Emotional Fitness Through the Steps of EQF

At the end of each section, I include practice sessions so that you can take concrete steps to implement what you've read. Simply put, the path I lay out here is this:

*Willingness + Trust + We Principles = EQ Fitness*

## STEP ONE: WILLINGNESS (PART 1)

Willingness is a linchpin of EQF. It begins with self-honesty. It's easy to stay on cruise control, but you've been dodging, or pushing down, or numbing those feelings of unease and self-accountability for long enough. That's what happened to me at thirty-nine. I finally stopped dodging my history. Life can be so much richer if you catch this earlier than I did!

Willingness simply means that to improve yourself starts with understanding yourself. It asks you to grow in self-awareness, which is the beginning of emotional intelligence. We become willing to work from the inside out, as Stephen Covey proposes in his *7 Habits of Highly*

*Effective People*, so this is old wisdom. Let's work from the inside out by identifying unproductive emotions, like anger and resentment, and bringing them out into the light so they can be dispelled before they come to work with you.

The path is an ongoing process; it's not a one-shot deal, because life just keeps on happening. The sooner you deal with unproductive emotions, the sooner you'll feel the freedom to forge meaningful relationships.

## STEP TWO: TRUST (PART 2)

Being willing feeds directly into building trust. Of the many rewarding emotions out there, trust is the best barometer of healthy work relationships. Many other emotions, like gratitude and hope and compassion, can rise up without needing reciprocation, but it takes two to tango with trust. It can be sustained only as long as it's shared.

It can be hard to open up at work and trust people. Many of us have experienced opportunists, cutthroat competition, and basic unfairness. Some people are just jerks, always trying to game the system for their personal benefit. Those you meet in this book will talk about having a willing heart, but also a shrewd eye. Some folks are just not worth the time it takes—and it does take time—to build authentic trust.

Trust is critical as Step Two because it requires emotional risk, which is a rigorous test of willingness, and is also an effective gateway to We Principles.

## STEP THREE: WE PRINCIPLES (PART 3)

Step Three adds the spiritual work that develops us into true leaders. It looks at how we use We Principles, which are *hope*, *generosity of spirit*, and *moral courage*, to moderate our self-centered inclinations. This isn't a judgment on anyone; we all want to know how things can be beneficial to us. As a leader who practices the We Principles, you prioritize your people and the greater good of the organization. You keep your ego in check. Let's face it, many high achievers have super-size egos, so I offer a whole chapter on managing ego and our tendencies toward self-aggrandizing behaviors. We Principles help you inspire more from your team. You build *purpose* into the culture. People want to work for something bigger than them.

By practicing We Principles, you can connect with people and get out of your own way. You've also gained an important perspective—that the emotional health of your organization is vital to its economic health.

## DOING THE NEEDED PREP WORK

### WHERE IT BEGAN FOR ME

I took on leadership roles by practicing some EQ basics without fully understanding them; I just came to work paying attention to others around me and responding in engaging ways, since I found it helped to get things done. But it wasn't enough. To get to the C-suite and experience success that was really fulfilling, I had to go deeper.

I had my first glimpse of what being EQ Fit is all about as I sat on the beach one weekend in Santa Monica. At the time I was a regional director at a popular TV network and considering a job transfer that offered me a bigger title and more money. In the stillness, I heard, *it doesn't fit.* The more I thought of it, the more my stomach hurt. I thought of my new husband, who loved Los Angeles and who'd have to saddle up and find a new job in a new city. I thought of my team, none of whom were trained to step up in my place. I thought of how much more I could still accomplish for my company in my current position. For the first time in my career, I made a choice for those who were in my life, instead of just for me. I decided not to chase "new" just for the sake of the chase, and on Monday morning I took my name out of the running. A fresh perspective had opened up when I allowed myself the time, and the willingness, to reflect on it.

## INFANT EMOTIONS

We bring many unproductive emotions to work, and fear tops the list. So many of our fears are rooted in two seemingly simple emotions that we're born with: the need to feel secure and the need to be loved. My conversations with psychologists, executive coaches, and executives for this book, and my years of experience as an executive and executive coach, have confirmed those roots. Fears bubble up in many forms, from performance jitters to blending well with teammates. More diversity and inclusion means employees are bringing anxieties about acculturation and gender identity to their jobs too. Many fears sweep in matters of the heart and, sometimes, the soul, all of which can muddy trust building. Step One of EQF asks that you confront and clear away all this confusing and uncomfortable emotional "stuff" as a precursor to authentic human connection. You need to do the prep work before you can build trust in any meaningful way.

## TRUST AND SPIRITUAL GROWTH

Being willing builds the bridge to Step Two: creating relationships of trust. We give our trust to those worthy of receiving it. It takes time, patience, and a little risk to open ourselves up to trust others, and to become trust*worthy*. We cannot give something we don't feel worthy of receiving ourselves. We can earn others' trust as we grow in self-respect, a foundational quality of EQ Fitness.

In Step Three, we begin to live beyond the surface of right *behaviors* to right *motives* with spiritual insight. This is a place of self-transcendence, the final and perhaps most challenging of the steps, because we're used to seeing things through a lens of our own needs. You might act like you're high in EQ, but if it's still all about *you*, you're not leadership material yet. EQ Fit leaders go from "me" to "we" and build healthy, emotionally rich, and profitable cultures. This is what happened to me at HGTV, and it can happen for you too, if you're willing to practice the steps laid out here. As our careers and personal lives keep evolving, we stay alert and ready for possible moments of emotional growth. Thus, emotional fitness never ends, and is a powerful tool throughout our lives. To be happy and productive, we need to stay vigilant and keep practicing.

We need *both* vulnerability and resilience working *together* to gain well-developed and mature emotional intelligence. Those in a steady, emotionally fit place have the necessary grounding to draw in both. This is a paradox that underlies EQ growth, and it may be hard for many of us just starting down the path. How can two seemingly contradictory things—vulnerability and resilience—*both* be needed? But they are. EQF opens our eyes to how often paradox plays a role in our lives. It's been said that the soul is the only part of us that can deal with paradox, so you'll see how having, or trying to gain, some spiritual depth helps with each of the three steps. You'll begin to see a larger truth emerge from seeming contradictions, and your life will expand with possibility.

## EQF AND TECHNOLOGY

For those who've grown up communicating through screens, EQ Fitness may be a challenge, but it's all the more necessary. Technology is a tool, but it can inhibit human connection when it becomes a barrier, a form of self-protection from encountering others face-to-face. That doesn't have to be the case; technology *can* become a healthy partner instead of an enabler of bad habits. I love my devices, but I try to guard against using them as partitions. Communication via technology is disposable, and people and relationships can become that way too if you're not careful. If you're on the receiving end of an email you don't want to deal with, you can just delete it. To dodge a confrontation or (my personal favorite) someone who likes to digress, you can press Send instead of talking it through. Face-to-face communication, although messy at times, is also heart-to-heart communication, and the foundation of building trust with another. When you breathe the same air, it's an opening to something new—maybe a spark of an idea or, if we're really lucky, a friendship.

In a 2017 commencement speech, Apple CEO Tim Cook told students that technology can do great things, but it doesn't want to. It doesn't *want* to do anything.[6] It's up to a company's leadership to make sound judgments about technology's deployment. Work and social relationships can be buffeted through technology, but only if those relationships are already intact. In other words, spend time with people, which builds real trust, before imposing an intermediary. You'll read about leaders who have learned how true this is, and who work to build interpersonal trust every day with their teammates and within the teams themselves.

Millennials will be the last to know what life is like with and without the Internet. Data shows that 25 percent of kids between the ages of two (!) and five years old have a smartphone. Child psychologists will tell you that face-to-face interactions are the primary way kids learn and *bond*, so what we do with technology matters more than ever. Kids who grow up communicating through screens are less intimate with human emotions; now there are even classes to help teach them how to read emotions, since they never learned how through natural processes. If that's standard for a seven- or eight-year-old, how will they experience the precious lessons we learn through looking someone in the eye, interacting face-to-face, heart-to-heart?

"When my kids were growing up, I encouraged them to join pickup basketball games, not the organized ones," explained **Dr. Robert Kelley**, Distinguished Service Professor of Management at Carnegie Mellon

University's business school. "It's the ideal place for kids to have to look others in the eye and read them. If you're a ball hog or otherwise not playing a team game, the others will punish you. You have to negotiate the rules with the other players in real time, and these rules can vary depending on the gym or playground where the game is being played."

Technology is amazing—but trust must come first.

## ESTROGEN VS. TESTOSTERONE?

When I told my friend Barbara about EQF and this book, she said, "Oh, that's great. Men really need this." That's partly due to biology and partly due to American culture. As psychiatrist Julie Holland explained in the *New York Times*, "By evolutionary design, we [women] are hard-wired to be sensitive to our environments, empathic to our children's needs and intuitive of our partners' intentions."[7] At about that same time, Dr. Melvin Konner, an anthropology professor at Emory University, published "A Better World, Run by Women" in the *Wall Street Journal*, arguing that testosterone is the culprit for men behaving badly and that women leaders have modeled more emotionally mature leadership time after time.[8] Culturally, women have been reared to have relational (read: emotional) identities—wife, mother, daughter—and are discouraged from having individual identities that aren't tied to those roles. However, stress around gender roles rears up for men too, given the deeply entrenched notions of what "manliness" means. Protector? Breadwinner? Linebacker?

It wasn't like I was showing any considerable emotional smarts as a woman moving into middle management and then leadership through my twenties and thirties. I was closed off, was anxious around others, and I had no self-compassion. But, I was observant and pragmatic, and I learned quickly that getting along with people worked better than anything else in getting things done. Maybe that was my estrogen talking, who knows? But what may have looked like EQ was only surface-deep. Many women leaders I know also demonstrate superficial EQ at work because—big irony here—as we rise in organizations, we're cautioned against opening our inner toolbox too widely. Heaven forbid a woman leader should cry! So we can be kind of a mess; shades of emotional richness inside, steel outside. Both women and men need EQF. All leaders and workers do. In my favorite workplace fairy tale, EQF is the ideal we *all* strive for, and benefit from.

· · ·

If you pay attention, there are always opportunities to grow in emotional fitness. When we're in a steady, balanced place, we can change and adapt and tackle new things. We begin to see life for what it is— often just our own shared, human predicament. Once we master the three steps, whenever we experience fear or worry, we will first pause to name it, then face it, and ultimately dispel it. Every time we go through that cycle we're ready for more emotional and spiritual growth. The cycle becomes second nature with practice.

You're about to meet many colorful characters, from a thriving entrepreneur who meditates regularly with her whole company to a well-known CEO who found the emotional maturity to overcome some tough teen years and find a new way to live and succeed. You'll meet the head of a food company who instituted a "ninety-day coffee break" for his new employees to get comfortable working there and to jump-start trust building. You'll learn how a woman who runs a $3 billion business expresses gratitude every day. And you'll meet a guy named Bobby, who simply bought a fellow worker a pair of boots, a gesture that had an enormous impact.

I'm guided by the wisdom of emotional fitness every day. It's become a meaningful lens through which I can see the trajectory of my career, and that lens informs choices I make in both work and life. I've gotten a little naked in writing this book—the willingness to do so gleaned from the transforming impact of these steps.

Emotional fitness continues to transform my life, and it can transform yours too. Practice has taught me that trust reaps great rewards—joy, peace, and purpose—if you're willing to open up and take some risk. And here's the bonus: you learn the best ways to manage the directives of your mind and your heart.

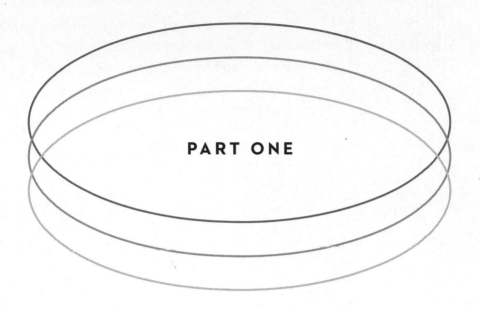

# PART ONE

# WILLINGNESS

*Work of sight is done.*
*Now do heart work on the pictures inside you.*

—Rainer Maria Rilke

You can't go forward in life or in work unless you know what's holding you back. When you become willing, you are compelled to do more than wanting or dreaming; you take action. When it comes to building trust with another person, it starts with just being willing to try.

Part one of this book is about self-discovery, which is how we begin to harness the power of emotional intelligence. Self-discovery is gaining insight into your own nature so that you can better understand and manage your emotions. Courageous people do this. They're willing to examine their thinking and how they understand and navigate the world. Confronting our beliefs, opinions, and emotional reactions is an act of bravery. It's easy to keep coasting on the versions of reality we've mapped out for ourselves, but the courageous have figured out that you can't truly move forward until you identify, test, and, if needed, let go of outdated narratives. For many of us, our reinforced behaviors prevent us from forming healthy relationships with others. That cruise control is often disguised in a cycle of high performance, achievement, and reward. This was my experience, and it might be yours.

I can't tell you how to become willing, but I can illustrate what a lack of willingness looks like.

John was thinking of buying a new car, and he told his best friend, Jimmy, his exciting news. Jimmy was quiet for a moment and then said, "Great, what's the first thing you think you should do?"

"Well, I've gone online and looked at some models."

Knowing John well, Jimmy then said, "OK. What else have you done?"

"I've looked at prices. And I'm thinking I might need to take out a loan. I don't know . . . lots of decisions." Jimmy was quiet again until John broke the silence. "*What?*"

"Sounds to me like you haven't given up your old car yet."

Jimmy sensed that John knew the "what" and the "how" to get that car, but he lacked the willingness to change his old ways of living. "Willingness" is an action word, and you need action so you don't stay stuck like John.

I learned this the hard way in my early years of being a mom. When our son, Drew, was three years old, he started throwing some major temper tantrums, and we often couldn't settle him down. I was worried he was becoming alarmingly obstinate. I called a friend who worked with young kids and asked her if she could evaluate what was wrong with him. She got out a phone number and read it to me. "This woman's great with parenting issues." *Parenting issues?* I didn't have parenting issues! *Did I?* She said, "Susan, he sounds like a normal three-year-old. But I think you could use some help." It was a blow to my ego, but her words nudged me to look at my reaction and then pray for more patience in rearing him. Such willingness actions—*seeing, praying, changing*—are formative steps in emotional growth.

Willingness starts in a singular way: by taking reflective moments to better understand how you tick and what your gifts and liabilities are. To peek under the covers at all that scary stuff you might not want to see. It's a challenge here in the United States, because popular culture promotes self-esteem at the expense of self-knowledge. But they need to be on parallel paths, because having a solid sense of self comes from understanding what makes you, well, you.

Organizations also need to have a willingness to grow and change a step ahead of their competition, which requires a workplace of willing people on board. The Latin root for "corporation" is *corpus*, or "body of." Corporations are bodies of people, but somehow we have separated the work from the people doing it. Leaders of the most remarkable companies are willing to put their people first and the work second. They know that if you get the people part right, the work follows.

We'll look at the kinds of things that can hold a person back from connecting with others in rich, productive ways, and what to do about it. We'll take the self-knowledge you gain from the first three chapters and apply it in the fourth chapter to the kinds of jobs that would be the best fit for you. Good job fit is tangible evidence of your EQ Fitness.

We'll explore ways to stay vigilant, with frequent reality checks. With prep and ongoing practice, your life *will* improve. Without them, you can start backsliding into the old ways that didn't work before. To be EQ Fit, you can never coast. It will become second nature to do these spot checks. When something inside feels out of alignment, you'll ask yourself these questions:

*What am I afraid of?*
*What am I angry about?*
*Why have I been hurtful?*
*What action step is needed to fix it?*

You'll learn how to name it, claim it, and let it go.

Willingness is about new beginnings. For me, it's brought hope and second chances, and I'll share a few of those stories here, along with the voices of many others who are model practitioners of willingness.

# CHAPTER ONE

# WHAT HOLDS YOU BACK FROM TRUST?

*Tear off the mask. Your face is glorious.*

—Apocryphal Rumi[1]

- **Jarl Mohn**'s life fell apart when he was eleven. They'd jailed his deadbeat dad for not paying child support to his mom, who was struggling to raise three kids on her own. His mother had a nervous breakdown, and Jarl and his younger siblings were sent to a children's home, where Jarl lived for several years. "I just kept saying to myself, 'When I get out of here, I'm going to start running my life,'" he told me. Jarl learned unrelenting self-reliance.

- **Anisa Telwar** began working for her mother at seventeen. I asked her if she had any self-awareness back then. "Yes," she said. "I was aware of all I lacked." She didn't look right; she didn't act right. Anisa was never "enough" of anything good, and if she ever forgot it, her mother was right there to remind her. Alcohol and drugs became Anisa's solution. At nineteen, she walked through the doors of Alcoholics Anonymous.

Today, both Jarl and Anisa run large, profitable organizations. Jarl made his way in media and telecommunications senior leadership and CEO roles, and today he's the CEO of National Public Radio

(NPR). Anisa left her mother's employ at twenty-one and started her own company, Anisa International, which has become an accomplished maker of cosmetic accessories. In 2017, it celebrated twenty-five years of excellence.

Not all of us end up running or starting companies, to be sure, and not all of us are impacted by such tough childhoods. Let's look at a few other examples of experiences that can hold us back from bringing our best emotional selves to relationships in and out of the workplace.

- James can't shed his feelings that he is stupid. He thinks it stems from an incident in third grade when he got a failing grade on a composition, and his teacher made him stand up in front of the room and show the class his paper with all the red marks slashed through it. "By high school I was hanging out with a bunch of losers like me, who were just barely getting by in school."

- A journalist named David found himself terrified of driving to unfamiliar places. Given how that made his work a challenge, he sought a therapist to better understand, and hopefully overcome, this fear. With her help, he recalled an incident when he was five years old, traveling with his family to Europe. While his parents were buying tickets for a show, he wandered off and got lost. An old woman took his hand and began leading him away, until two police officers intercepted her. Reunited with his parents, he remembers the police telling them that they'd seen this woman try to take children before, in her mind "borrowing" them because she'd lost her own child.[2]

- Prince Harry went public in 2017 about beginning therapy for the grief he still carried from losing his mother, Princess Diana, two decades earlier.

All these examples reflect inner scars and wounds that need to be dealt with—healed—if you're to bring good mental and emotional health to work.

My story goes like this: What I recall as a child was feeling invisible. This was likely some sort of "middle child" syndrome, but, oh, I also happened to be born with supersensitivity. My sisters and brother pestered me and nicknamed me Sensitive Sue. I wrestled with this tension of both demanding *"someone pay attention to me!"* and quickly shying away if someone wasn't being gentle and kind. This played out in multiple childhood dramas in which I had the starring role, like faux–fainting spells during church service or on the playground. I ran away from home a bunch of times. In high school, I found alcohol, which would catch up with me later on. When I finally got to college, I dropped out in the third semester of my freshman year—*I've had enough of THIS!*—and moved across the country to live with my sister. I did eventually go back and finish, but my ride into adulthood was rocky.

## STOP. LOOK. BECOME VULNERABLE.

Everyone wants to be safe, secure, and accepted. This is completely natural, but work and life don't always cooperate. We've all had experiences and memories we haven't dealt with because we don't understand them, or they're just too painful to integrate and learn from. It could be a divorce or being fired, where we feel paralyzed by toxic shame. It could be a betrayal or a stubborn resentment. Emotional blocks can be from things that happen in childhood or in adulthood. They're from all the cards we're dealt, and each of us gets plenty of losing hands, which can live on to slow or stunt our emotional growth. The willingness to act and gain self-understanding begins with identifying those blocks that keep us from forging healthy relationships. We need to do it because, as we grow up, the human capacity for self-deceit is astonishing.

Child psychologists say we begin to form a self-image by seven years old. The DNA we're born with (like my ultra-sensitivity) and our environments meld together as we grow. The three biggest influencers to our emotional makeup, psychologists will tell you, are our instinctual needs to feel *safe*, *accepted*, and *in control*. When a person or an environment threatens any of these, we react in predictable ways, such as shutting down and exiling parts of ourselves, or living in fear, or lashing out. These are immature reactions, but they're also how we protect ourselves. How we survive.

The need for safety might be our biggest driver, at least it has been for me. As young adults, we go off to work full-time, where we're asked to meet strangers and play nice and increase some company's bottom line. We're asked to trust these strangers to be on our side, and to trust this company to do right by us. But many of us can't recall a day in our lives when we've felt truly safe. If we don't deal with our past, we carry this "wounded child" with us every day.

To some extent, we are all wounded creatures, carrying into work the monsters Constantine Peter Cavafy refers to in his poem "Ithaca":

> *You will not meet such monsters*
> *if you do not bear them in your soul,*
> *if your soul does not set them before you.*

We can be the leader of our *own* lives if we're willing to step out from behind the walls we've erected and open ourselves up to being *vulnerable*, and name what might be getting in our way. A well-quoted adage says that holding on to toxic emotions like anger is like drinking poison and expecting the other person to die. We need to integrate all our history, whether personal or professional, so that trust building becomes possible.

· · ·

**EQ Fitness is about forging healthy and mature human relationships,** but many of us aren't ready to do that when we arrive at work's door. I know I wasn't. By thirty I felt like life had drop-kicked me.

I wrote about two seminal experiences in my last book, *New Rules of the Game*. First, I was assaulted in my hotel room and, four years later, my work partner murdered his wife before taking his own life. A third happened between those two events. While on an international trip, I was pulled from the security line, taken to a private room, and strip-searched while another agent watched, which felt like another physical assault. I felt humiliated and powerless. These events all happened before I turned twenty-nine. It would take another decade before I could begin to feel safe at work or build genuine, honest trust with others.

I no longer felt safe, but that instinct for survival kicked in big-time. My gut reaction was to lock everything down tight, to repress it—a mechanism we'll go into later in this chapter. Repression makes every relationship superficial. It was not only self-limiting, but it also ate away at me. The fear was always there just beneath the surface. The good news is that I found it's possible to break the gravitational pull of fear. Fear is like a shadow boxer: if we're willing to confront it, it disappears in the light. (In chapter two we'll describe how all that works.)

## HOW OUR INSTINCTS DO THEIR WORK

Let's look at some examples of how our instincts—those qualities nature gave us to stay safe and secure—can impede our emotional development when they're threatened. Our response to any menace is to add more layers of self-protection that block us from others. Some examples might be

- experiences from our past that still have a grip on us,
- something we've done to another that needs to be reconciled, or
- our temperaments—how we're made, like my ultra-sensitivity.

| INSTINCTS | TEMPERAMENT EXAMPLES |
|---|---|
| Safety | Ultra-sensitivity |
| Love & Approval | Unrelenting Standards |
| Control & Pride | Introversion |

FIGURE B: Instinct and Temperament Considerations When Confronting Threats

See if you can identify with any of the instinct and temperament examples from figure B. Even if none of these applies to you, I'm sure you're working with someone like us, those people who are slow to warm up, leery to trust. They don't act arrogant, just reluctant. Understanding others is part of engaging fully in relationships, which is the essence of emotional intelligence and EQ Fitness. As we gain these new understandings, we can behave in a way that's genuine to who we are and that's compassionate to others we meet along the way.

## FEELING SAFE

Father Greg Boyle—or Father G to me—works with kids from gang-heavy parts of Los Angeles to repair their broken parts. He offers them a sense of family, safety, and purpose. He teaches them catering, silk screening and embroidery for custom T-shirts, and other trades. Father G is a Jesuit priest who founded Homeboy Industries, one of the largest and most effective gang-intervention programs in the United States. He's turned around many young lives.

He wrote about his work in his bestseller *Tattoos on the Heart*. In a 2015 interview with Krista Tippett on NPR's weekly program *On Being*, he said that most of his kids arrive feeling unsafe. "[Their] mom was frightening or frightened. And you can't really soothe yourself if you've never been calmed down by that significant person in your life."[3]

He told the story of one of his boys, José, who is now in his twenties. He and José were giving a training workshop, and José spoke of his early life:

"I guess you could say that my mom and me, we didn't get along so good. I guess I was six when she looked at me and she said, 'Why don't you just kill yourself? You're such a burden to me.' . . . I guess I was nine when my mom drove me down to the deepest part of Baja, California, and she walked up to an orphanage and she said, 'I found this kid.'"

Psychologists will tell you that the biggest fear in people's lives is not of dying, but of being abandoned. This makes José's story all the more remarkable. He not only survived that, but after working with Father G in the substance abuse program of Homeboy Industries, today he is clean, sober, and purposeful. He's gone from that shaky precipice of trying to stay alive, to wanting to live.

## CONDITIONAL LOVE AND APPROVAL

Gangs are bastions of *conditional* belonging, Father G wrote in *Tattoos on the Heart*—one false move and you're out. You may have felt that way growing up. Developmental psychologists who study attachment theory say that close to half of US infants are insecurely "attached" because of early experiences with their parents or caregivers, who may have been dismissive, unreliable, absent, or threatening. In many cases, the parents' affections were contingent on some behavior from their child. This leaves children anxious into adulthood.[4]

In his classic bestseller *The Road Less Traveled*, psychotherapist M. Scott Peck tells the story of his patient, a brilliant tech guy in his early thirties:

"You can't trust a goddamn soul." He described his childhood as "normal" and his parents as "average." In the brief period of time he spent with me, however, he casually and unemotionally recounted numerous instances during childhood in which his parents had let him down.[5]

Once they promised him a bike for his birthday, but they forgot about it and gave him something else. On another occasion, they forgot his birthday entirely. Not trusting people became the "map," as Peck terms it, the patient used to see the world. The only way he could learn there were folks he could trust was to make himself vulnerable. But in the end, that was too big a hurdle, and Peck couldn't help him.

When the love we experience as kids or adults isn't consistent, or is predicated on our performing in a certain way, trusting anyone can become a mountain too high to climb. *The issue with not taking that risk is that you never emotionally grow up.*

## CONTROL AND PRIDE

A common reaction to needing control is making a move to dominate someone or some situation, which often manifests at work as arrogance or puffed-up pride. Pride in its finest form is self-respect and a strong self-identity. But while pride is healthy, puffed-up pride is not. It shoots holes in your tent of healthy, reciprocal relationships. It's usually about protecting your ego, and often driven by fear or sometimes failure, the ultimate expression of a lack of control. The thing about loss and failure, which you learn after having a few birthdays, is that they're teachers. Being fully human, even in its pain, is the gauge of a worthy life because it jump-starts emotional growth and durable long-term relationships. Victory is a quick high, then it's gone. We'll dive more deeply into pride, control, and ego in chapter eight.

## TEMPERAMENT

There are many personality traits that we could examine here, but in my experience, the following most often get in the way of our success.

## Ultra-sensitivity

Early in my career, I tried denying my tender nature because it's really hard to be a kick-ass businessperson and be "sensitive." It's stressful on the inside, and it can undermine how you conduct yourself on the outside. I didn't want to come across as weak, especially in negotiations, which I've always done in my work. So I stuffed down feelings of vulnerability. I have an agile mind and did my best to see the negotiating as a mental chess game, nothing more. Ultra-sensitivity might play itself out for you in undesirable ways, which others can take advantage of.

Ultra-sensitivity may also reveal itself by pulling in others' needs to a point that's not productive for you. Sometimes I felt like Sookie, the lead character in HBO's hit supernatural series *True Blood*, a telepathic waitress who can hear others' thoughts—like how she's a slut for sleeping with a vampire—and struggles to block them out. I don't recall sleeping with any vampires (well, maybe in college), but I could relate to "hearing" others' thoughts. That quality is great in sales, which I did for my whole career and was always successful at, but it's brutal when you have to make hard decisions, like needing to let go of an employee; you pull in all their heartache.

Having self-awareness helps you understand these things better. We need to put names to our most primal characteristics, which helps us stay grounded in the best of what we are, while managing as well as we can with the rest. Just being willing to try—step one—is over half the battle!

## Unrelenting Standards

Anisa Telwar, who was never "good enough," told me, "Because my awareness was focused on what I lacked, I felt that I had to overcompensate. I felt that I had to be perfect, and I knew I wasn't."

Surely some of you can relate. Many of us strive for unrealistic standards of perfection like they're a badge of courage. It's a self-limiting quality because we don't learn how to delegate, any work-life balance is elusive, and we're always exhausted. We look around and see others turning in a B- project but getting an A+ in networking. They don't turn themselves into slaves, like we do. It's easy to fall into the "martyr" routine with these unproductive emotions.

As Anna Quindlen says in *Being Perfect*, "The thing that is really hard, and really amazing, is giving up on being perfect and beginning the work of becoming yourself."[6] The work of becoming yourself—the best version of yourself—is what EQ Fitness provides. It's a design for work and life that is about progress, not perfection. When we chase perfection because we loathe our imperfections, we're locked in a never-ending struggle to resist "what is." Those unrelenting standards exhaust and deplete you.

### Introversion

My husband, Bill, seemed concerned. For a few months, he'd been writing music with his partner, and after brainstorming images for the cover of their new CD, they came upon one online they especially liked. Bill "friended" its owner on Facebook to ask about getting the rights. One morning he was feeling fed up that he was being bombarded by the guy's updates.

"Why won't he stop?" he asked me. I tried for gentle. *Honey, you only have one FB friend. This guy. Don't sweat it.*

Bill is an introvert. Knowing whether you're an introvert or extrovert is critical self-knowledge to have when you arrive to work each day, because your style in getting things done might be dramatically different from others'. The way introverts recharge their batteries, for example, is through time alone. Extroverts do it by being with others.

At about forty, I noticed that I, too, was behaving in a more classic introverted way, needing time alone, enjoying friends who were introverts—excellent listeners, more perceptive and aware. I'd always been a strong "E" (extrovert) on the Myers-Briggs Type Indicator (MBTI), a widely used personality inventory, so I took the test again for the heck of it. It showed me straddling E and I (introvert). Do our temperaments change with age? Maybe. I'm reading more about ambiverts these days: those who live close to the middle of the temperament spectrum. Perhaps many of us are ambiverts and we just don't know it.

**Angela Teague** is a midcareer professional at a large media company. About ten years ago, at a work retreat, she took the Myers-Briggs test and found that she was one of only a few introverts among her colleagues. "I went home and cried because I felt exposed and not fit to work in a corporate environment," she said.

Angela was echoing a myth perpetuated by our culture: those who are more gregarious, *loud*, and make their work more visible to others have a better chance at success. But Angela, one of the bravest people I know, pushed through her fear and not only arrived at a place of self-awareness, but also learned how to better navigate her career with this fresh perspective.

"I had to realize that I could be successful, contribute, and lead without becoming a manager of people. My focus is to make the project successful, not on people management. I can lead, motivate, inspire, and encourage others without the pressure of supervising my teammates in their daily jobs."

We're conditioned to believe that leadership *must* require the managing of people. Angela is a wonderful example of the many forms of leadership available; it doesn't mean formally running teams. There are people in your organization today just like her. They offer compassionate guidance. They have the technical skill or expertise you want to learn. They're always worth seeking out and cultivating as informal mentors. When you get to part two, which is about building trust, you'll see how bringing an open mind to work each day is a guiding principle of EQ Fitness. There are so many who can help us improve if we're willing to seek them out.

**Dr. Barron Patterson** is an associate professor of pediatrics at Vanderbilt University Medical Center. He divides his time between treating children and dealing with administrative matters. Barron, in his midforties, described himself as very much an introvert: "It was hard to come to terms with becoming a physician, because I knew it would mean talking and engaging with families. But I felt it was right, about more than me, so I chose this profession."

He often brings teams together in his leadership work, and he uses his innate listening skills to keep the conversation productive. "By my nature, I take more time," he said. "It may seem as plodding, but really I'm just trying to understand others' thoughts before contributing."

While leadership still doesn't come as naturally to him as it might to an extrovert, he learned the importance of getting comfortable with it. "I've been asked to be a leader here, and so I need to lead. It makes it easier knowing others depend on me to do it," he said.

The fact that **Leroy Ball** is a self-proclaimed introvert hasn't stopped him from becoming the leader of the billion-dollar-plus carbon-products company, Koppers. Leroy grew up in steel country, in a small town not too far from Pittsburgh. He was one of four kids and the first to attend college. He was always shy: "I spent a lot of time alone in my room. I was less comfortable around crowds." He graduated with a degree in accounting and began working in that field. He wanted to make more money, so he applied for a sales position with his employer. He was turned down. "I heard it through the grapevine: Management said I couldn't do the job because I was 'socially backward.' It was a real soul crusher," he said.

Leroy worked on his social and interpersonal skills, even when it was uncomfortable. "I'm not good at networking or backslapping," he admitted. "I'm not a dynamic speaker, and I know it's easier to fall under the spell of extroverts. My guiding light was always that I wanted to make a positive impact on others."

Today, Leroy tries to make a positive impact on his 1,800 employees and their families. "I hired an executive coach who works to keep me balanced. And I read *Quiet* [Susan Cain's bestselling book on introverts], and it clarified a lot. The only real change from when I didn't get that sales job and today is [that] I own what I am. And I'm proud of it."

When we learn what we're made of and what our life experiences have done to shape us, that is powerful information! It will allow you to better navigate your choices in all aspects of life.

# SELF-LIMITING REACTIONS

All the monsters: Fear. Rejection. Betrayal. As the stories above demonstrate, life is chock-full of them. Traumas hit hard, for sure, but so do the small, everyday disappointments. These can build up, and we'll do anything to avoid facing these painful experiences, so our reactions play themselves out in three self-limiting ways, which are all forms of escape. We **shut out**, **lash out**, or **numb out**.

These three reactions limit our ability to grow. The goal of EQ Fitness is to become secure and capable of *directing* your life, rather than just *reacting* to it. Having coached countless colleagues over the years, and now in my professional coaching work, I've found figure C to list the most common reactions to tough situations.

Almost all these reactions come from a place of fear, even if you don't consciously know it, and almost all compromise your self-

| SHUT OUT | LASH OUT | NUMB OUT |
|---|---|---|
| Repression | Noise | Escape |
| Physical Illness | Anger | Malaise |
| Fanatical Self-Reliance | | Substance Abuse |
| Codependency | | |
| Shame | | |
| Playing Victim | | |

**FIGURE C:** Common Reactions to Instinct Challenges

esteem. Untreated fears will block you from any self-understanding, and you'll remain emotionally adolescent. EQ Fitness is about showing up at work as an adult.

## FEARS, PERSONAL AND SOCIAL

Two kinds of fear get in the way of living an emotionally healthy life. One is personal to the individual; the other emerges in social situations.

Personal fear is often the dread of having something taken away. Those things are not just a promotion or money or the next deal. You can have your dignity stolen, too, if you're humiliated or put down. As with most of these limiting emotions, you need to look beneath the surface.

Let's examine a common work fear: the fear of failure. Say, like **Mary Ellen Brewington**, you are asked to sell something. Brewington, along with her family, owns Cherokee Distributing, a sixty-year-old beer distributor with more than four hundred employees covering sixty-one counties in Tennessee. "In my twenties I was afraid to make one sales call for Cherokee," she told me. But here's what she admitted next: "I was the baby in the family. I didn't feel anyone had confidence in me. In a family business, you struggle with the fear of making someone you're related to mad."

*Ah.* Mary Ellen wanted her family to trust her, and she wanted them to love her even if she failed. I've coached many family-company executives, and I believe it's heroic work they do trying to make a living side by side every day. All those emotional trip wires!

Anisa Telwar had this to say about fear: "I knew I loved business, and knew I had to improve myself to succeed. I used a lot of self-help books, because I wasn't grounded and I had a lot of fear. They gave me something to anchor to that was not fear."

Little by little, fear hacks the cords of emotional fitness. **Erin Wolf**, a Duke and Harvard graduate who is now executive director of women's leadership at Kennesaw State University, in Georgia, and an executive coach, told me imposter syndrome was a major hurdle for her clients. "Imposter syndrome, the feeling that you got somewhere by luck or chance, is a big fear. I'm coaching a female equity partner. I asked her what her biggest issue was, and she said she didn't feel as deserving as her colleagues of being an equity partner. So I asked her to recite her credentials, and she did. Then I asked her if there were others at the firm who had credentials and expertise more impressive than hers. She reflected on that and said no. So much of fear is stuff we make up."

The "made-up stuff" are the stories we tell ourselves when our natural instincts feel threatened. If we've been made to feel unworthy at some point in our lives, we often react with fear.

Forty million adults in the United States suffer from anxiety disorders rooted in social fears. The most common form is social anxiety,[7] which covers everything from public speaking to giving presentations to small teams to just speaking up in a one-on-one meeting. Worries include being scrutinized or judged, being found to be wrong, or having a blank mind. An anxiety diagnosis does not prevent anyone from achieving EQ Fitness, especially if you are willing to take action steps to better understand it. Prime emotional health is no different from physical health in that way; no matter what ailments we're born with or develop, we can always take action to get better.

**Jerry Fried**, LCSW, BCD, a full-time clinician, works with adults from companies like DeRoyal, Pilot Flying J, and Scripps Networks Interactive (SNI), the larger media company that HGTV merged into, who are experiencing social anxiety and panic attacks in their workplaces. Jerry most commonly treats them with cognitive behavior therapy, which retrains the brain's response when symptoms of anxiety rise up. "If someone wants to grow but is too fearful to take the risk to do what's needed," he explained, "I step in and we work together on new behaviors."

In chapter two, you'll learn some of the ways Jerry helps his patients who have social anxiety.

## SHUT OUT

### *Repression*

I never knew pain could scream. I needed to quiet mine, so I buried it. This is repression: you just keep stuffing down the hurts and disappointments until they're locked down tight. This is what I did; never once spoke to anyone other than my husband and my sister about the traumas I'd experienced. The long-term risk of repression is that you keep burying stuff until you run out of room in your underground bunker. That's when you have to sound the battle cry, or whimper, of willingness. Don't wait until you're thirty-nine like I did.

### *Physical Illness*

I wonder if you can relate to this: When I was working like a maniac, I'd get sick on just about every vacation I allowed myself. (On my honeymoon, I hacked for ten straight days, which made the whole affair a bit challenging.) But when it was time to get back to work, I'd feel healthy again. Those of us who live high on adrenaline, juggling travel and meetings like we're invincible, find that the first moment we let our body stop, it shouts, *Enough!* We've ignored the symptoms of physical and mental duress, and now we pay the price.

### *Fanatical Self-Reliance*

While there are moments in our lives when we need to go it alone, at the heart of things we're built for community. This doesn't mean we should always be with other people, but it does mean we should always consider them in our decisions. Self-reliance is a survival skill, but in too large a dose it is a lonely way to live and work. I'm sure you recognize these folks from the office: they never delegate anything, not really, and even when they do, they micromanage. They try to keep the whole world in orbit by sheer force of will. If someone has ever turned to you and asked, "Hey, little god, what's big God say about that?" it's pretty likely you're that person in the office. Self-reliance is often a cover for keeping others at a distance so you won't get hurt. The problem is that it's not sustainable. Muscling through life this way is like forcing the wrong piece into a puzzle. It's exhausting and unnatural, and it works for only a while. Even Jeremiah Johnson, the isolated mountain man who was made famous by a 1972 Robert Redford movie, ended up with a friend and a wife. We need others.

## Codependency

Some people can wear you down so much that you become a master at shutting out conflict just to survive, and you affix yourself to them or, equally stupefying, you hide from yourself. This is the opposite of self-reliance, and it allows others to completely take over your life through guilt, bullying, or the carrots they may dangle. If you're in this type of relationship, you are passive. You cosign the other person's poor treatment of you. This person can be a supervisor who's made you believe your future is completely up to them—which is never the case. When you practice the steps toward emotional fitness, you will begin to see a larger playing field of possibility.

Codependency can also exist in spouse and partner relationships, especially if your partner controls the money or has a substance abuse problem. Programs like Al-Anon teach participants how to unshackle themselves. It's a heroic moment when you take action to stop this form of emotional dependence.

## Shame

Radio host Krista Tippett calls shame the black holes in life; when that toxicity gets internalized, it obliterates all your self-worth. The word "shame" comes from a European origin that means "to cover." No surse, because when you feel shame, you feel like you want to curl up in a ball and sink into the earth. You might have been let go from a job and are horrified for having "come up short." In your personal life, if someone repeatedly shames you, you're in a destructive relationship. It often starts in childhood, when parents hold all the power. Shame is always cruel. There's no place for it in a healthy relationship.

## Playing Victim

When you're not the leader of your own life, it's easy to fall prey to self-pity. Some of us really have been victimized in one way or another, but we've found a way to go from victim to survivor—to *thriver*. If you find yourself throwing yet another pity party, use this trick: think of the car behind you. I used to get so angry when drivers tailgated me, until one time I looked back and noticed that the guy behind me was being tailgated by a car behind *him*. My tailgater was just trying to get out of his guy's way, so he could zoom ahead and jump over to the right lane too. In other words, I wasn't the target at all. *It wasn't about me.* Most things aren't, but if we keep our world small and obsessively self-focused, we can believe they are.

## LASH OUT

### Noise

Nonstop people and parties and frenetic activity can be signs that you're running from something. If solitude and stillness terrify you, pay attention to learn why.

### Anger

Activist Parker Palmer has said that "violence is what happens when we don't know what else to do with our suffering."[8] It's easier, and in some perverse way more satisfying, to be angry than to be mature. It vents what you're carrying around, like those instincts and temperaments in figure B. If you're prone to detonate, that trait can be marshaled for good; even Mother Teresa was said to have had a temper. But most use anger as a response to inner pain. Wherever rage lurks, under it is often fear or profound sadness. This is why willingness is such hard but *noble* work. As we peel away the layers, we begin to see our patterns of behavior.

## NUMB OUT

### *All the Escapes*

"I was so career-driven, I was addicted to my work," Angela Teague told me. "All my self-worth was tied up in it." I asked, "Isn't it a positive thing, women taking charge of their careers and identities?" Angela's reaction was mixed. "Yes and no. I ended up divorcing my first husband because we needed to move from our small town if I was going to advance, and he wouldn't move. Then getting a divorce made me feel like a failure."

You might be a workaholic, or a shopaholic, or an exercise-aholic. Substance abusers fall here too. As of this writing, approximately twenty-one million Americans suffer from substance abuse, and one in three households has a family member in active addiction, in recovery, or who's been lost to an overdose.[9] One in *three*. We've all read the daily accounts of the ongoing opioid crisis; overdose has become the leading cause of death for Americans under fifty.[10] Yet government funding remains paltry compared with funding for other health crises like cancer and AIDS, despite more people suffering from addiction than all cancers combined.[11] I'm well aware of all these facts, because I suffered from substance abuse for many years before getting help.

Many of us type A personalities live hard-charging lives. We're adrenaline junkies and want *more* of whatever we already have—a bigger job, a sleeker body, going for wasted instead of just buzzed. These escapes and compulsions can dull the anguish of the emotions we don't want to feel, or the confusing history we don't want to face. But *more* doesn't get rid of the problem itself; it still needs to be named and brought into the light. We often need help from professionals, like therapists and counselors, with resetting our default from *more*. This includes the critical need to get help for substance abuse, because addiction is deadly. I tried tackling it alone, and it never worked until I opened myself to others who had the experience and generosity of heart to guide me.

Having the self-awareness to see these patterns, and to confront them, is important to your peace of mind and serenity. Taking action toward finding more balance is foundational to peace and emotional sobriety.

## Malaise

In some ways, this reaction is hardest to manage, because it creeps around the edges and feels nonspecific. Unlike the distinct feelings of anger and shame, it is general, like feeling rudderless. Or hollow inside. Malaise often presents itself as a background hum. *Is my discontent a bunch of things or just one thing?* You keep ignoring it, becoming numb to it. Maybe that's what philosopher Hannah Arendt called "organized loneliness,"[12] feeling lonely even when you're working in and around teams of people. Often malaise is related to a bad job fit. I had no heart for selling CNBC, a financial network, but loved selling HGTV, a network about home.

Or it could be the company itself and its "leadership" practices. I can't imagine working every day at a place like Wells Fargo, where employees were commissioned to create fake checking accounts with customers' personal information, or at Mylan, which has been repeatedly warned about pricing abuses with its EpiPens. Leaders at these places created and reinforced those practices and environments.

We'll look at "job fit" in depth in chapter four. If feelings of unease are giving you a wake-up call, explore why.

## LOW SELF-ESTEEM

Low self-esteem is the product of most of the self-limiting reactions we've covered.

When Amy Schumer was interviewed for the release of her film *Trainwreck*, she told a reporter she was afraid to accept love and didn't feel lovable.[13] Low self-esteem does that to you, and it's especially common in women. I've seen it in many women I've coached. It's one thing to think, *I made a mistake*, and then learn from it and move on. It's another to think you *are* a mistake. Nothing decent, productive, or nourishing comes from feeling *less than*. In her book *The Art of Memoir*, Mary Karr wonders if maybe it takes a lifetime to occupy your own body. Gads, I hope that's not true! We need a little swagger well before we're eighty. Or forty.

Executive coach and leadership expert **Jim Emerick** cofounded a chip design company, sold it, then began working in leadership development and coaching. He told me, "I've dealt with someone's fears of not being technically proficient enough in a job and holding the false belief that technical command or experience correlates with their self-worth."

When I spoke with Angela, Anisa, and Mary Ellen, they all told me that it had taken decades to feel on firm, comfortable ground with themselves. For Anisa, it happened in her thirties: "People liked my work. That gave me the ability to look at myself less critically and gain confidence."

Mary Ellen made me laugh when she said, "In your forties, you start flying. In your fifties, you go stinkin' berserk!" She sees all this moving up a decade with her younger employees. In other words, start flying *now*.

The goal of all the work we're doing in Step One: Willingness, is to become grounded in healthy self-esteem. This means honoring all our gifts and potential, along with accepting our limitations.

## STILL WITH ME?

I wonder what you're thinking now. Maybe it's *I don't know where to begin*. In which case I would say to you, *You already have*. Maybe it's *I don't need any of this!*—which only you can judge. But let me make one last introduction in this chapter.

Meet **Joe Zarantonello.** Joe is a spiritual teacher who at any given time has over thirty mentees, ranging from their late twenties to their eighties. Most are working, many in leadership roles. Full disclosure: I'm one of them. He's a Notre Dame alumnus who did postgraduate work in Ireland, studying the Irish poets. Later he spent fifteen years studying in the Gethsemani monastery, where contemplative monk and author Thomas Merton lived sometime before Joe arrived. He's an average guy, married with kids. His chosen career is teaching middle schoolers. (*Are you nuts, Joe?!*) Where he differs from most of us is in the *vast* spiritual life he embraces, which he chooses to share with others. He runs Loose Leaf Hollow, a cozy retreat house in Kentucky, where many come to gain clarity of purpose, or just to find some peace. When you enter the house, you see his Zendo (Japanese for "meditation place") on the right. Photos of Buddha, Jesus, Mother Teresa, his grandmother, and others grace the walls; they are all his teachers.

We were sitting in the Zendo one morning and I told him I was beginning to write a book about trust and leadership. I asked him what "leadership" meant to him. "Great leaders are fully human, Susan."

He explained further: "It means you've gone from your first half of life to your second. This isn't chronological. It's how you view the world and interact with it. It usually requires having life fall apart on you. If you're willing to hang in there, it vaults you into a more open way of living. You become more grounded and aware. We can seek grounding, or we can seek escape."

An image came to mind of flowers with strong roots. I recalled that the deeper the root, the higher the growth.

"At some point it helps to have those roots grounded in some sort of spiritual practice," Joe continued. "If you're lucky, you can convince your ego to adjust its mission statement from just keeping you safe to managing the directives of the heart. You enlist your ego in the service of the heart."

EQ Fitness enlists you to bring alive all dimensions of self, which blend to make us fully human. The Sufi mystic Rumi said that the wound is the place where light enters. You must let it if you want to heal, and that means peeling away all the self-protections so we get in touch with the spiritual dimensions of who we are—that spark of divinity we're born with. The soul work of EQ Fitness wants us to tell the truth about ourselves. It craves staying rooted in hope and kinship. These are the ways we form lasting bonds with others.

On occasion, Joe reminds me that the only thing that works better after it's broken is the heart. My life fell apart in my twenties, like Jarl's did at eleven, and Anisa's at nineteen. Maybe yours did too. Through hard work—by becoming willing to square off with the pain—things finally began to make sense, and we got our grounding. For me that meant unlocking the armor to grow a fuller life, one that melds the whole hot mess of me together with others and creates meaning.

Wonderful things can come to you. The first is self-acceptance, which morphs into unwavering self-respect—the foundations of emotional growth. Honesty and trusting relationships—floodlit by heart, not ego—follow. It's like what Thomas Merton described one day on the streets of Louisville, when he looked around at all these strangers. What he felt was . . . complete connection. "There is no way of telling these people that they are all walking around shining like the sun."[14]

This is emotional intelligence at its best and most mature; it's emotional fitness.

I hope you *are* still with me. While having an experience like Merton's may seem improbable for the rest of us, the steps of EQ Fitness are practical and actionable, and they can help you to frame life like Merton did that day. I know it's possible, because I have experiences like his too—not every day, but enough days to look forward to the next.

The most productive way to light your future with promise is with willingness. Willingness is a tool you'll pick up throughout your life, discarding what no longer serves you well and replacing it with new skills. These skills will free you up to live more expansively.

Think of a companion, someone you trust implicitly and you want along with you on the ride to willingness. Now turn the page.

# CHAPTER TWO

# THE DARING TO SUCCEED

*I have a thousand brilliant lies*
*For the question:*
*How are you?*

—HAFIZ

What's familiar is safe, but it keeps you small. I once read of a woman, Janice, who was a talented artist. Whenever she finished a painting, she'd carefully wrap it up and store it in her attic. There were over a dozen paintings up there, never seen by anyone. If no one saw them, no one could reject them; no one would reject her. She kept her gift small. One day her brother challenged her to hang just one in his home, where their friends gathered often. She agreed, and their friends couldn't believe she had been hiding this talent!

Being willing to push through fear is a challenge that dares you to succeed.

**Joe Zarantonello** calls the way life plays out order-disorder-reorder: "You marry your sweetheart. Everything is perfectly fine (order) for the first ten years, then the marriage falls apart (disorder). What happens then is key. If a couple can hang in there through the months of therapy, which feels like hell, sometimes their marriage will be reborn as an entirely new and better marriage (reorder). I know this is possible because that's what happened to my wife and me."

For much of my twenties and thirties, I stayed in disorder. All my secrets were making me sick; I just didn't know it. I recall one particularly challenging day when I felt I'd lost my mind, and I thought,

*Could this be genetic?* I decided to count all my relatives who were crazy, or at least deeply pathological. There were eight. Three had had nervous breakdowns, and the other five, well . . . were just not well. Clearly, I'd inherited the crazy gene too. I wonder how many of us carry such beliefs around because we just don't know any better. We haven't been given tools that can help us, like the EQ Fitness tool kit.

## THE CHAIN OF PAIN

To quiet the din of my mind, I dove into nonprofit work. Because I had so much free time—I was only building a monster business, raising a toddler, and trying to stay married. The organization I chose was Childhelp, a group that works with sexually abused children who are brought in from local and county service groups. I was applying to be an advocate, which means you sit and play with the children until a doctor or child psychologist takes them in for consultations.

The director who was training me explained about the chain of pain. Freud called it "repetition compulsion." Often, the child of an alcoholic grows up to marry one. Or a child who's sexually abused might end up carrying on the pain with their kids. Through early intervention, Childhelp was there to break that cycle, while healing the broken parts of the child. I found that sitting in someone else's pain, especially a child's, put mine in perspective, and helped me too. It was like giving and receiving came from the same place, and the paradox that my young adult mind couldn't fathom was that in offering compassion, we ourselves are one of the greatest beneficiaries. What I learned most of all was that nothing was so heartbreaking as a child's ferocious pain.

## A GAME OF SUBTRACTION

EQ Fitness is about shedding things that inhibit emotional intelligence, not taking on more. For some of us, the hardest thing to let go is that part of ourselves that always feels unsettled. After all, who are we without the chaos we carry around? A lot of this happens unconsciously. You wear a pair of shoes that chafe, and eventually your skin hardens and you just keep wearing them, when the smarter thing to do would be to toss them in the Goodwill bag.

In our culture, we're taught to accumulate things, to take on more, not less. How many senior leaders do you know who've moved all their busywork off their desk so they could concentrate on vision, if just for one day? Who has been empowered to do that? It's not how we're trained. It's not how we get our next raise.

Having a life of joy and purpose means letting go of what no longer serves you, like resentments or shame or the word "blame." It's remarkable what you can uncover in yourself when you're willing to let go of these unproductive emotions. It's like the story of a man who took an old rocking chair to an upholstery shop to replace the worn-out cushion. The shop owner said he could do that small repair, but first he offered him $350 to buy the chair. The man was shocked. "What would you want with this old chair?" he asked. The owner said, "I can see that if I tear off all this cloth and pull out all the tacks and varnish the wood, it'll be a beauty." The man had no idea what was lying underneath.

EQ Fitness pulls off those things that form barricades to emotional fitness. Tibetan nun Pema Chödrön describes it as a gift of fearlessness when "we share what we have learned about taking down sunshades and unlocking armor, about being fearless enough to remove our masks."[1]

And guess what we find? Someone, *you*, who's brave and strong and willing to be seen just as you are.

## THE CYCLE OF DARING

This chapter takes the self-knowledge you've investigated in chapter 1 and offers a process and a set of tools to move forward. In this way, emotional fitness is not only a state of *steadiness*, but a place of *readiness* too. It's a readiness to take actions to get unstuck. It starts with giving voice to our fears and discomfort through a process like this:

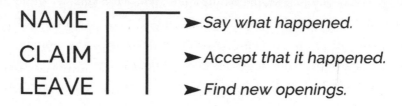

NAME IT ➤ *Say what happened.*

CLAIM IT ➤ *Accept that it happened.*

LEAVE IT ➤ *Find new openings.*

You engage the cycle by first trying to *name* how you feel. Is it anxiety? Deep sadness? Emptiness? Are you carrying resentment, or is someone carrying a resentment toward you and you just *know* you need to fix it?

When I was working college summers at my dad's direct-mail shop, one of the other seasonal workers, John, asked me out. I declined. One morning I was telling a work friend how John wanted to go out but what a nerd he was! His mother, who also worked there part-time, was right around the corner and heard the whole conversation. In my early twenties I couldn't put words to what I was feeling, other than wanting to ball up and hide. Today I know it was shame. She and I danced around each other for several days until I finally apologized.

This phase of describing your discomfort can take a while, and you may need help. Naming it gives it form and begins to take the air out of it. With trauma, this is the hardest part, because naming it is facing it all over again. Giving it a name makes it real. *That really happened.* The good news? When you face things you want to keep hidden, you find new ways forward out of the dark.

Homeboy Industries' José confronted the traumatic abuse he experienced by putting it into words: "My mom beat me every single day. In fact, I had to wear three T-shirts to school every day." He wore three T-shirts even into adulthood because he didn't want anyone to see his scars. "But now . . . I welcome my wounds. . . . How can I help the wounded if I don't welcome my own wounds?"[2]

José shed his extra shirts, became vulnerable and brave by acknowl-edging his past, and *claimed* the pain. This is how acceptance happens, a huge step that slays the monster called denial. *Whew, that pressure is finally off my chest!* It's when you look your pain in the eye without blinking. In the acceptance phase, you move from escaping yourself to accepting the whole of who you are. You also start to see the bigger picture and to understand what little control you have over the cards you've been dealt in life. To grow up emotionally, it's critical to leave these things behind so that you don't bring them into work each day. It's a process of dismantling fear and shame and other long-held beliefs.

In the *leave it behind* phase, you begin to heal. When my mom and sister unexpectedly died within a month of each other, I went to a grief counselor. He told me the holes in my heart would scar over in time; they'd close up, leaving a memory, which would soften as the scar faded. I'd always carry the scars, but I'd leave the jagged edges of the pain behind. I've since learned he was right.

A woman I coached, Barbara,[3] was a highly paid executive whose com-pany was bought out. She was being given warning signs from the new employer that her job was in jeopardy, and I gently pointed them out so she would be prepared. She was the breadwinner, with young children, so she needed to be emotionally and practically ready when it came time to move on. HR called her one night as she was driving home. She called me right away, very agitated. "Susan, I don't understand a word they were saying to me. What are they saying?" I told her. And I recall *her* finally saying it: "I'm being fired, aren't I? I'm being let go." Afterward, she sounded a bit dazed, but calmer. I told her our job now was to nego-tiate an excellent exit package, which she did, and which allowed her to stay home for many months. She actually enjoyed having free time to spend with her kids and her husband. Yes, her ego was bruised, but she became open to new options. Today, she sits on a couple of boards and consults, and she talks about how much she grew with that experience.

We can numb out, lash out, or shut out real life. Or, we can find possibilities for growth, even if it sometimes means kicking and screaming our way there. My friend Lisa puts it well: "Oh, great. AFGO" (another f'in' growth opportunity).

New openings *can* be wonderful; they look you in the eye and dare you to succeed! They expose available space in *all* parts of you—head, heart, and body. Carrying a lighter load makes it easier for your heart to feel passion about your work and to be compassionate toward others. Your body loosens up too. Athletes know that when your muscles are tight, you don't perform as well, so they limber up by stretching. We carry those unproductive, self-limiting thoughts and feelings in our bodies, which is why we often need some physical release when things build up. It's a sweet moment when we can travel more nimbly.

This healing cycle *grows our self-worth*, a critical foundation of EQ Fitness.

## WAYS TO RELEASE THINGS

There are four ways to name, claim, and release. Unfortunately, none of them are available in the app store. The work gets done only through human relationships as we marshal our emotions to do their finest work.

### COMPANIONSHIP

I ended the last chapter by suggesting that you think about asking someone to accompany you on this phase of Step One. Call this person your companion, sharing partner, or chief cheerleader; you're looking for someone you implicitly trust, someone who you know—without a doubt—has your back. They may hold your hand if you need it, but more than that, he or she is emotionally mature enough to hold your confidences. (When we get to trust building in Step Two, you'll see how important it is to keep confidences.) Here are some examples of who this person might be:

- a best friend
- a family member
- a spouse or partner
- a spiritual teacher, friend, or member of the clergy
- a work coach
- a therapist

You're not asking this person to "fix" you (unless it's a therapist or coach), but just to be there as a shock absorber as you give voice to some inner truths. Parker Palmer frames it as a journey "toward inner truth" that is "too taxing to be made solo: lacking support, the solitary traveler soon becomes weary or fearful and is likely to quit the road."[4]

When we're at work, trying to solve a puzzle or bring a project to the next level, it seems obvious that we need to rely on others, but we sometimes still insist on being solo travelers. When I was COO at HGTV, we needed to build the entire infrastructure, including human resources. The first thing I wanted to do was to gather the best practices other media companies were engaged in, especially regarding flextime, shared jobs, and parental leave. I was calling around when Julie Cookson, our sole HR employee at the time—already overloaded in her role—offered to help. She shared my passion that HGTV would be a friendly place for our young workforce as they transitioned into being parents. Of course I needed her help! And not just from a time-crunch standpoint; I needed her fresh perspective.

"The path is too deeply hidden to be traveled without company," explains Palmer. "Finding our way involves clues that are subtle and sometimes misleading, requiring the kind of discernment that can happen only in dialogue."[5]

It's up to you to establish the rules before you begin. For example, your sharing partner can weigh in if you want them to. They might even suggest that you take certain actions. That happened to Matt, who asked his companion for guidance on some inner demons he kept obsessing over. His companion listened and suggested, "How about tomorrow you go out and help any elderly person you see who may need help?" Matt, who lived in New York City, was flummoxed—he had never noticed any older folks in need of assistance! His friend responded, "Well, great, then you won't need to do a thing." The next day, Matt started looking around and found seniors in need *everywhere*: getting on the subway, crossing Seventh Avenue, carrying bags. It felt like a grand conspiracy—until he realized what his companion had done: he'd distracted him from self-pity and given him a different way to see the world.

Of all the qualities you're looking for in a partner in this process, being a good listener is the most important. It can be hard to ask a friend to do you this incredible favor of listening, but the listening itself—that's the really hard part.

## Find a Listener

**Brenda Moyers** listens for a living. Brenda works at a southeastern substance-abuse rehabilitation center that uses the Twelve Steps as its foundation for its patients. In step four, the participant writes down all their pain and the instincts that have led them to hurt others. In step five, they share these things with Brenda, or someone like her.

She told me, "In order to be helpful I listen with my heart as well as my ears. I need to hear what lies beneath the words, where the early wounding occurred and how that wound has shaped and informed their responses to life. It doesn't matter what their beginnings, I often see parts of myself reflected in their stories."

A good listener knows it's easier to connect when you look for the similarities, not the differences. A good listener receives what you share with compassion.

The work that Stephen Ministers do is to listen too. Headquartered in St. Louis, Missouri, Stephen Ministries began in 1975 and is now in over twelve thousand Christian parishes. Founder Kenneth C. Haugk, a pastor and counselor, didn't have enough time to offer pastoral care to everyone in his community who needed it, so he began training members. Six hundred thousand laypeople have since completed more than fifty hours of training each, learning to listen compassionately to those who are struggling, grieving, or lonely. Anne Donahue, a trained minister, said, "We're not there to solve everybody's problems. We're there to get them to open up . . . to release some of this, whether it's anger, frustration or confusion. That's how you heal."[6]

### "All" You Do Is Say It

"Just" saying it takes the air out of the balloon—the power out of the circumstances holding you back. The language itself matters. The more specific you can be, the easier it is to release things, and then, if they're needed, to take action steps. Psychologists call the ability to be precise with your emotional language "emotional granularity."[7] Feeling "righteous indignation" about how someone has treated you is more precise than feeling "uncomfortable," and may spur you to confront the person to seek an apology. EQ Fit people do their best to use clear emotional language.

When you name what's causing discomfort, you defuse it. I can't explain why this happens, I only know that it does. A few years into our marriage, Bill and I flew to Romania and adopted our son, Drew. When Drew was about two, I went to a seminar for adoptive parents. The speaker asked the group, "Have you told your child yet that they're adopted? If your child is older than two, it can become a problem. Do it now."

My stomach dropped. Was I too late? The Packard family was doomed!

He explained that telling them isn't for the sake of the child, but for the sake of the parents. The sooner you use those words "you're adopted," the easier it will be for you to say them naturally. That way, your child won't pick up on any undercurrent of unease or feel different from the other kids.

So when Drew was two and I was still carrying him around, I'd say, "I'm so glad we adopted you!" It felt a bit silly, but I did feel better, like I was letting little Drew in on a secret. Bill and I showed him Romania on world maps, so that where he was born wouldn't be clouded in mystery either; instead he could feel proud about it. When he was around three, he began saying to strangers, "Hi, I'm 'dopted from 'mania!" He never seemed to have an issue with being adopted, whereas a friend whose son was not told about his own adoption until he was four years old ended up needing counseling with his adoptive parents. Who knows everything that went into his behavioral issues, but the counselor felt that he was acting out because the parents had bent over backward to make him feel "normal." In short: secrets make us sick.

There's so much power in just saying it—whatever "it" is. I met **Jana** at Serenity, a temporary home for women fleeing abusive situations. Jana was volunteering while earning her graduate degree in social work. She listened to the women's stories and allowed them to express their anger or hurt: "I asked one woman to journal about her issues. The next time we met, it took us an hour to get through her first sentence. She struggled to describe what she was trying to say in that first line. It was still all trapped up there. Talking it through helped her to release it."

Journaling is better than doing nothing, but it's not as powerful or effective as saying aloud what's inside. Also, there's the reward of human connection in sharing a brave and sacred moment with someone else.

A woman I worked with would invariably talk about her unhappy marriage by way of her "selfish stinkin' husband." I'd first remind her I'm not a marriage counselor, then nudge her to look at what solutions were available. She would become quiet then, and we'd move back to her workplace issues. I guess we must have done this scene enough that one day she surprised me: "I asked him for a divorce." She also sounded surprised when she said it! It was her first step in a gold star practice of EQ Fitness: living in solutions instead of problems.

## WORK COACHES AND THERAPISTS

You're now entering the world of writing a check. Sometimes your company will cover these costs, but not always. If you don't currently have the resources to hire someone, skip ahead to "Share Circles" below.

### Coaches

Work stress has bred an industry called executive coaching. That stress is typically brought on by workplace tensions, and sometimes by the need to bounce questions of business strategy or culture off someone without a dog in the fight. A warning: if you hire a former business-person (versus a psychologist), they might move into problem-solving mode too quickly because that's what we've been trained to do. Be sure your coach is first and foremost a good listener.

Many coaches who are hired by an HR department have an assignment that is limited in time, say six months. I don't agree with that approach, because a big part of coaching effectively is knowing someone well—better than you can accomplish in a short period of time. I used to do those kinds of gigs, but they always felt incomplete, so I now engage only for a year or more. (If one of your duties is to line up coaches for your organization, please consider offering this benefit for at least a year. It can take three to six months before someone is willing to feel safe and open up!)

When I was at HGTV, our senior leadership team brought in two partners in a coaching firm with a nice roster of executive clients. Being coached was the last thing on my mind, but enough of the rest of the team was excited to contract them, so I went along. Danny Frankel was my coach for several years. Danny held a PhD in clinical psychology and had a private practice too. He was an excellent listener, and when I'd ask, he'd offer guidance. He was on board when my mother and sister died in 2003. I took a thirty-day leave to just sit in the quiet. In that time, I envisioned other careers that wouldn't entail sixty-hour workweeks. When I returned, I began to change my work habits in small gradations, cutting down on travel and dinners. One day over lunch Danny was uncharacteristically bold and told me, "You know you're pulling back from the job, right?"

Life unfolds moment by moment and you must pay attention! I never would have seen the full picture if not for Danny. He understood that I was pulling away before I did, because he knew me well enough to see it. A year later, I asked the board to revise my job description, reducing the line responsibilities and taking on duties that required less travel. A few years after that, I left.

Good coaches are good listeners, counselors, and fixers too.

## Therapists

At Homeboy Industries, all three hundred of Father G's kids are in therapy of some sort; he has four paid therapists and forty-one volunteer therapists on staff. Father G believes in the power of therapy because he has seen how it's worked for his kids.

We may not all come from neighborhoods afflicted by violence, but by the time we reach adulthood, all of us carry shards of painful experience. Therapists can help those dammed-up memories break free and lose their power, which leads to healing. Regretfully, therapy is still surrounded by some stigma, which doesn't serve anyone. The parts of you that are injured become stronger through therapy, just like going to physical therapy helps you recover after an injury. England's National Health Service has been running a psychotherapy-for-all experiment for the past few years.[8] I hope that in our son's lifetime, therapy in all forms will be commonly accepted.

Clinical social worker Jerry Fried, whom you met in chapter one, most frequently helps clients "fix" four things: social anxiety, panic disorders, post-traumatic stress disorder (PTSD), and obsessive-compulsive disorder (OCD). Social anxiety takes up the bulk of his time.

He's worked with everyone from businesspeople at multimillion-dollar companies to engineers in the US government. Most have a marked and persistent worry about situations in which they'll be observed or evaluated, and where embarrassment may occur. Jerry treats them with cognitive behavioral therapy (CBT), which focuses on incorporating remedial ways of thinking and behaving so you can manage unwanted thoughts.

Another kind of therapy that can be helpful is psychoanalysis, in which a doctor and patient work toward finding the unconscious meanings behind troubling behaviors. A lot of these meanings have been deep-sixed by your brain, so the work is to pull them out. It can take profound courage to enter psychotherapy. Walking in is the hardest part. Once you begin, life will start to make a whole lot more sense.

## SHARE CIRCLES

After many years of trying to conceive, thirty-one-year-old **Jesse Sutherland** had had enough. She knew there were other women in the same boat, and she needed them. So she did a very courageous thing. She sent out a note on Facebook sharing her story, and she got over one hundred responses in the first hour. This eventually morphed into two communities she has led: an in-person share circle and an online support group. Her share circle met for the first time on Mother's Day.

"I thought the day was fitting. It was amazing. It was me and three other women, which was the perfect size for starting out. I feel so much more connected, understood, and empowered. There's a weight that seems to be lifted every time I'm able to share my story and listen empathetically to others' stories."

Share circles come in all sizes, themes, and shapes. The universal feature is being together, in one room, for the collective purpose of naming, claiming, and letting go of the demons so that you can reclaim your life. Former soldiers share their nightmares. Cancer patients share their fears. Widows and widowers prop one another up.

Those abusing substances—booze, drugs, food, whatever else—find others wanting to get well too.

I once heard that the only difference between "illness" and "wellness" is changing the "I" to "we," and share circles can help you work through even the hardest of moments together. One muggy summer night, my sister Linda was brutally raped in Ypsilanti, Michigan. She'd left her first-floor window open because of the heat. Her assailant raped and cut her. For the longest time Lin didn't talk about it, but we urged her to get help, and she reluctantly joined a circle of survivors. Three years later, the police got the guy, and Lin had the courage to confront him in court. The sometimes agonizing work she had done in the circle gave her the strength to show up, which helped convict him.

When I, too, joined a share circle with others in recovery, I immediately felt safe. In these groups, you feel less alone because everyone in the room has lived a common experience. The room itself provides a "container" for your pain, and the acceptance and understanding you encounter there leads to self-acceptance. You also are inspired by folks who have found new and productive ways to live and work. They're pretty easy to spot by their gratitude and how they keep showing up to help others. The rest of us just want what they've found. They'll become your heroes.

Do you know that brilliant last scene in the first season of *Game of Thrones* (SPOILER ALERT!), where Khaleesi emerges from the fire unharmed with her baby dragons? That's how I felt after participating in a share circle. Except for the dragons. And not being blond. Or naked. Just listening to others who've gone through similar experiences revealed that I hadn't been singled out in some cursed or Gothic way.

It was just life. The raw honesty is palpable, and, surprisingly, there is lots of laughter. In naming things, you often see the unproductive ways your mind can work. *Ha, we're all crazy together!* When you reach that understanding, you can begin to really take care of yourself and enter the next phase of self-discovery: learning what enriches you.

Above all, in a share circle, there's hope.

## JUST YOU

There will inevitably be moments when you're alone with your feelings, and you can still work on gaining emotional strength. Maybe you're physically alone or feeling alone in a crowd. There will also be times when you *need* solitary moments to process and reflect, or to grieve.

When Bill's dad, Stuart, passed away, we each grieved in our own way. He was so dear to all of us, and he was Drew's last living grand-parent. Grief is a very personal and often a very solitary thing. How you express it can be surprising. I remember driving to the funeral home after the service to pick up Stu's urn. The very somber funeral director handed over this heavy, blue, bell-shaped urn that must have been twenty pounds. I asked, "What have you got in there with Stu, a German shepherd?" It seemed bizarrely funny to me that she re-mained somber.

We're often our own best audience, and humor can lighten tough moments, or ones that just hit on a nerve.

Tears can be cleansing, and stress relievers too. Likewise, you might journal. You don't need to recount something bad that happened; you can write about anything and still reap the benefits. Joe Zarantonello writes poetry, which, he says, is "not about rhymes or turns of phrase. It's about what's killing me, or what's keeping me alive."

Don't underestimate the power of movement. You can hit the gym if you need to work off anger or frustration. Endorphins are your friend. I once read about a man who'd grown up with a beautiful mother who'd left her husband and young son for a life of drugs and partying. He was raised by an emotionally distant dad; he hated his mother, who hap-pened to be a gifted dancer. After many years, she sobered up, got off drugs, and moved to where her son was now living. She kept reaching out, trying to rebuild their relationship. He ignored her calls. Weeks and months passed, and ever so slowly he began to soften. He learned she was teaching modern dance at a studio not too far from him. So one day, he walked in and saw her alone, eyes closed, dancing. He watched her. She opened her eyes, saw him, and froze. Then, tentatively, she reached out her hand, and as the story goes, they danced together.

## EXCEPT, IT'S NEVER JUST YOU

*Unless you want it to be.* At heart we're emotional beings, so human connections enrich us. We're spiritual beings too. We're meant to do soul work, which enlarges and completes us. For those without a sound inner foundation, chasing the next deal or better ratings—and even getting them—can bring more fear and worry. Our culture rewards only the milestones we can see, which means we start worrying about the next big thing without taking a breath, feeling real gratitude, and recognizing the intangibles that went into that moment. While there's no participation trophy in emotional fitness, here's what you do get—a strong body, a sharp mind, and a grounded inner life. These, together, make us *feel* fully alive. Fully human.

Many of us have trouble with the idea of some exalted god sitting high on a mountain thundering down on us. I did too—that was the god-image I had growing up Catholic. I've since come to understand there's a difference between spirituality and religion. Religion can be exclusionary and rigid for some. Spirituality is all-inclusive, going beyond a set of institutional beliefs and doctrine to a feeling of loving connection to something bigger than you. I believe in a spiritual presence I call God, but the name doesn't matter: Great Spirit, Higher Power, True Self. Sufi poets often call it the Beloved. In some recovery share circles, "GOD" stands for "good orderly direction." By any name, your spirituality drives purpose and meaning beyond just you.

In growing a spiritual dimension to self, an inner life, you gain an awareness of where your control over life begins and ends, and make peace with it. You find yourself praying for others instead of your own list of things. You feel nudged toward service and away from selfishness. Those nudges are the presence of grace, a spiritual strength that helps awaken the most fundamental parts of ourselves.

# NEEDING TO MAKE IT RIGHT

When we stay too much in our heads, we hurt others. Nudges of grace make it easier to say "I'm sorry." Pema Chödrön asks, "How do I communicate to the heart of a person so that a stuck situation can ventilate?"[9] I think she means, How do we find compassion, and acknowledge our own responsibility, so that the other person can start to heal? How do I unlock us both?

In *New Rules of the Game*, I shared a story about a pitcher and his good sportsmanship. But as I reconsider the story in light of my own emotional growth since writing that book, I can see it was about so much more: remorse and forgiveness. At a Major League Baseball game in 2010, a young player named Armando Galarraga almost pitched a perfect game—until the last out. Looking at the tape later, Jim Joyce, the first-base ump, knew he'd blown the call and cost Galarraga a chance to go down in baseball history. The next time Galarraga saw Joyce on the field, he walked out of the dugout and approached. Everyone took a deep breath. What would he do? Then, on national television, Galarraga shook Joyce's hand. *No hard feelings.* In a stadium of thousands and on a telecast to millions, Joyce broke down and cried. *I'm sorry.*

Sometimes tears say "I'm sorry." Sometimes actions do. It can happen in a letter, over a meal, or through a peace offering. It can be a living amends, which means you realize after someone has passed away that you owed him or her an apology and take constructive action in their honor. After I lost my mom, I wrote her a letter, which I've saved, and I try to honor a quiet promise I made to her the day before she passed away. It's been a source of comfort to do so.

What matters is that you own your part and *initiate* some sort of action to make it right. With forgiveness, we can meet again, heart-to-heart. This will help you most of all. It builds moral strength and emotional resilience. It's cleansing to be forgiven—you carry a lighter load, and in that moment, you begin to forgive yourself. A clear conscience is a soft pillow at night.

# GROWING YOUR SELF-WORTH

In her bestseller *Gifts of Imperfection*, Brené Brown writes about how many of us run around "hustling for worthiness."[10] It's an epidemic among women in particular, but I know plenty of men like this too. Once we work to release the past and the negative baggage we've been carrying, we get "returned to ourselves," as Father G writes in *Tattoos on the Heart*, and find we're worthy. You'll find you start liking this looser, lighter you—a lot. Shedding those layers of self-protection, you'll move closer to touching the divinity that's within all of us, and honoring the basic humanity of others. It begins with honoring ourselves; we can only give what's within us to give.

Until then, though, you'll live closed off, in a house with the windows shuttered and the doors permanently locked. The cycle of daring allows all of us to unlock our lives bit by bit—and for those of us who need it, to rebuild them, stone by stone. This is the work of willingness, from which we gain new measures of self-respect and a firm foundation to weather the pain that inevitably comes to our threshold. We add doors to welcome the good. We add windows to let in the light. By doing these things, we're building a framework for unshakable emotional maturity.

We're becoming emotionally fit.

# CHAPTER THREE

# WHY PEACE OF MIND MATTERS

*Ends and beginnings—there are no such things.*
*There are only middles.*

—ROBERT FROST

Peace of mind is a competitive advantage. In our current "attention economy," skills like focus, problem-solving, and working fast are valued most. Having a clear head, free from the storm clouds of worry, allows you to show up focused and alert. Your ability to concentrate is a skill as valuable as any technical ability you may have, especially in a leadership job where vast amounts of information need to be absorbed. It's our best problem-solving resource, allowing solutions to arise more easily and naturally. All these skills can be enhanced through the practices of **mindfulness** and its first cousin, **meditation**.

You'll hear them buzzed about in leadership articles, but there's confusion about their origins and practice. Some may use the terms interchangeably, believing they are the same thing (they're not). While their origins are Buddhist, they are practiced by many other faiths, including Christianity and Islam. In fact, while they can be used in spiritual practice, they are marshaled in various secular ways too; it depends on your intention.

I've meditated for almost ten years and am now certified to teach it. Let's look at each of these practices, how they can help you on the path of EQ Fitness, and—the real one-two punch—the power of working them together.

# DEFINING MINDFULNESS

## MOMENTNESS

Mindfulness has been practiced for thousands of years. It has many definitions, but the simplest one is the state of mind of attending to the moment. If I were a marketer of mindfulness, I'd rebrand it "*momentness*" because that's precisely what it is: being present, all in, *in this moment*. (Plus, mind-*ful*-ness—who wants a fuller mind?) Regardless, mindfulness matters because our lives are always in motion, sometimes insanely so, and the work is to stay present in a given moment. Our friend Suzanne Moody's holiday card last year wished us an "ecologically-sound, morally-centered, physically-fit, stress-free, and mindfully-considered" New Year, which about covers it. Mindfulness gives us the perspective and the practice to slow our pace enough to see things, so they won't pass us by in the frenetic pace of the everyday.

During a trip to Alaska, Bill and I flew out on a small plane with a guide to fish for arctic char. After we hauled in a load, the guide set a fire and cleaned and cooked our catch. He was quiet doing his work, but while we were eating, he looked at both of us inquisitively and said, "I don't understand most Americans. Look around. What do you see?" I looked and saw blue water and enormous mountains capped in ice. "So many race around, when they could be sitting right here. Looking at this," he said, sweeping his hand wide. That was the beginning of mindfulness for me, although I wouldn't call it that until many years later, when I attended my first retreat and learned to slow down enough to observe all my senses.

Jon Kabat-Zinn is an MIT-trained scientist who brought mindful practice into popularity in Western culture in the eighties, using it to help others manage stress and physical pain. Kabat-Zinn describes the practice as life itself, and "minding" all our senses moment by moment.

During the meeting in which E.W. Scripps Senior VP of Television Frank Gardner and Ken Lowe recruited me to join HGTV, there were many sensory-rich moments—some hilariously awkward in retrospect. When I knocked on their suite door at the Candy Cane Hotel (the *Candy Cane?*), a young woman opened it. She wore a miniskirt, fishnet stockings, and five-inch heels. "Is this the Scripps suite?" I asked, getting slightly nervous that I had taken a wrong turn. Then I saw Ken and Frank, with sheepish looks. They ushered me in. I sat in a chair, and it was . . . sticky. Like sitting on candy cane juice. They explained that they had been late in registering for the Western Show, a national cable industry trade show that was held annually in Anaheim, California, and this was the only hotel available. The "hostess" was some tangential friend's idea, and they didn't know what they were getting either. Their awkwardness was endearing, and I felt a human pull toward them. They were new to the business, and they were trying.

My brain was amped up, and I can still recount every moment. While it was the lowest-tech presentation I'd ever been to—on poster boards, held up by a rickety wooden tripod—what was on the poster boards was vibrant: home magazines with splashes of color and welcoming design, photographs of men and women putting their hands back in the dirt and taking up gardening, warm images of families coming together in homey spaces. I could almost smell the bread baking. *They're onto something*, I thought. In fact, it felt like a home run of an idea. At the end, Frank asked me, "Do you want to build a culture you can call your own, from the ground up?"

I was theirs.

If you don't know the language of mindfulness, you might not realize you're in it. Think of a normal day when suddenly every thought and sensory detail came to life. A time when you were mentally alert and spiritually aware. This mind-set is an appreciation of "what is" at a given moment. That's mindfulness.

## NO JUDGING

Mindfulness also means being nonjudgmental. Consider this: joy is this very moment, minus your opinion of it. Being nonjudgmental is really hard and takes a lot of practice, especially if you've made a habit of judging *yourself* harshly over every little thing. It's also hard if you're working with another person as their mentor, boss, or coach and trying to provide counsel. Once, I was coaching a young woman who had started a business, and she told me she'd brought her husband onto the payroll. I almost blurted out, *You did* what? I flashed back to the disaster of trying to work with Bill at his yogurt store; we were like that old southern saying "Don't get your money where you've got your honey." Thankfully, I remembered to take a few moments until my snap judgment dissipated. We can't ever know how marriage works for others. At times, it's baffling that our *own* marriages can work. Being mindful helps us pause and not act out impulsively in some self-centered, hurtful way.

Rumi most gorgeously captured this idea of being present without judgment:

> *Out beyond ideas of wrongdoing and rightdoing*
> *there is a field. I'll meet you there.*
> *When the soul lies down in that grass,*
> *the world is too full to talk about.*[1]

Living mindfully helps us stop sleepwalking. It offers awareness of whatever's being served up to us. It is a crucial part of wonderful moments, and tough ones. With emotional fitness, we face them all with courage and grace.

## WHY MIND THE MOMENT

### Productivity, Leadership, and Our Place in the World

Gloria Mark, professor of Informatics at the University of California, Irvine, has found that office workers are interrupted, or self-interrupt, every three minutes.[2] Businesses are starting to get the message and teach their employees mindful practices to improve productivity, stay focused, and reduce stress. At the World Economic Forum, where global business leaders convene to learn and teach their best practices to others, mindfulness was one of the hottest topics in 2015.[3] In the past decade, companies like Intel, Keurig, General Mills, SNI, McKinsey, and BlackRock have incorporated it into the workday. Aetna has, too, having seen how it reduces health care costs in the companies it insures.

In 2016, in partnership with Michigan State University, I created and facilitated a three-day mindfulness retreat for women leaders at St. Mary's, a retreat house on beautiful Monteagle Mountain in Sewanee, Tennessee. Attendees came from Texas to Georgia, Michigan to DC. **Lisa Parker**, my MSU partner and the senior director of alumni engagement, describes them as "a group of career-focused women who, in many cases, had never invested in self-care as a means to be effective leaders." We interspersed meditation with more mainstream business subjects, like resilience and building sturdy cultures. It was funny—even though the agenda had been explicit, some of the women were baffled. *What, we're going to meditate?* We talked about ways that we, as leaders, could grow our self-awareness and understand our responsibility to a larger world. We practiced yoga and had hours of quiet time. When we were in dialogue, we learned how not to rush to fill the silence with words, but to allow it to unfold. In our own ways, we prayed for the stamina to bear the stillness and the patience to find how opening to the quiet often leads to a more open mind.

As Lisa observed, "By the end of the second day, the shift had occurred. Quiet reflection no longer triggered restless energy. The women were beginning to understand listening to themselves and reflective time were of value, like listening to Susan was." At the end of the weekend, many women let us know that they planned to take these practices back to their workplaces.

Omaha, Nebraska, is home base for Gravity, a Center for Contemplative Activism. Gravity hosts two retreats each year, and in its first three years had more than two hundred people from over fifteen countries attend. The median age of attendees was thirty-three, and over three-quarters were under forty years old. Gravity's founding partner Phileena Heuertz finds that silence and stillness provide "correction to the imbalance and depletion many of us are experiencing in our crowded, overly-consumed, hyper-active, digitally-addicted society."[4]

Likewise, Father Richard Rohr, the founder of the Center for Action and Contemplation, often works with millennials who "feel like old souls" and are "seeking a fuller and farther vision of who they want to be and how that is distinct from what they want to do."[5] These young adults are our current and future leaders. They weren't raised anchored to large institutions like church, government, or big business, so the transition to adulthood breeds many more questions. Sure, they love their friends and their busy lives, but device distraction for many has stopped working as an escape. They welcome stillness as they unfold the layers of their own identity to grow an inner life and find a deeper foundation of meaning. Mindful practices teach us to access the parts of us that can see wide-open, limitless possibilities. These tools both grow and enhance our ability to lead in all areas of life.

## Hitting Pause

Learning to pause, an outgrowth of mindfulness, has become a best friend to my marriage. Where I used to react, now I take a moment and say a quiet prayer to be patient and listen. It's made a huge difference in my communication with my husband, especially since patience has never been my virtue. It has also helped me observe how I might normally react in a situation—and to interrupt that habit.

A huge benefit of these practices in the workplace is that you don't show up spring-loaded; you learn how to take a breath before instinct takes over, or defer to silence when cutting words are ripe for unloading. This is hard stuff, pressing pause when you might otherwise respond with heat, but it gets much easier the more you practice. Moreover, you become a better listener and a more creative worker. Often we jump to "solutions" before understanding the problem, or without having dreamt enough in a brainstorm meeting.

We're human beings, not human doings, and pauses give your brain a breather. We make our brains run marathons at work, when the science says that humans can focus for only 90 to 120 minutes before we need a break.[6] When we don't fill up our invaluable brain space with endless chatter, our minds don't get so caught up in the noise and chaos. Mind chatter is its own form of dodging accountability to yourself, and your life.

Pausing first thing in the morning, instead of diving right in, will help you organize your day. At the end of the day, it'll help you untangle the challenges you encountered. *Did my boss really mean she wanted more customers, or more sales volume? I'll clarify tomorrow.* It helps you assess—*what did I do well? what could I have done differently?*—and refresh and calm your mind before heading home, which can be a danger zone. Home is where many of us deposit our daily frustrations, unless we learn how to detach from them before cranking up the car.

### Seeing Time as Friend, Not Enemy

As I built businesses, time was always the enemy. A leader's job is to stay at least one step ahead of your consumers, and it's a relentless push. In the early 2000s, when I was at the peak of growing SNI, an article in a business magazine caught my eye. Matthew J. Christoff had been a high roller with executive jobs at Procter & Gamble and Mc-

Kinsey, and later as a partner at Spencer Stuart, a top executive search firm. A sudden diagnosis of metastatic testicular cancer, emergency surgery, and many rounds of heavy-duty chemo brought him to understand that *time* was the real gift. I'd never read something written by a business leader that was so personal and vulnerable. Now I see that what he was really preaching was mindfulness. My copy of the article has coffee stains and is dog-eared, but I've kept it as a reminder of what matters: what's happening *today*. The only thing we can't replace is time.

Mindfulness is slowing down enough to use time in a precious and patient—not perfunctory—way with others. We can be plenty impatient about goals we need to meet, and that's OK. It's another thing entirely to make it part of your MO with the people around you.

## MINDFULNESS FOR STRESS RELIEF

In a stressful mind, full of fear, we lose all sense of the moment, because fear focuses on the future. No one knows this better than our college kids, who are fighting battles with stress and work overload. Many leave home without the emotional equipment to cope with the increases in workload and social expectations, which results in anxiety, depression, and extreme stress.[7] Universities like Michigan State have instituted mindfulness and meditation programs for incoming freshman that have become wildly popular. At Smith College, an initiative called "Failing Well" awards a "certificate of failure" upon entry—*Hey, this happens in college!*—and offers workshops on perfectionism and imposter syndrome.[8]

Stress relief is just as important for postgraduates beginning professional lives, especially in certain industries, like the legal profession. Drinking problems and mental health issues are at disproportionate levels among younger lawyers in particular. In one study, over 36 percent of respondents qualified as problem drinkers, while 28 percent experienced depression, and 19 percent showed symptoms of anxiety.[9]

The Tennessee Bar Association devoted its fall 2016 publication to mindful practices, and for good reason; research shows that mindfulness-based programs can help treat anxiety disorders.[10] Firms that support mindfulness and meditation for employees are combatting the stigma against asking for help and reversing the trend of higher risks faced by the profession.[11]

# MEDITATION

When I first heard about meditation, it made no sense. The very thought of sitting in silence for more than twenty seconds made my skin crawl. I didn't get it—until I began practicing.

Sometimes it's enough to *just start*. I know now how a quiet mind has enriched my relationships with others. I know that it helps me to discard useless, self-limiting thoughts, to see a bigger picture, which has given me a bigger life. But my ever-active left brain had to be convinced. So let's start with the facts.

## HISTORY TO MODERN SCIENCE

The roots of meditation trace back to ancient spiritual practices in China and India. Fast-forward five thousand years to the 1960s, when Western society was in the throes of a cultural revolution. Many disillusioned young (and not-so-young) folks ventured east to "find" themselves and brought back Transcendental Meditation, which flourished over the next few decades. Today there are over twenty types of meditation, including Buddhist, Christian, Hindu, Islamic, and secular. Most use breath and/or a mantra, which is a repeated word or sound.

Meditation has a clear and immediate effect on our bodies. Scientists have found lower levels of cardiovascular inflammation when comparing participants pre- and post-meditation. In other words, healthier hearts. That part's impressive, but what I find most fascinating is what happens in the brain, where meditation can have the same effect on the flow of neurotransmitters as talk therapy does.[12] In one study, those who did yoga and meditation together showed improved moods and emotional well-being over a control group.[13]

The work of researchers like Stanford University neurosurgeon James Doty has demonstrated neuroplasticity, the ability to change the wiring and the structure of the brain, through meditative practice.[14] The news gets even better for long-time meditators, whose amygdalae—the fight-or-flight part of the brain triggered when we're in fear or survival mode—actually *shrink*. Our brains are mutable! In as little as two weeks of meditating, Doty's patients showed decreases in inflammatory markers and blood pressure.

Advances in neuroscience in the past few years have given scientists a new perspective on our brains. Instead of them withering away with age, our brains change and shift if we keep them active. Dr. Andrew Newberg has demonstrated that meditation in particular can help slow the brain's aging process. Wow! Not only that, but his brain scans show that those who meditate stimulate the anterior cingulate, a small structure in the part of the brain where we experience feelings of compassion—or, as Dr. Newberg calls it, our "neurological heart."[15]

Meditation can be a path to better peace of mind, which will help us become thriving workers and leaders, find more connection to others, and reach fulfillment in work and life. It's a critical piece of the puzzle for gaining emotional fitness. Jon Kabat-Zinn has said that the scientific evidence suggests that "when you choose life" through mindfulness practices "your brain changes both in form and function, your immune system changes, your body changes . . . we start to really take care of what's most important."[16]

An active practice of meditation can help us leave behind negative thinking and take control over our minds; every little annoyance doesn't have to become some grand drama. We can stop believing the small, boxed-in thinking our minds and egos want us to. Best said, with a practice of meditation, you don't believe everything you think.

## HOW MEDITATION WORKS

Almost all forms of meditation teach you ways to calm and stabilize your mind using your breath. In its simplest form, you close your eyes, you feel and listen to your breathing, and when thoughts arise, you acknowledge them and just as quickly let them go. When I teach meditation, I use the analogy of watching a boat on a river slowly go by. Put your thoughts in that boat and allow it to drift by. Here's the big reveal: YOU WILL ALWAYS HAVE THOUGHTS. To be a "good" meditator doesn't mean having a blank mind. The key is learning to *detach* from unproductive and self-limiting thoughts, to let them float down the stream of consciousness—and move on. As you practice, you'll find it comes much more naturally. If you've never meditated before or are looking to improve your practice, try your hand at the guided exercises in "Your Turn" on page 95.

| STAGES OF MEDITATION | | |
|---|---|---|
| Stage 1 (surface) | Surface Left Brain & *Ego*/Mental | CHATTER Time, static, repetitive story lines *I want to quit!* |
| Stage 2 (deeper) | Left Brain & *Ego*/Mental | THINKING Doing, words, gripping, calculating, concepts |
| Stage 3 (deepest) | Right Brain *Soul*/Spiritual | AWARENESS Peace, no time, creativity, inner silence, deep grief, paradox, presence |

**FIGURE D:** From Surface to Deepest. Courtesy of Joe Zarantonello

## RIGHT-BRAIN BENEFITS

Meditation is a right-brained activity. Your right brain is where connection and compassion reside, and freeing it up has both practical and spiritual benefits.

### ιother Way to Let Things Go

We think nothing of making space for a new chair in our den, but it can be hard to imagine taking control of our mind and opening up some space in the same way, and just as easily. This is what meditation allows. Serenity comes in those moments—not always, but more and more as you practice. Meditation is another form of willingness. There's a parable about a truth seeker who visits an old monk to gain wisdom. The young man tells the monk about all his studies and travels, and the monk nods, listening. As the young man keeps talking, the monk boils tea and brings out two cups. The man *keeps* going on as the monk begins pouring tea until it overflows—and he keeps pouring. "Stop! My cup is already full!" the young man says. The monk demonstrated that you can only teach someone who is open, listens, and has a receptive mind, not one overfull. In that moment, the young man becomes enlightened.

I cannot say this enough: meditation is not about having *no* thoughts. You will always have thoughts. By learning to detach from them, you can see more objectively who you are, and who you have the potential of becoming.

### Learning to Breathe

Whether you're an executive, a manager, or an employee, meditation offers the same benefit and applications. It lets our right brains—where creativity, problem-solving, and active listening reside—breathe. As a leader, you'll spend more time on vision and less on putting out fires. Meditation opens mind space for learning, as well as opportunities for compassion, connection, trust, and gratitude.

Anisa Telwar meditates with her whole company at least twice a year. On one occasion, I led the sessions at a local yoga studio. She told me her team felt closer to one another afterward, and it helped them to slow down when they later found themselves under stress. Anisa meditates daily and she finds it indispensable to starting her day grounded and focused.

## More Self-Awareness

*Watch your thoughts; they become words.*
*Watch your words; they become actions.*
*Watch your actions; they become habits.*
*Watch your habits; they become character.*
*Watch your character; it becomes destiny.*

—ANONYMOUS[17]

Your opened mind allows you to see . . . *you*. By detaching from your thoughts, you can see yourself more objectively. You can see who you are more clearly—literally watch your actions in a given situation—and how you might improve managing your emotional instincts.

A story to that point. In the spring of 2017, I was in Los Angeles keynoting an event for a client. I was to speak about the lessons I share in my book *New Rules of the Game* in front of a hundred or so. As the room was being set up and attendees began to filter in, my contact turned to me and said, "I'd like to tell them that your book is new. It is new, right?" And I heard myself—watched myself—respond, "Sure. The average life of a book is thirty years and mine is two years old." *What?* I have *no* idea what the average life span of a book is, or if books even have one. I just made that up. Completely. What I really wanted to do was reassure her that the session would go great, and to demonstrate some sort of (imaginary, in this case) expertise. It's times like those when I'm sure one of my eight pathological relatives has just hijacked my brain. It was a harmless fib, but showed me I needed to better practice the pause, instead of letting ego play a wild card.

## Building Trust

Given the scale, fast pace, and relentless drive of our workplaces, we need tools to ease stress and build trust. It's hard to do one without the other. Meditation and breath work ease stress. Mindful actions build trust. Both open up mind space to pay attention to those around us, to know them better and learn how their skills complement our own. They facilitate building reciprocal, supportive relationships. Having a wider perspective also makes those you *can't* trust come into focus more clearly. (We'll discuss those scoundrels in chapter five.)

# CENTERING PRAYER

## History

What do I know of spirit or soul? I went to a Catholic school where the nuns said you carried a soul inside you, where God lived. It was a kind of mini deity, which in my mini mind sounded like I had superpowers—exciting! But then they ruined it by saying God is no fun at all; he punishes you with a lot of disapproval. Who needed that? I had parents for that. Many of us have had similar experiences where we're taught that we humans are "less than." My work in share circles and with a form of spiritual meditation called Centering Prayer (CP) have changed those outdated notions for me.

Centering Prayer has Christian origins. Since I was raised in a Christian home, it felt familiar, and I quickly gravitated to it. Christian meditation goes back centuries and has its roots in "contemplation," which in a religious context is a life of deep reflection and a quest to grow in relationship to the divine. Ascetics like Saint Teresa of Ávila lived contemplatively, as do contemporary monks who reside in monasteries. In the twentieth century, contemplative prayer gained prominence through the writings and modeling of Thomas Merton, a bit of a wild seed who chucked the material things of the world to become a monk, writing over forty books and working with figures of other world religions—like the Dalai Lama—until his death in 1968.

In the 1970s, Father Thomas Keating, a monk who'd attended Yale for a time, was living in St. Joseph's Abbey in Spencer, Massachusetts, when he set out with a couple of other monks to make contemplative practices accessible to all. Keating is known as the father of CP, and he, too, has done much inter-spiritual work with Jews, Muslims, and Buddhists. He teaches that we all have the same spark of divinity within us, which represents our good, and advocates Centering Prayer as an ideal vehicle for connection and enrichment. He wrote in *Manifesting God* that, "For human beings, it is the most daunting challenge there is—the challenge of becoming fully human. For to become fully human is to become fully divine."[18] Father Keating passed away in the fall of 2018 at the age of ninety-five.

Today I teach CP in leadership retreats, like the one I did in partnership with Michigan State. Learning it took time for me, but I mostly needed a willingness to practice. The first step is to spend a few moments of quiet time choosing a "sacred word," which is sacred not for any specific religious affiliation, but because it signals your intent to access the divine. (More on this in "Your Turn" at the end of part one.) As with breathing or other mantras, a sacred word has the purpose of clearing the decks, if you will, of moving your thoughts down the river of consciousness. Whenever unwelcome thoughts arise, return your attention to your sacred word by saying it to yourself very gently, as gently as a drop of dew on a leaf. Teacher Shunryu Suzuki said, "Leave the doors and windows open. Let your thoughts come and go. Just don't serve them tea." It helps to remember the 4 Rs:

1. Do not **Resist** thoughts.
2. Do not **Retain** thoughts.
3. Do not **React** emotionally to thoughts.
4. When caught up in thought, **Return**, ever so gently, to your sacred word.

Keating says, "Silence is God's first language; everything else is a poor translation."[19] You might think of CP as a listening prayer.

## Divine Therapy

To learn CP, I spent many weekends at St. Mary's, the mountaintop center in Tennessee, culminating in an eight-day silent retreat with about thirty other attendees. The first few days were an enormous struggle. I kept future-tripping about how long eight days of silence was going to be. At work, I was known for getting things done quickly. If it could be done in four, I did it in two. *What was the point of eight days? Why was I even here?* My thoughts wandered from jumping in my car and hightailing it home to meditations on pepperoni pizza.

But then, about halfway through, something happened: I settled in. Without daily distractions, your mind stops causing you trouble. With nothing to feed its craving for frenzy, it begins to embrace the quiet. I also experienced another form of share circle, where we meditated together in one room. You have to experience this to believe it, but here goes: as you spend time in CP with others, *even in complete silence*, the circle gets closer, tighter, more fiercely bound together. Even in silence, we reap the benefits of community.

I learned, too, how CP can help us let things go, much like the other methods I discussed in chapter two.

Father Keating calls the process *Divine Therapy*, and he represents it as a spiral (figure E). Over time, with regular sessions, we move closer to our center, which is the good, the soul, divinity. Merton calls it the "true self." To get to it, you have to peel away all the layers of self-protection you've taken on to survive and function. We all have that armor because our natural instincts, or "programs for happiness"—to feel secure, to feel esteemed, and to feel control over our lives—are all threatened at one point or another. CP moves us gently through removing those layers, but it still can feel hard because it involves unloading stressful thoughts and memories that we've repressed.

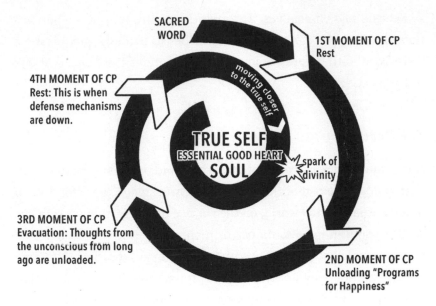

**FIGURE E:** The Spiral

This is the phase between "disorder" and "reorder" Joe Zarantonello spoke of earlier, when the "hardest part is hanging in there with the process when everything seems dark, dead, and hopeless." Similarly, Father Richard Rohr calls the unconscious where "all the garbage lies," and this prayer heals the unconscious.[20]

I had a lot of unexcavated garbage around the deaths of my mom, dad, and sister, all of which hit me in a four-year period. I cared for them at the end of their lives, and in the case of my sister, was tasked with making medical decisions I had no experience with. It was very sudden, she had no will and was on life support, and while all the doctors told me there was no hope, I still was the one who had to give the nod to end life support. Unknown even to myself, I'd carried an unconscious image of me as a hand of death. One day, with "divine therapy" at work, that image came visible in my mind's eye. I could then move it out and let it go. I felt peace in that moment.

Grace is spiritual strength, spiritual muscle. I've opened myself up to it through CP—and if I did it, I know you can too. It prepares your inner ground to be a welcoming place for grace, and grace, in turn, awakens our divine selves. Through Centering Prayer, we get "returned to ourselves," as Father G describes it, to all the goodness we were born with before we lost sight of it under the burden of our self-protections.

## The Best Trust

As a leader, you're surrounded by a whirlwind; you must tend to staff, shareholders, your monthly P&L. In the workplace, we often live so much in the external world, on the surface of things, that we may not realize something feels empty or displaced—until the symptoms emerge loudly enough that we can't help but pay attention. After two years of almost daily CP meditation, I found myself paying attention in a big way. When you practice enough, all you're left with is you, and the bare, unavoidable truth (more on this in chapter ten).

Emotional fitness is about bringing the *whole* of you to work each day. The practices open up new dimensions in you, and in turn you can offer them—your fully human self—to the work you've chosen to do. We live in our heads at work. Can we bring along our hearts too? The best way I've found to do that is by moving out unproductive, self-limiting thoughts and memories to make space for what's good and nourishing and most alive: all the right-brained emotions that bind us together. Growing the whole self is prep work for Step Two, building authentic trust. Trust is, at its essence, an emotion, but we think of it too often as a transaction, especially in the workplace. The best trust is binding, not usury.

# MINDFULNESS AND MEDITATION AT WORK TOGETHER

What we do in our minds is nothing short of brutality. Thomas Merton said that to "allow ourselves to be carried away by a multitude of conflicting concerns, to surrender to too many demands . . . is to succumb to violence."[21] **Meditation is the engine that fuels a mindful life.** Mindfulness is being focused, being aware, and attending to the present moment, instead of drifting off. It teaches us to be present to one purpose or person at a time. Meditation helps us release things so we have mental space and heart space to do just that, so the two complement and reinforce each other. Qualities like attentiveness and mental rigor can be *taught*, and mindfulness and meditation, working in tandem, facilitate that learning. Meditation and mindfulness promote mental agility, too, so we can weave in and out of meetings and navigate diverse issues smoothly. We can condition our minds in the same way athletes condition their bodies. I think that's pretty cool!

The work to become EQ Fit is not for the faint of heart. It's brave work, and most of us are braver than we think. When Pema Chödrön was first married, her husband told her that she was one of the bravest people he knew. When she asked why, he said because she was a complete coward but went ahead and did things anyway. A woman I coach, who has flourished building a multimillion-dollar business, recently told me how scared she was about an upcoming work initiative. It wasn't stopping her though. That's what us scaredy-cats do—we act *even though* we're scared. We find ways to get unstuck from the self-limiting thoughts that want to take over. I still feel fear, but many of its root causes have been expunged through the healing tools of a listening friend, a share circle, mindfulness, and Centering Prayer meditation. These tools help us gain precious self-awareness so that we can settle into ourselves, accept who we are, and recognize the gifts we can offer in our workplaces.

They help us to become all we were meant to be.

Now you're ready to parlay your newfound self-awareness into the kind of job, and the kind of work culture, that best fits *you*.

# CHAPTER FOUR

# GOOD JOB FIT

*But, if you have nothing at all to create,*
*then perhaps you create yourself.*
—CARL JUNG

When John Clark was in high school, he really liked chemistry. "But I hated foreign languages. I found out that if I got a chemical engineering degree in college, I wouldn't have to take any language classes. So that's what I did."

Freshly degreed from the University of Tennessee, and following his passion for environmental issues, John worked as a chemical engineer in hazardous-waste cleanup for over twenty years, fourteen in San Francisco. "San Francisco is a food and wine mecca, and there were small coffeehouses everywhere. I loved good coffee," he told me. John then took a job in Knoxville, Tennessee, where there was no good coffee anywhere. "Starbucks hadn't even come to Knoxville."

So John did something about it. "I started roasting coffee in our popcorn popper. It started out as a hobby but became a passion." He began buying coffee "cherries" (the fruit coffee beans grow in) online, the best he could find. Then he bought a used commercial roaster on eBay and began roasting coffee in his garage. "I got a glimmer that I could make this into a business," he said.

"It was my worst nightmare!" his wife, **Sue**, exclaimed. I'd invited her to the interview. "My father had left his corporate job at forty to open a print shop, and I lived through all that growing up. I thought I'd married a man with financial potential. John was telling me he'd be leaving behind a VP job for one with zero income," she said. "It was so scary."

Sue was working for me at HGTV at the time, and she recalls how she came to discuss all of it in my office. "If we were going to pull this off, I had to negotiate with you. It was my first salary negotiation."

*How did you do?*

She laughed. "Well, more than anything I heard a vote of confidence from you and the company that I had a future there."

The Clarks cut up their credit cards and put themselves on a strict budget. Twenty years later, Sue is still at SNI, which HGTV morphed into, and John founded and runs Vienna Coffee Company, one of the biggest coffee labels in the Southeast.

How do you ever know if you're in the right job, the best job, for *you*? How do you know it's worth taking a leap of faith to try it? As with everything else, it starts with self-knowledge.

The rubber is about to meet the road. This chapter will show you how self-awareness translates into a paycheck—and, even better, into a job that lights you up.

## SELF-KNOWLEDGE IS POWER

In many cities today, start-up accelerators and incubators offer stipends and grants to enterprising young adults, who, in turn, grow their business there. One evening, after I gave remarks at an event in Detroit, a young woman, no more than twenty-two years old, raised her hand. "I'm really good at new ideas and working to get them off the ground," she said. "But I'm not great at process. How do I get to be a complete CEO?"

My knee-jerk reaction was to say, *Who'd want to be in charge of process? Get someone else to do that!* I was just like her; I've hated process my whole career. But I took a mindful moment and instead offered encouragement and praise for her self-awareness, remarkable for someone just starting in their career. I then explained that we generally fall into categories of builder-entrepreneur or process-systems person. Our job in developing ourselves is to first identify which one we are, then to work on developing the other skill set, especially if we want a leadership position, because great leaders need both.

I've met very few CEOs who are really skilled at both process and start-up. If you manage others, it helps to add team members with skills not native to you. But *first* you need to know what you're good at, and what you love to do. **Process person** (a term that sells short what this skill set really entails) versus **entrepreneur** is one choice that can become clear with self-knowledge. You can follow the path I did to **intrapreneur** work, in between the two—building new brands and divisions within established parent companies. Stephen Covey says that private victories precede public ones, as he pushes the reader toward self-discovery, and I've always found that to be sound guidance. Whenever I checked in with my heart and my stomach, two "private" gauges of calm or anxiety, I found intrapreneur work fit best.

Before you identify which label best fits you, start with a simple question: What makes you smile after you've done it? Use that as a gauge of possibilities. It could be taking your eye for detail and becoming an architect or city planner. It could be using your curiosity about people's lives and becoming a journalist or joining a human resources department. It might be marshaling your empathy into a caregiving role as a nurse or other health care professional. Or using your rhythmic ear to play and perform music. If you wonder how things are made or why they're purchased, that might be fodder for engineering work or a career in brand management. Over the past few years, as I've written books and interviewed fascinating people, I've found the process truly inspires me. After speaking with Sue and

John Clark, I hung up the phone and smiled. *How cool! They made his dream real.* That kind of response is your heart telling you something. Listen to it.

Consider, too, how high you want to advance in an organization. You might recall Angela Teague, our introvert who chose not to manage people. That decision was born from self-awareness. Another friend, Babs, works at an enormous aerospace company, and she describes how her boss will, about every year or so, walk toward her cube with a certain look. She knows what's coming. The boss is looking for someone to fill a newly vacant management position. Babs said she and her colleagues all put their heads down, pretending to be engrossed in some project. None of them want to manage anyone.

In most companies, advancing means managing larger and larger teams. You may want to hightail it up the career ladder and be happy to take on reams of people. I loved challenge and high achievement, so I was happy to keep climbing. Until I wasn't.

My HGTV boss, Ken Lowe, and I were working side by side as CEO and COO, respectively. He got a corporate nod to take over the parent company, E.W. Scripps, and wanted to know if I wanted his job as CEO. I slept on it, and surprised him by telling him no. But the answer didn't surprise me.[1] I knew myself well enough to know that his job wouldn't be a good fit. Being CEO is all-consuming, with a responsibility to shareholders and employees alike. I needed some work-life balance for myself and my family, and knew I had to stop at number two—even if it meant diminished opportunities at HGTV or another company in the future. Saying no opened up other opportunities and interests that were more important to explore, including growing a variety of business areas at SNI and running the New York City Marathon, which took training and prep. There will be key junctures in your life, too, and practicing the three steps of EQ Fitness will provide sound guidance.

These questions of job fit may confront you many times over the course of your career. Practicing with the EQ Fitness tools allows you to stay alert and vigilant, and fresh self-knowledge arrives all the time.

## OWNING YOUR LIFE

The best job fits are a combination of the following:

- knowing which gifts you can offer, because you're made that way;
- the things that interest and stimulate you, like whether you'd rather be with people or work by yourself to problem-solve big questions; and
- the place itself; what kind of company culture draws you in.

Finally, there's the matter of—and you know I'm going there—whether you've done the soul work to inhabit your life, not someone else's version of it. Approaching your career in an integrated way may reinforce what you thought to be true—or your heart may tell you what your mind doesn't want to hear.

I've coached many executives in family-owned businesses, and I always try to discern if they really want to be there, or if they are there by obligation. All I know is that when I've asked, every single one has said, "Yes! I want to be here!" It seems to me that a family business is, by definition, about more than one's personal choices. You're there for a lot of people, including future generations. Working in a family business may be the most obvious example of a veiled motive behind taking a job, but you can imagine others: a paycheck even though you're bored senseless and could live on a lot less; the prestige of working at a big-name company even though you're surrounded by people you can't relate to at all; or the power a certain job commands, even though you butt heads daily with other leaders over values and ideology. In these scenarios, you haven't started thinking about job fit with *all of you* in mind.

Over the course of our working lives, we'll come to many crossroads, as our professional identities unfold and unpredictable opportunities arise. It takes courage and integrity to absorb the big picture when it comes to job fit. Emotionally intelligent people see job fit in its largest sense, because it means taking ownership and accountability over choosing wisely, taking into account where your heart is guiding you. This means going beyond considering what you *can* do, to what you *love* to do, so that "can do" doesn't become a life sentence.

To get the most out of this chapter, I'm going to ask you to suspend disbelief. Don't think of the practical limitations that may hold you back from seeking your most "sick" job (as our teenage niece Rachel would say). Dream big.

## SELF-KNOWLEDGE TOOLS

Most work coaches will ask you to take a self-awareness survey so that they can gain a better understanding of your personality, temperament, and management style. One is the Enneagram.

### THE ENNEAGRAM

Our personalities are made up of three things: temperament, childhood experiences (whether our instincts, as we saw in chapter one, have been satisfied), and the choices we make every day. The Enneagram—"number" and "gram" in ancient Greek—is believed to have been created by the Sufis, who were Islamic mystics, over one thousand years ago (see figure F, page 75). It was brought to Europe by the Russian mystical teacher G. I. Gurdjieff in the 1920s and arrived in the United States in the early 1970s. The Enneagram surveys and charts your temperament. Once you understand it, you can learn how to manage it to find happiness and success.

Some use the Enneagram as an interpretive tool to point out our limitations. Others use it to better understand our potential. I'm squarely in the latter camp. Influential psychiatrist Carl Jung, also a believer in a more positive view, said that we don't help the psyche by villainizing its shadows, but by integrating them.[2] Like all self-knowledge tools, the Enneagram's value depends on the interpreter. I use it for coaching because it goes much deeper, with multiple dimensions, than other survey instruments, and it lines up well with opportunities for emotional and spiritual development.

"Unevolved," or immature, number types are people who, fundamentally, haven't done their self-awareness work yet. "Evolved" number types bring all dimensions of self to their decisions: mental, emotional, and spiritual. They have a balanced perspective, and if a decision involves a team or an organization, they will prioritize "we" over "me."

Knowing your temperament is a first step, and it throws light on who we can most naturally build trust with, and with whom we need to work harder. With its spiritual roots, the circle of the Enneagram also urges us toward transformation and interdependence by seeing everyone as part of a whole; no type is left out.

The Enneagram identifies nine temperament types, which are our most elemental selves—the DNA we're born with, if you will. Our type represents our core motivation, and we each have one. Practitioners use various names for the nine categories, but they're all variations on the same idea. Here are mine, developed after years studying the Enneagram and using it as a coaching tool.

1. Perfectionist
2. Kind-hearted
3. Self-Tester
4. Romantic

5. Puzzle Solver
6. Loyalist
7. Fun Lover
8. Power Broker
9. Peacemaker

Of course, we all have each of these tendencies, but we also have a dominant temperament. This is your individuality. You can find plenty of free Enneagram surveys online, or in books (please see "Your Turn" for suggestions). If you work with a coach who understands the figure, they'll be able to offer more customized guidance.

### Interrelationships and Wings

Figure F shows the arrows that go to and from each personality category. Think of this as an anatomy chart. All of us in the general population can use this as a guide. Once we know which number we are, either through a survey or a coach, we can see how we interrelate with

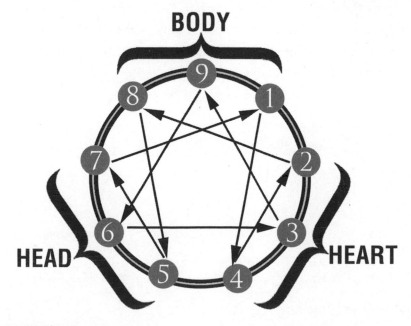

**FIGURE F:** The Nine Types

other number types. The arrow represents how you relate to another temperament, which is particularly helpful when you're building any kind of relationship, including work rapport. The arrows that don't connect show the types that are not compatible with your inner nature, which is equally important information when you're trying to understand why you might have a difficult relationship with a boss, peer, or report. Each of us has four of these "incompatible" types. Finally, the "wings," or numbers on either side, reveal a deeper and wider perspective on the additional qualities that make you *you*. We refer to the wings as the personality types that we "lean" into.

## Energy Groups, or How We're Powered

Each of the nine types is clustered into one of three energy groups— Body, Heart, and Head—which is our "fuel supply," or how we're empowered by our temperaments to respond or react to things (see figure G). When you understand your energy, you are fully charged up to reach your potential.

I'm a 3, "leaning" 2. As a Self-Tester, I'm very competitive with myself, and when emotionally and spiritually out of whack, I can easily become a workaholic who is driven to excel with no bounds. Self-Testers can also be "shape shifters"—in the dark about their own emotions but attentive to others' if it helps them reach their goals.

| ENERGY GROUP | TEMPERAMENT TYPES | WHEN UNDER STRESS . . . | EXTREME REACTION TO EMOTIONS |
|---|---|---|---|
| Body | 8–9–1 | Show aggression and are quick to ignite | *Life is a full-body blow* |
| Heart | 2–3–4 | Seek attachment | *Feel everyone else's feelings* |
| Head | 5–6–7 | Pull away | *"Think" their feelings* |

**FIGURE G:** Energy Triads

Unevolved 3s often stay in "me" mode. An evolved 3, on the other hand, can be visionary, adaptive, inspiring, and an effective builder of organizations.

The wing type I lean into is a 2, Kind-hearted. This means I am drawn to others, but if someone's needs are in conflict with a deadline, I might communicate in a terse fashion. As with all EQ Fitness, the goal is to find balance in order to weave through work and life fluidly. As I'm in the triad of Heart (2–3–4), I react instinctively with a heart-to-heart kind of connection. As a 3, I have a direct touch point to 6, my husband Bill's type (phew, a coincidence?), and none with 8, 7, 5, or 1, which basically means these people will more easily drive me crazy.

Back to my husband, Bill, a 6, or Loyalist. Even though we have connecting points, it doesn't mean our communication styles are always compatible. The Enneagram helped me to understand him, so I wouldn't get offended by or impatient with how he sometimes reacts, especially his instinct to pause and really think things through. Once, when I suggested a vacation spot I was excited to visit, instead of reacting enthusiastically, he pulled out the computer to do some research. Our friends John and Barb had been there, so he also wanted to reach out and get their opinions. See what I mean? *Let's just go!* But that's Bill: he prefers to check it out first. Another benefit of doing mindfulness work is that I now know how to pause, too, recognizing that this is how he's built, and we're just different. And truth be told, all the research time he puts in, which I'm unwilling to do, makes our trips better (as hard as that can be to admit).

## MORE PERSONALITY INVENTORIES

The most popular personality test is the Myers-Briggs Type Indicator, which is how most of us learned of "introverts" and "extroverts." Others include DiSC (Dominance, Influence, Steadiness, Conscientious-

), the 360 reviews, Hogan Personality Inventory, Influence Style
cator, Energize2Lead, and Birkman. Most are available online for
a fee.

Executive coach Erin Wolf uses the DiSC. "With the Myers-Briggs
or Birkman, you learn about yourself," she said. "With the DiSC, I help
clients understand themselves but also read others. That way they can
learn how to identify and interact with others according to a style
defined by DiSC, which solves part of the puzzle." Like the Enneagram, DiSC is of great help to understand the people you meet and
might work with.

Executive coach Jim Emerick finds Energize2Lead especially helpful in a work context; he feels it's the best assessment of leadership
potential. It asks questions to discern three things: what we like to do
most, what we have been conditioned to do, and what we need to do
based on our instincts. The results come in colors that represent the
energy levels we expend in various situations. We use energy when
we're pushing up against areas that don't come naturally, so the more
energy expended, the more stress.

Jim asked me to take the test. I was high red (independent) and
blue (inquisitive and visualizing). "You fit the perfect entrepreneur
profile," he told me. His notes said, "Avoid telling Susan what, when,
and how to do things." Oh yeah, there I was, the bossy dreamer. This
tool can help coaches get a fuller picture of your leadership capabilities and goals.

Empowered with self-knowledge, it's time to consider the personality, or culture, of the companies you're considering.

## CULTURE, OR HOW TO AVOID
## DYSFUNCTION JUNCTION

When we were in the maniacal building phase of HGTV, I hired someone for a senior position. She'd come from a media company and had

excellent strategic skills—I could tell just by our conversations. About three months into the job, she came into my office and closed the door. "Could you please give me the org chart?" she asked. "I can't figure out how to navigate this place. It was so much easier at my last company." As we talked more, I realized she wanted something HGTV couldn't give her: clear lines of authority to the senior staff; a sense of hierarchy. In that moment I saw that I'd failed her, because cultural fit is so key, and we hadn't even discussed it. We were a matrixed organization, and in those first years, all senior people were on board and accountable to the full enterprise, even for things that didn't officially fall into their department.

For example, our head of advertising sales was also spot-checking ads; while we craved every dollar of revenue, we didn't want to put on the air something like compostable toilets that can swallow eighteen golf balls, or ten-minute face-lifts. Once, he brought a spot for Master Lock to the senior team's attention. It showed a hand firing a gun, and then a Master Lock barely dented by the bullet. *A great demonstration of durability, right?* The problem was we were building a brand about shelter and sanctuary, not guns and bullets. We vetoed it, and he walked away from his commission. He was as emotionally invested in what went on the air as our programmers were, even though he wasn't responsible for the ratings.

As for the exec I'd hired without giving good color on our culture, she stayed for a while, but the fit was always uncomfortable for her, and those who interacted with her.

I can't say enough about the importance of cultural fit. It's as critical as having the right technical skills, maybe even more so, because you can learn those things on the job. The challenge with cultural fit is you don't always know what you're getting until you sign on.

Susan McLaughlin was a C-suite executive at Kodak, and later president of BellSouth, then a seven-billion-dollar company. She is now with Pierce Consulting Partners, a boutique executive search firm, a small shop that engages in the highest level of searches. She suggested some questions to ask HR when considering a job, and if you can meet or speak with some future colleagues, that's great too:

1. *How do decisions get made?* This gets to whether it's a collaborative culture.
2. *Does leadership speak with one voice?* This gets to whether there is unity around the company's vision and strategy at the very top, because if there's not, the whole culture of the place will be disjointed, and long-term success is in peril for the organization, and ergo, you.
3. *How do you get ahead there?* Take a look at the 4 Cs under "Company Culture, Domestic and International" on page 82, for why this matters.
4. *How do people in the company talk about their colleagues?* Ask to speak with a potential coworker, and have them describe one or two others they work with. If they respond with gossip or negative words, that's a huge red flag.

She also recommends going to job search sites like Glassdoor to look at comments. It's not foolproof, as disgruntled employees can post there as easily as anyone else, but it might offer some insight. Finally, she suggests learning what employees do for fun. Some have a casual approach that may or may not work for you. Susan shared that one company had Pajama Day on Fridays. Do you want to go work at a company that has Pajama Day?

In the last couple of years, more and more offer letters contain "non-disparagement clauses," which breed a culture of secrecy, although these are most prevalent in separation agreements. If you see one of those clauses, proceed with caution: you might be heading to Dysfunction Junction.

## JUST BECAUSE IT'S SILICON VALLEY . . .

. . . doesn't mean every culture is the same. When **Mark Hale** was executive vice president of global operations and chief technology officer at SNI, he traveled to Silicon Valley several times a year with his team. Their purpose was to find companies launching products that made sense for SNI and to offer guidance in turn. "It dawned on me how the various cultures of these places was so different," he said. "On one trip we visited HP [formerly Hewlett-Packard], Google, and Apple. At HP, we met in one of the first places they built there when starting out. There were pieces of the original founders' offices that had been preserved. Everything smacked of rich heritage and a reverence for the past. Those we met with had been there a long time."

At Google, the contrast was startling. "It was mass chaos. The receptionist didn't know who we were or recognize who we were supposed to meet." They were finally led to a small cubicle. A young woman rushed in, disheveled and sleepy, and apologized for being late.

"She said she'd been there until 4:00 a.m. working on something. You could tell that even though she was tired, she was excited and energized by the project. It felt like the whole place was alive and bubbling with new ideas."

Apple, their final stop, was just the opposite from Google with its over-the-top organization. "They had access badges waiting for us with our photos already imprinted on them. The whole day was scripted and organized. They had our nameplates in front of the chairs we were each to sit in. It's like when you walk into most Apple stores, you have a really orderly experience."

No industry is homogenous, whether it's tech in Silicon Valley or the media world from which I came. When I was at HBO, the atmosphere was very social; NBC was filled with lawyers, and our discussions revolved around our legal "leverage," or power; and SNI was a rollup of HP, Google, and Apple. The SNI start-up team came from either entrepreneurial companies or places where process and order were prized. While we were a start-up, we were owned by E.W. Scripps, a 150-year-old newspaper company rich with the Scripps family heritage, as well as journalistic roots, and thus we put a premium on accurate content. Our own emerging "history" mattered too, and we tried to keep it alive with big celebrations every five years, including a ten-year anniversary book with fun memories and stories of why our core values mattered.

The companies in any business sector come to life each day in their own ways. A unique combination of each company's history and growth, and the EQ Fitness tools deployed by its leaders and managers, trickles down to its workers.

## COMPANY CULTURE, DOMESTIC AND INTERNATIONAL

It can be helpful to think of the 4 Cs, developed by *Fast Company* co-founder Bill Taylor, when evaluating corporate cultures: company as **community**, company as a **constellation** of stars, company as **cause-driven**, and **compact** companies.

The first kind of workplace prioritizes trust, teamwork, and peer-to-peer loyalty. In the second, folks are hard-driving and competitive; it's sink or swim. But superstars can be built there. The third category focuses on collective impact and buy-in to the overarching mission. The fourth culture is labeled as "compact" because it is not driven by scale to succeed. Of the broad categories, Taylor wrote, "what matters at work is whether the value proposition that drives your company is in sync with the values that motivate you, whether the culture that defines life inside an organization is compatible with your personal style, and whether the people with whom you work make you think, grow, even laugh."[3]

At HGTV, we were a blend of community and collective impact, and I think that was a prime example of EQ Fitness: the work mission rose above individual self-interest. Or, said another way, when an individual's self-interest is in sync with a company's mission, that makes success much easier for *both*. Those at HGTV who really "got" our brand lived it. They spoke fondly about their homes and how their weekends were often spent at home-improvement stores ferreting out gizmos and materials for a new project.

The last time we met, an executive I coach named Paula gave me some essential oils she personally uses, and the packaging read: "Seed to Seal. It's not a slogan. It's our calling." This company aims to be a "good steward of the planet." Its commitment to sustainability is part of its DNA, the way home was part of HGTV's. Research studies show consumers want brands to take a stand on social issues, and to communicate their values with words and actions.[4]

Only you can judge job and culture fit. Organizations are made up of people who, ideally, move together toward shared goals. Find out if there is a "together" there, or if the place is full of independent operators. Employees at organizations rich with EQF move in rhythm.

If you're considering an international job, or working for a foreign-based company, make sure you try to get a handle on that country's culture. *Harvard Business Review* provides a basic overview of what you might find in various countries and regions:[5]

- *Consensual and egalitarian*: Everyone is urged to have input, but it can take longer to get things done.
- *Top-down and egalitarian*: If you want to stand apart from others, speak up, politely, even if your opinion differs from another of higher rank. Once a decision is made, move on and support it.
- *Top-down and hierarchical*: Decision-making resides at the top of the company.
- *Consensual and hierarchical*: People are asked their opinions, but eventually the highest-ranking person makes the decision.

Understanding the different ways things are done wherever you end up is key to your success and fulfillment.

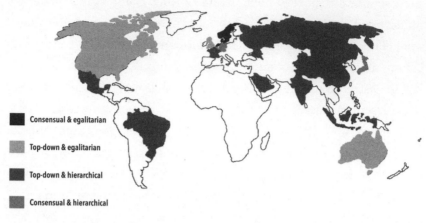

**Consensual & egalitarian**

**Top-down & egalitarian**

**Top-down & hierarchical**

**Consensual & hierarchical**

**FIGURE H:** International Work Styles

## MOVING YOUR CAREER ALONG

It takes time to work out our professional identities. Our lives are constantly opening up and expanding. Admitting that you need a change, or transitioning from one job to the next—or one industry into another—can feel like a step sideways or, heaven forbid, backward. That couldn't be further from the truth. Growing pains are growing signs of EQ Fitness. You've become mindful of what your heart wants.

I've heard people say, "My work is what I do; it's not who I am." It was always hard for me to divorce my self-worth from something I spent most of my waking hours on. Sure, some of us get in, get out, go home, and have a beer. That may even be the job you have, or want. It all depends on what phase of life you're in when considering a job, and your temperament.

### EARLY-CAREER MOVES

The first few years of working rely on a decent amount of trial and error. How can you possibly know all the things you want from a job in your twenties? There are plenty of famous examples of people who found their real passion in their thirties, forties, and beyond. Julia Child had no interest in French cuisine until she was in her late thirties—and then, as we know, she changed the world. Do your research, but then dive in. Finding the right fit is born of taking a little risk.

When she was twenty-two, author Leigh Ann Henion worked as a receptionist at a corporate law office. She was bored stiff. It felt like her soul was being sucked out of her body each day. So she finally worked up the courage to quit. Her boss, a lead lawyer, was indignant. He told her to grow up. She'd never find a job to make her happy, he said, because it didn't exist. "You think *I* want to be here?" he challenged her. His identity had merged with his checking account.

But she wanted a job where her heart could sing. For half the wage, she started working at a seasonal shop that sold stained-glass kaleidoscopes. She loved engaging with the locals who strolled in, and really loved holding these tiny, expensive treasures in her hand. She couldn't afford any of them, but she could be among them and marvel at their beauty. Her previous job reminded her to never become someone who resented her work, and to be true to herself. She could choose to feel alive.[6]

When I was about Leigh Ann's age, I got a summer internship working at General Motors. This was a high-class internship for a Detroit girl. *My first corporate job!*

The first thing I noticed was how quiet the place was. I thought maybe sound was absorbed by the thick carpeting that lined the hallways, but no, it wasn't that. People talked in hushed tones, like they were in a library. Almost everyone had an office, and they generally stayed in them. My job was to balance some guy's checking account— not exactly the riveting stuff I had pictured. CEO Mary Barra is challenging all those outdated ways, and GM is much different today, but at that time it wasn't just autocratic. Employees were expected to be reverential toward the white, old, all-male management. Yuck.

When I went on an interview at HBO for my first media job, the place was *noisy*. People were milling around. I fell in love.

If you're at a place and it's not quite right, honor that. Millennials have a reputation for moving around more than prior generations did, and I think that's smart. Most companies aren't showing loyalty to them either; it's hard to give back what you're not given. And you'll never know if you don't try. A young neighbor of mine set up a storefront business to troubleshoot computer issues. But about six months in, he closed up shop and was planning to open a pretzel venue in the mall. He'd been staring at computer screens for ten years and had just had enough!

This is why having the willingness to pick up the tools in this book is so important. They're a shortcut to job satisfaction. It wasn't until I was thirty-nine that I began truly enjoying my work. You don't have to wait that long.

## MIDCAREER MOVES

CNBC hadn't been a match for me because of its culture, but also because I couldn't get excited about being a human barker for a financial news product. At HGTV, all that changed because of the culture we built, because of my teams, and because HGTV was about home— rootedness. I needed that grounding, and I was all in.

I was at SNI for sixteen years. *How had that happened?* I believe I stayed there longer than anywhere before because I was able to wear a lot of hats over the years, starting with getting distribution for HGTV and Food Network, then launching our international sales arm, and then starting our video-on-demand division. These roles filled my need to stay entrepreneurial. SNI was outgrowing our space, so we underwent a two-year construction project to house all of us in one place. One Friday afternoon, we gave employees and their families a sneak peek. They streamed in from all over the city, laughing and talking excitedly. I stood in the lobby of that shiny new HQ and watched it all with a smile. And thought, *I'm through here.*

The place was thriving, and I knew it would live on quite nicely without me. It was time for fresh leadership to take charge. But knowing something and being willing to act on it takes constant EQF practice. It was hard to envision not coming to work there each day! But, like the game of subtraction we talked about in chapter two, it's important to let go of things when the time is right. I had to do it if I was going to explore the opportunities waiting in the wings. All organizations need to bring in leaders with fresh eyes at some point too.

To know when the time is right for you, follow your gut. Today, I write books, speak, and mentor. John Clark left his longtime career to open a coffee-roasting business. CBS entertainment chief Nina Tassler, who's brought us such great fare as *The Good Wife* and *The Big Bang Theory*, had an extended contract through 2017, but in 2015 she had a yearning to leave. "I know I'm done," she said in an interview.[7] Doing the inner work helps you make the right choices. I'll say it once more: our hearts often tell us what our minds don't want to hear.

## CAREER AND SOUL WORK

The word "vocation" is rooted in the Latin word for voice, *voce*. Work can be a calling if you have the ear to listen. The bestselling author David Whyte worked as a naturalist guide on the Galápagos Islands until he knew it was time to transition to a "larger language than science. Somewhere out there beyond the islands was another work and another life."[8] Today Whyte is an internationally acclaimed poet. I can only tell you, from many of us who have done it, that transitioning careers midlife begins from the inside. It's a feeling that keeps yanking your chain. For some, the motivation is to find a job that's a truer expression of your passion. With deeper self-knowledge, you just know there's a better fit out there. You're looking to have a more integrated life, something that merges your personal identity with your professional one.

Whyte describes the need to open up a part of himself as "some energy other than that which comes from the constant application of effort and will."[9] He was describing a job that moves your soul. Nourishing your inner life will provide these moments of discernment.

## REFLECTING ON BUSYNESS

The wanderings of my career inspired me to create a weekend retreat for a group of women looking to remake their lives, women who were seeking a way back into the world through meaningful work. The attendees were from all over the country and from all walks of life— businesspeople, community organizers, teachers.

The first thing we did was to slow down. I held the retreat at my favorite place, St. Mary's in Tennessee (the same spot I hosted that Michigan State University retreat, which has over two hundred acres of walking paths and panoramic mountaintop views). This retreat, however, would serve a very different purpose; my hope was that it might lay groundwork for new forms of self-expression. I explained that we needed to move to a speed other than "busy" for this weekend. Busyness can be a reflection of your need to feel, well, needed. There's the joke about the CEO who hails a cab and the driver asks, "Where to?" And the CEO says, "It doesn't matter! I'm needed everywhere!" The thing about busyness is the faster you go, the faster you'll keep going as the momentum ratchets up to overdrive. Suddenly everything is urgent. When, really, very little is. I recall my first financial planner writing that "family, friends, faith" is what a paycheck is about. I thought about it for maybe two seconds and told him my paycheck was about paying off the mortgage. We were both right, but at that moment I didn't have the ability or tools to take on his perspective.

At the retreat, we spent the weekend in a more reflective mode. We did Centering Prayer. We wrote down our favorite childhood activities, those things that always brought a smile. We drew images of how we spent our time at ten, twenty, and thirty years old, and what our ideal *today* would look like: How would we prefer spending our time with hobbies and work?

These exercises revealed a whole lot. For some, they reinforced their hunches. For others, the exercises opened up new ways to consider their choices. I got in touch with a childhood memory that felt like a harbinger of my work today. Growing up, I loved to act, but I couldn't sing or dance, and was gawky, so that ruled out leading-lady roles. Once I was Pigpen in *A Charlie Brown Christmas*, and in *How to Succeed in Business Without Really Trying*, I was a mop woman with no lines; I walked across the stage mopping the floor as the crew changed the set behind me. I kept telling myself *there are no small parts!* It doesn't surprise me that today I love to work with and speak to groups. Our childhood selves play an enormous role in our work choices, even though you might relate to your work in different ways over your lifetime. You keep evolving, and your work comes along for the ride. At times it's the driver, and other times, the friendly passenger. EQ Fitness gives us tools to see the whole panorama and respond with our full humanity.

## BECOMING EQ FIT

I don't have to tell you the weight of practical matters when it comes to a career. Matters like a paycheck. Sometimes our work is chosen for us because we need to pay the rent or the mortgage. But I also want you to dream. Make sure you're choosing wisely and authentically when you have the freedom to do so. Work to separate your truth from how you've been conditioned and how others' expectations might weigh in. Think of it this way: The people in your orbit, who are voicing an opinion on what's best for you? You'll be no good for *them* if you make work choices without integrity, because you'll just be stressed and unhappy.

EQ Fit people have the ability to discern what's right for their lives. Good job fit leads to peace of mind, and so many moments of real satisfaction in work! From there, it's easier to build relationships based on trust, and to find what you're meant to become. What your soul sets up in plain sight.

# WILLINGNESS
## Dropping Your Emotional Armor

Habits can be hard to break. You are going to need support in the form of practices that help you learn willingness, and resources you can turn to during this process of opening up. Your mind—and body, including your nervous system—needs to get on board. In my experience, it's faster, easier, and more comfortable to use proven approaches, whether from eastern or western tradition.

Below is a small sample of practices that work to foster willingness. No need to do every single one: if a couple resonate, make them into regular routines, continue to explore, and see where they lead you. This is your time, your life, and your emotional fitness. Make the support suit *you*.

## PRACTICE:
## Managing Social Anxiety

### BE IN COMMUNITY INSTEAD OF ISOLATED.

So often our anxiety comes from our own busy minds. When we meet up with others, we shift the focus from ourselves to them. Get out of the house and read in a public place like a coffee shop or a library. Just being around other people can start to settle your anxiety.

Ask a friend to come along for a walk in a pretty place.

Join a club that interests you, like a book club or a chess club or a choir. Look at local community centers, churches, or sites like Meetup .com to see what's in your area.

## BECOME AN ACTIVE LISTENER.

If your anxiety tends to make you distracted, practice being present with other people. Take a breath. Put down your phone or close your computer. Make eye contact.

Especially in big-picture or difficult conversations, pay attention to what the other person is saying and note their key points. When it's your turn to talk, summarize what they said, beginning with something like "So what I've heard you say is . . ." By mirroring, you acknowledge their perspective before stating yours. Once you've restated their point and they've agreed that you understood correctly, then you can respond. Done well, active listening slows down our distraction and weakens our tendency to react without processing. It is key in building relationships of any kind.

# PRACTICE:
## Managing Anger

## TUNE OUT THE NONSENSE.

When someone at work or at home says something thoughtless, follow Ruth Bader Ginsburg's advice. She says that in any relationship, it helps to "be a little deaf." Take a deep breath, and return to what you were doing. Reacting in anger, however justified, will only lead to bad consequences.

## BE THE FIRST TO MAKE THINGS RIGHT.

I recently had a testy phone conversation. We both hung up unhappy with nothing resolved. The next day I took a deep breath and called back. I started by saying, "I was really tired yesterday so I may have been short with you." This second call was productive. Try taking the initiative and accepting responsibility—if you own any part of the issue, acknowledge it. You'll win loyalty and trust by reaching out first, and being vulnerable enough to admit your part.

## COUNT TO FIVE.

When you feel yourself about to react in anger, count to five. Press the pause button. This will help you to regroup emotionally and avoid blowing up.

# PRACTICE:
## Self-Acceptance and Self-Love

## WRITE A LOVE LETTER TO YOURSELF.

This can be one paragraph, or many. Start with something you tackled and overcame as a child. Include at least one example each of a personal and professional accomplishment. Then include what your best friend would say about you, and any other uplifting things people may have said of you. Now, it's your turn to say something good, from the heart, about you. Keep it somewhere handy. When you are feeling vulnerable reread it.

## TALK YOURSELF UP—TO YOURSELF.

Before a meeting, remind yourself: "My voice is worth listening to." Speak up at least once in the meeting. You'll feel more confident when you both prepare and take action.

## DREAM DAILY.

Give yourself the gift of thirty minutes a day to go within. You can be writing, drawing, browsing Pinterest, doing spiritual reading, or just paging through your favorite magazine. Move your mind away from your daily demands for this time. If you dream enough, insights will bubble up that may guide you in a whole new direction!

# PRACTICE:
## Managing Stress

## BREATHE CONSCIOUSLY.

Maybe you've already noticed how *key* breathing is in most of these exercises. Breathing consciously helps slow down our swirling thoughts and soothe our tendencies to react. When we breathe deep into our bellies, we calm our nervous system and make room for new thinking and wisdom.

- Sit straight up on the back of a chair or on a cushion on the floor. Inhale deeply.
- As you exhale, squeeze breath out until your lungs are completely empty. Sit and repeat for at least five to ten minutes if possible. (If that seems like an unfathomably long amount of time, try one minute—or thirty seconds. Whatever your hesitation, just *start*.)

## MEDITATE.

Most forms of meditation try to lessen chaotic thinking, also known as "monkey mind," through interrupting thoughts with a "mantra," some repeated word or sound. To begin, sit with your eyes closed and back straight, bringing your attention to your inhale and exhale the same way you do in conscious breathing. It can be helpful to listen to some audio guides. Visit the UC San Diego Center for Mindfulness or the Insight Meditation Society to find guided meditations.

- Sit straight up on the floor (you can use a cushion or two) or erect in a chair.
- Close your eyes. Take a few deep breaths.
- Notice your body where it touches the floor (or the cushions) or the chair. Notice the weight and heat, tension or lightness of your legs, arms, torso, skin. If your stomach is tense, let it soften.
- Open your mind to the present moment, exactly as it is, good and bad. Don't fight against it.
- If thoughts and judgments come up, use your mantra, like the word "steady." Don't engage them.
- Resist the temptation to judge yourself for whatever thoughts and experiences you are having.
- Return to noticing the present moment exactly as it is.
- Practice daily for small amounts of time, and gradually increase the length of your practice to twenty minutes or longer.

## ACCESS DIVINE AWARENESS
## WITH CENTERING PRAYER.

- Choose a sacred word as a symbol of your intention to consent to Spirit's presence and action within you.

- Sit comfortably with your eyes closed.
- Introduce the sacred word into your consciousness by either saying it silently or seeing it in your mind's eye.
- When ordinary or worrying thoughts come up to distract you, don't resist them, just let them come, and if you're engaged with them, return your attention ever so gently to the sacred word. In this practice, the focus is on releasing, not resisting, thoughts.
- Over time, aim to do this for twenty minutes per session. At the end, remain in silence with your eyes closed for another few minutes to allow the practice to settle into your system.

Some of the more than twenty forms of meditation are **chakra** (focusing on energy centers, done during yoga), **Zen** (with roots in Zen Buddhism), **Transcendental Meditation** (focusing on a mantra), and **loving-kindness** (focusing on empathy and compassion). Try anything that sounds interesting until you find the practice that best suits you.

## VISUALIZE.

Release stress or other unwanted behaviors or thoughts by visualizing them in a balloon you're holding, then slowly release the balloon into the air. As the wind takes it, your hand is empty and open, palm up, ready to receive something else.

## MEDITATE IN MOTION.

Moving meditation is walking while concentrating on the slow, steady rhythm of breath. Daniel Headrick, who leads weekly meditation groups, says that he steps with intention to the earth below him, picturing a flower, which blooms whenever he lifts his foot. The benefits are similar to those from other forms of meditation: moving into a place of calm and gentleness with yourself, nature, and those you may see as you walk and later around you.

## DO YOGA.

Yoga helps connect our minds to our bodies. Our spirit too; some say yoga lets your soul catch up with your body. If you're hard-driving or full of nervous energy, you probably spend a lot of time in your head. You may neglect or even abuse your body. Believe it or not, this is not helping you advance in any sphere of life, much less the workplace. By connecting mind and spirit to body, you can access an entirely different intelligence. People often figure out the solution to big problems when their monkey minds take a back seat and their unconscious mind is allowed to work on it.

Yoga feels great physically too. You *don't* have to be flexible to do it. Get out of your head and into the flow. If you've never done yoga before, find a workshop for beginners that will show you the basics.

The *Yoga Journal* and Yoga International websites explain the different kinds of practices available and demonstrate poses to suit your level of ability. Team up with a friend so you have someone to explore with—which has the added benefit of being a part of a community as well.

## SIGN UP FOR A RETREAT WEEKEND.

As you've probably gathered by now, my favorite place for a recharge is St. Mary's retreat house in Sewanee, Tennessee, and anyone can go. Find a place that appeals to you for a weekend getaway. Time away in a healing space is important.

# PRACTICE:
## Letting Go

We often hold tightly to our opinions and beliefs. This is left-brained thinking. You can't open space for new ideas when you're clinging to old patterns. You can do this one alone, but I usually do it when I'm leading a group.

- Put your right and left hands flat on each thigh.
- Pick up a pencil with your left hand and grip it, with your fist down.
- Flip your right hand open and faceup, resting on your right thigh.
- Grip the pencil even tighter.

Reflect on what you feel physically: Tenseness in your left arm? Your neck? How does that compare with your right side? This exercise is a physical representation of what happens when we live just in our left brains. The left hand, all tight, represents our left brain. The right hand, loose and free, our right brain. This exercise shows how good it feels to access our right brains.

# PRACTICE:
## Talk It Out

### FIND A THERAPIST.

When you decide to talk to a therapist, you will need to make some choices. Do you want to see a psychologist, psychiatrist, social worker, licensed counselor, or even an art therapist? Trusted friends can provide recommendations, so ask for guidance. Then do some research.

The American Psychological Association (apa.org), GoodTherapy.org, and even WebMD.com have tips on how to find a trained professional who can help.

## JOIN A THERAPY GROUP OR SHARE CIRCLE.

Group therapy helps you put your problems into perspective. In hearing others' experiences, you'll begin to see that you are not the only one struggling, and you will learn how others handled similar issues. There are groups for people in the grips of fear, worry, or regret; for people dealing with PTSD, grief, abuse, and addiction, just to name a few. Check with your local mental health associations or search *Psychology Today*'s website (www.psychologytoday.com).

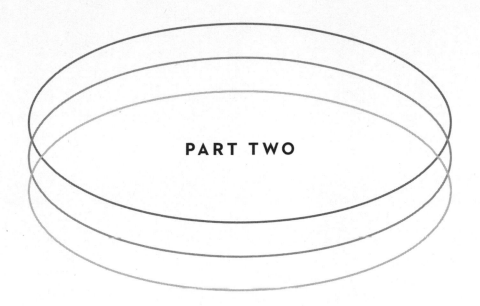

**PART TWO**

# TRUST

*The way to make people trust-worthy
is to trust them.*

—ERNEST HEMINGWAY[1]

t's uncanny how certain memories stay with you. Ten months into my role as COO at HGTV, first-time budget projections were due to our CFO, **Jim Clayton,** by midnight, and I was working from home to finish everything. I pressed Send at about 11:45 p.m.

Afterward, as I reviewed them one last time, I began to hyperventilate. I'd made an enormous error, one that would cost my groups necessary funding. At my former company, NBC, something like this would have had my management railing and the finance people in a snit. I didn't really know Jim yet, and I was unfamiliar with Scripps corporate finance, because he managed those communications. I called Jim at about 12:30 a.m. and told him what I'd done. This is the part I'll never forget: He said, "No sweat, Suz, let's you and I get in early tomorrow. We'll fix it together." My trust-o-meter shot up to the sky. I knew that he had my back, and that I could trust him to work with me, not against me.

Jim's response was highly EQ Fit, and a model for how emotionally fit leaders can dramatically change their workplaces. The harsh reaction I'd come to expect at my former company would have been unproductive, especially since I already knew I had messed up and took ownership of my mistake. By moving directly to a plan of action, Jim offered a solution that included collaboration, as well as forgiveness (a powerful trust emotion we'll touch upon in chapter six). While he made me feel happy and supported, and that's essential, it was also important that we immediately moved to fix it—together—since my mistake could have had a negative ripple effect through the organization. EQ Fitness considers practical things like accountability to a company's economic health, and it has a higher purpose too: the emotional health of the larger community it serves—its employees, consumers, and customers.

We could marshal any number of emotions to develop our newfound willingness into EQ Fitness. I chose trust because it was hardest for me. People could trust *me* to follow through because I got cooperation when I did. It was just more efficient that way. But trusting someone else? That was really hard. So I figure if this self-reliant soul could learn how to trust people at work, you can too. You'll have to relinquish some control, but here's the honest truth: complete control is an illusion. Life is so much bigger than you. Trust is a practice of humility—something all leaders could use more of.

I also chose trust because it means letting people in, building the community we need to feel whole and fulfilled as we work. And I chose it because of the returns it pays for your career. Trust makes your job easier because you let others assist, and it helps you work faster because there's no time spent stuck in the muck that distrust breeds.

Trust starts as an inside job. You have to foster enough self-respect to know that you add value to a team or company, that others need you, and that they can benefit from what you offer. This isn't arrogance. This is trusting yourself.

There is a wide spectrum of what it looks like to trust others. It could simply mean believing enough in someone to get out of your own head and listen. Or it could mean a willingness to take a leap with someone by your side, even when neither of you can see ground below. It's like faith that way, because when you believe in something bigger than you, you've jumped off a spiritual ledge.

What I love best about trust is that it instills the one emotion that always inspires us to press on: hope. Trust is hope with a track record.

Even if you don't trust me, I hope you'll listen to Adam Bryant, a journalist who collected more than *five million words* over a dozen years writing Corner Office, the *New York Times* Sunday column on leadership. In his final column, he wrote, "If you were to force me to rank the most important qualities of effective leadership, I would put trustworthiness at the top."[2]

Let's look at this tricky but powerful emotion and how to deploy it for success and job satisfaction.

# CHAPTER FIVE

# TRUST IN ACTION

*Be humble, for you are made of earth.*
*Be noble, for you are made of stars.*
—SERBIAN PROVERB

M ary Ellen Brewington, who opened up about her fear of failure in chapter one, told me this story about a beloved member of her work family.

Bobby Hood worked with me at Cherokee Distributing for a long time. Suddenly, he passed away from cancer, and a wave of grief flooded our company. What made him so great? He was authentic, reliable, trustworthy. He never said much, and you could never get Bobby on text or email. He'd only call you or talk to you person-to-person, because he never wanted to misunderstand someone, or be misunderstood.

A few days after his death, a coworker told me a story about Bobby, who one day saw a new deliveryman at Cherokee working in cold conditions. Bobby told the delivery guy his shoes weren't proper shoes for a beer man. The driver said he couldn't afford new shoes right now. A few days later, the deliveryman had new work boots. Bobby had quietly gone out to purchase these new boots. No fanfare.

People say the Sampsons [Mary Ellen's family] built Cherokee. People like Bobby are the ones who built Cherokee. Show up, do your best, lend a hand. Bobby did this not with his words, but with actions.

## WHY TRUST MATTERS

Trust building is an exercise in willingness, and the next step in your program to strengthen your EQ Fitness. Bobby Hood built trust quietly through actions that drew others to him.

Trust building expresses itself outwardly as action. Inside, it's an emotion, a feeling of safety with someone or a team. People build relationships of trust for lots of reasons. It makes our jobs easier, because you feel more comfortable taking calculated risks or learning new things with those you know have your back. You work harder because you're emotionally invested. You can have more fun with those you trust, too, as you're looser with them. Trust allows you to focus all your mental firepower, without worrying about the disruptive noise that can invade our relationships. It takes time to build, but the payoff is in the quality of and satisfaction with your performance. You work better and you're happier doing it. We *could* stay surface level with our colleagues; in fact, it's prudent to do with the scoundrels you'll meet in this chapter. But the way I figure it, we spend a huge part of our waking hours at work, so why not try for an experience that's a little deeper, a little richer, with a profound promise of fulfillment?

Trust binds you to teammates, and it can transform a regular company doing regular business into a market leader. It was, without a doubt, the force that drove HGTV into its top position in lifestyle TV. Most of us had experienced cutthroat corporate cultures and brought that experience to the start of something new. But more important, we brought a collective hope that this time, we could forge a company with enough humanity to attract others.

The seven of us who started HGTV "confessed" in one of our first meetings together that our old workplaces were just different shades of hostile. Those with a few more birthdays than I had worked in multiple companies with ruthless "every man for himself" type cultures. I had been on both sides. At my first company, HBO, relationships of trust were common, whereas in my six-plus years at NBC, the corporate people treated the rest of us as slow-to-learn children. My HGTV teammates shared their relatable experiences with honesty, which, as we learned in part one, is so important to growing in emotional fitness.

Trust is fragile; it takes work every day to earn it, and it can be damaged in an instant. EQ Fit people know to watch for signs of disconnect and to check in one-on-one so you don't go akimbo. You can only do your part; if your colleague doesn't also work at it, there's no foundation of mutual respect. They're accountable too.

**Trusting a *colleague*** gives you an emotional safety net if a situation turns challenging. With that person by your side, you're empowered to press on and not give up.

**Trusting your *team*** means that whenever you all convene, it's not a waste of time; something constructive will result.

**Trusting your *leaders*** gives you cover to take risks with the confidence that they'll keep steering the enterprise in the right direction, so that you can be a part of something lasting. You trust the guidance and learning they provide too.

While trust is an emotion, trust *building* takes action. The great news about being EQ Fit is that we can all get there. I never thought I'd learn how to trust others, especially men, but it turns out that the guys at HGTV were amazing teachers. They were open and willing to initiate trust building with me, like my CFO Jim did, and they'd often use humor, including the self-effacing kind, to cut tension during high-stress moments. EQ Fitness is a mind-set, but also a skill set available to all.

# INHIBITORS AND FACILITATORS OF TRUST

## CAN YOU TRUST A SCREEN?

Bobby Hood's policy of no texts or emails won't work for most of us, but technology *can* get in the way of understanding. At dinner one night, my friend Lynn said, "I no longer text words when I want to share an emotion. I text emojis. A whole sentence can be emojis. What's happened to me?" What's happened to Lynn has happened to all of us who use technology to communicate. We look for shortcuts. We substitute images for words. We substitute screens for looking into someone's eyes. We use empty or trite words instead of what we really want to say.

Technology helps get things done today that were unimaginable just a few years ago. Yet technology keeps us separate too. You can't build trust on an iPhone. You might be able to *sustain* trust through judicious and deliberate use of technology, but the spark gets ignited when you're in the same room.

One of the reasons HGTV was so grounded in trust was that we met almost daily to problem-solve as we built the business. With today's speed of change, holding daily meetings is unrealistic, even imprudent. But *some* physical, face-to-face contact is critical. Skype and FaceTime help, but there's no getting around the fact that you are miles apart. With those you care about, virtual hugs are a little bittersweet.

Remember what it was like to call someone on the phone? It's not the same as being in the same room, but hearing a person's voice, excited or sad, is still hugely gratifying. Hugely human. In fact, being able to identify someone's emotional state forms the *basis* of emotional intelligence. Sending texts or emails can also shirk personal confrontations, which just gets you into more hot water when you have to explain yourself later.

University faculties across the country are teaching their students how to get comfortable interacting as human beings, in person. Carnegie Mellon University has classes devoted to teaching students how to interact as a team and how to become self-observant (the keys to willingness we discussed in part one). Many of the kids have had little experience building face-to-face rapport versus through social media or over the phone. They're teaching them how to put down their devices and to feel safe enough to engage, head-to-heart, with others.

Whatever we do as technology advances, let's be sure that our kids, our students—our future leaders—are EQ Fit enough to know how to build workplaces of community. This way they can experience the gift of *belonging* with others and walking shoulder to shoulder with them.

The tools of modern technology grew up at the same time emotional intelligence did, in the 1990s. These two remarkable phenomena work best interdependently, side by side.

## WHAT TO DO ABOUT THOSE SCOUNDRELS

Emotional intelligence helps you read people, so you can quickly find colleagues to trust—and also recognize the scoundrels. You might have the most earnest intentions, but then Frank shows up. Fast-talking and slick, he's quick to assure you he's there for you, but your intuition says it's a con. Or John: handsome, polished, bitingly polite—and oh so superior. Maybe it's Larry. Larry's just smarmy. He offers inappropriate, too-personal compliments to every woman on the team. Or there's Jenny, who spreads her negative, depleting energy around the office. It's not so much that you can't trust her; she's just a downer. These scoundrels are not EQ Fit!

Look, there will always be people you can't trust. At HGTV, we called them assholes and we tried to avoid hiring them, but a few slipped through. The best you can do with these people is to be vigilant around them. Do not be vulnerable. Do not socialize, but be polite. Don't talk about them to someone else, because who knows, they may have a relationship that you don't know about. Be alert around them, and keep in mind their bad behavior is on them, not you. Don't take their bait; they can't score against you if you're not playing their game. If there's a coworker who likes to disparage others or the company, have an excuse ready when they start in with their spiel, like "Big project with deadlines. Talk later!" Come up with solutions to get things done with a different team member. If a scoundrel is the only resource you have, vet your options with your manager. Ask for their thoughts about how to work well with someone like "X," "X" being a personality type. You can describe a person's style and your conflict with it without naming them—something that could get you into dangerous political territory.

What if your boss is a scoundrel? Ugh! It happens often enough, sadly. Explore your mobility potential—will there be opportunities for you to move into another job within your division? If you need your boss's sanction to switch positions, look for lateral opportunities outside their purview. Or maybe it's time to look outside the company. The sad fact is that if you find a few jerks running wild, you're likely to find more. It reflects poor leadership from the top down.

It may be that you're not in a position to leave because you need the paycheck. Go back to the actions of willingness and name what you're feeling with someone you trust, so you can free it from being bottled up. Reframe the situation so you get more breathing room to live and work there, like finding gratitude for what you *do* like about the place. Pray for guidance, or meditate to move those unproductive thoughts down the stream of consciousness. Finally, consider what you learned in chapter four about job fit. If, after running through these willingness tools, you still conclude this company is just not right, start mapping your exit plan.

And don't forget the lessons from part one so you can remain emotionally healthy. Resentments will just hurt your peace of mind. Name them, claim them, and let them go.

## VULNERABILITY IS TELLING THE TRUTH

An enormous *facilitator* of trust is vulnerability—being willing to admit that you're not perfect, or you're stuck, or you're unsure. Like all our emotions, vulnerability is not gendered. However, I've worked side by side with men my whole career, and if I had said to one of them a few years back, "Hey, John, you look down. It's OK to be vulnerable, you know," he'd look at me like I'd lost my mind. Today, it is more socially acceptable for both men and women to admit feeling vulnerable at work, which is a sign that both are open to EQ Fitness. A recent study showed that men are, in fact, more likely to open up about their emotions at work than women (probably because women are sometimes punished for showing the same sort of emotional range that might earn a man accolades for being so sensitive).[1] Only a quarter of eighteen- to thirty-four-year-olds surveyed found it hard to open up at work. This suggests that the majority of our rising workforce feels that it's A-OK to admit their feelings—and that's awesome! For anyone working with young employees, it's important to know that they may express themselves more than you're used to doing, including their feelings of vulnerability. Honor what they're telling you with an in-person meeting, active listening, and quiet assurance.

Vulnerability is entering into public discourse more too. At the 2017 Grammys, Adele got nervous performing a George Michael tribute song and had to start over to get it right—and the millions of viewers *loved* it. Men are also learning to let go; even Prince Harry has been open about his near breakdowns.[2]

People often ask me if I get nervous when I speak, because apparently it doesn't show. The answer is absolutely! Every time. I do the willingness steps, naming my anxious stomach, saying a quick prayer, and moving into acceptance; I know it will be what it will be because I only have so much control. Although I've rehearsed, the AV might still break down. I could tell a joke and not get any laughter back. I remind myself I'm pretty brave to do this *at all*. And then I walk onstage. (Who knows, maybe Adele does that too!) Actions will always trump emotions, and taking the right actions regardless of fear is EQ Fit behavior. With practice we can act ourselves into right thinking.

Being vulnerable is being relatable, and you're inclined to want to trust a person who shows you that side of themselves. At the same time, we know that people are not always trustworthy. Being vulnerable feels like a high-wire act between self-protection and openness. I've found power in letting myself be vulnerable in five words: "I don't understand. Help me." That's as simple as the willingness to not be perfect gets. Being vulnerable is feeling safe enough to tell the truth. Here are five more words, like the ones I said to my former CFO Jim Clayton: "I made a mistake. Help." If you have a history with people being unreliable or deceptive but you want to be brave, you might acknowledge to someone that in the past you've had coworkers you made the mistake of trusting, but "with you, I'd like to try." Being EQ Fit helps you say those words, and move forward with action.

"For years I put a wall between me and my coworkers, but I came to see this was self-defeating," admitted Angela Teague, our introvert from chapter one. "There was minimal advancement in my career because I wasn't willing to show my teammates and managers who I was or what I had to offer. I started slowly letting my guard down. Today I have trustful, supportive work relationships with people who know my strengths and weaknesses. I'm honest now about that, and it's allowed me to excel."

Being vulnerable doesn't mean baring *all*. God knows, when I arrived at the doorsteps of HGTV, I didn't share my personal past with the team, but I did start to gradually ask for help, starting with Jim. As I became comfortable, I opened up with others too. I recall one particularly treacherous negotiation with the largest cable distributor at the time—big, bad TCI. They wanted us to grant them 3-D rights. This was 1994, a world with no streaming, no video on demand, no high-definition. I called the lawyers and my CEO, Ken, to ask their thoughts.

They said, "What do *you* think we should do?" "*I DON'T KNOW!*" I screamed into the phone. My vulnerable side emerged then, and it wasn't pretty, but it was a big moment nonetheless. It was freeing, like jailbreak. *Please help me.*

It's a powerful moment when you can kick down the barricade you erected after appointing yourself in charge of the universe. Remember that little thing called fanatical self-reliance we looked at in chapter one? Believing you need to do it all yourself can lead you to believe you're the only one who *can* do it. But we actually do our best work when we can rely on others. And asking for help moves us away from self-centeredness, something we self-reliant types know a lot about.

Allowing others on your team to really see you, to expose yourself as someone who genuinely needs and wants guidance, is a risk worth taking. It's not weakness; it's an equalizer. It makes you accessible as the fully human being you are.

## TRUST AND RELATIONSHIPS

Since trust building takes work, let's look at more examples and stories of how it grows in relationships.

### BUILDING TRUST WITH YOUR BOSS BY STEPPING UP—AND DOWN

In David Whyte's *Crossing the Unknown Sea: Work as a Pilgrimage of Identity*, he recounts the harrowing experience of being at sea as a sailor. Reflecting years later, he finds that he and the rest of the crew should have supported their captain more. "We had given up our own inner sense of captaincy," he writes. "How we long for that parental image of a captain or leader to carry the burden."[3]

Even the most traditional-chain-of-command organization you can think of, the military's Special Operations Forces (SOF), has shed its hierarchy in favor of a network model with small, elite teams that connect themselves to a broad network of units. They call it a "team of teams."[4] "Instead of leading a top-down bureaucracy, we began to lead ourselves as a network," explains former Navy SEAL Chris Fussell. Notice the words "lead ourselves." When everyone feels accountable, you work more efficiently, and your outcomes are better.

Many start-ups within large companies, as well as completely independent ones, are structured this way. We used this "team of teams" idea as we built HGTV, as the founding members sometimes functioned in interchangeable roles. If Ken was traveling, I would run the weekly meetings, or sometimes another one of our colleagues would do it. Our titles mattered for understanding our general responsibilities but were not there to make us territorial or competitive. In fact, when Ken and I were the only employees at first, I asked him what I thought was a simple question: "Will your title be CEO?" "I believe, yes," he said. "Does that sound right to you?" "It's your idea! You started this business! Yes, it should be CEO!" I said in my not-so-gentle way.

Great leaders instill pride in their teams, and Ken was a great leader. In turn, I was a proud follower. When I turned down an opportunity to become numero uno at HGTV, I had to trust that he'd choose someone I could respect for that job. I was willing to risk it, and was rewarded when he chose Ed Spray. It fit with our philosophy of keeping the viewer first, and Ed had done a marvelous job as the executive vice president of programming. He was Midwestern, down-to-earth, and not one to put on airs. Ken made the right choice because he knew his team well.

Winning teams maximize what each member adds, and your boss also needs your accountability to the whole team. She needs the confidence that you have her back, and your colleagues' backs too. She needs you to be a leader at times and a follower at others. We all play a lot of roles—leader, follower, mentor, student—sometimes within the span of one meeting! EQ Fitness improves how well you play these many roles.

## WHY FOLLOWERS ARE KEY

I met **Robert Kelley** in the spring of 2017, when I spent the day at Carnegie Mellon University to see what they were teaching their students about technology and human connection. Dr. Kelley is the Distinguished Service Professor of Management, and as we were walking to lunch he mentioned a book he'd written, *The Power of Followership*.

"I was doing leadership research and it struck me that no one was talking about followership. No executives I worked with had ever been to a 'followership seminar.' The only programs like that were boot camps for the military.

"We've created a whole mythology around leadership. Leaders get the spotlight as our star performers, while followers are unmentioned. But in industry after industry we found you have leaders and followers all up and down the chain. In my and others' research, leaders exert 15 to 25 percent on successful outcomes and followers exert 75 percent. Followers make or break success. Our research shows that when you change the leader of a group, the outcomes don't often change much for the better. Leaders often have a greater capacity to do harm to an organization than to do good."

Wharton professor of organizational psychology and author Adam Grant says the most frequent question he gets from readers is how to contribute something to a group when you're not in charge. Likewise, bestselling *Quiet* author Susan Cain finds that "the biggest disservice done by the outsize glorification of 'leadership skills' is to the practice of leadership itself—it hollows it out, it empties it of meaning."[5] We need "leaders who are called to service rather than status," she says. EQ Fit people use their gifts for the overarching good. They're drawn by intrinsic goals, like their moral compass, and they're the strongest, most emotionally mature among us because they have a rock-solid foundation of self-worth. They are your prime trust builders.

On the flip side, sometimes these people seeking status are just scoundrels and—not to put too fine a point on it—assholes. Sometimes, there's a different story: they lack self-worth. Maybe they weren't safe growing up, or lacked love or consistent affection—things we looked at in chapter 1. Seeking status can be the MO of someone very lonely and/or very wounded, and if left untreated—if they don't practice the actions of willingness—it can translate into their trying to fill that hole with a big title. I write this from personal experience.

EQ Fit leaders and EQ Fit followers integrate all team members and amplify others' voices, not just their own. This is how you build trust. You prod the quiet people gently until you get their input, so you learn their points of view. If you don't know what someone thinks, how will you know if the team is unified around a strategy?

## BUILDING TRUST WITH YOUR PEERS AND REPORTS

I recently picked up an article about how to "step up" to your emotional best self with any person, in any meeting. It boiled down to these four basic approaches:

1. Show enthusiasm!
2. Offer a compliment.
3. Look for common interests.
4. Say someone's name when you're addressing them. And remember their name!

Let's look at five practical and, might I say, more meaningful actions to build trust.

**TRUST BUILDING** *is*

**Interdependent**

**Social**

**Respectful**

**Time-intensive**

**A meaningful path to finding purpose**

The skills each of us brought to HGTV added value in different ways. We were dependent on one another to perform our own duties well if we were to succeed, and that was all the more reason to have one another's backs. **Alana Lawson**, director of IT services at the University of Tennessee Medical Center, offers a creative way to structure her team with interdependence:

"[Well-balanced] teams have a good mix of qualities like being hardworking, dependable, and following through. When I first started a new job a few years ago, I was given a Herculean-type project. My team and I were getting to know one another. I asked the team to divide themselves into three separate groups, [and they were] each dependent on the other. I still to this day am in awe of what they were able to accomplish."

When the circumstance warrants it, roll up your sleeves to help your team, even if the specific project is outside your purview. It helps them to see that you want to understand their jobs and aren't above pitching in. **Jan Johnston Osburn**, formerly a manager at SOC, LLC, told me about a time when her team was in crisis mode to staff a contract of nearly one billion dollars that her company was at risk of losing. "You have to know when you need to get in the weeds, the trenches. Now was not the time to sit in my office and direct; now was the time to work *beside* my team, lending not just a hand but two hands, to prevent the team from being overwhelmed. You need to set the example by being beside them. You should never ask of someone else what you yourself wouldn't do."

## Build Interdependence with Your Peers

In many ways peers are the hardest to build trust with, because you both compete for limited resources like capital and promotions. Some of your colleagues may have bulldozer personalities; some are scoundrels. I've worked with all types, and I bet you have too.

When we're managers responsible for budgets, we know resources are precious and headcount is finite. In response to the anonymous survey I hosted about trust, one woman shared that, from the moment she started at a new company, she wanted to show her colleagues that she could be trusted. When she was given an open staff position to manage, she transformed that job into one that would support her peers as well as herself. It was a big risk—she didn't know how her peers would respond to this gesture—but it paid off, because not long after she did that, one of her colleagues did the same, and all benefited.

## Enjoy Social Time with Peers and Reports

Some organizations are highly social. People wander around the office and come together spontaneously. My first media job at HBO was like that. I worked in regional offices but spent a lot of time at the corporate headquarters in New York City. Most of us were just out of school and single. A gang of us might go out to a club on Friday night or run together on lunch breaks. When Monday morning rolled around, these people weren't strangers to me. I got to know my New York colleagues personally, outside the confines of the office, which helped since I wasn't permanently located with them.

**Sheli Cordero**, director of marketing at First American Title, told me she likes using social time to build trust: "I recruit my husband, who's a great sport and very outgoing, and take a colleague and their spouse or partner to dinner." Both Sheli and the colleague benefit, because they get to know more about each other at the front end of their relationship, which can enable trust more quickly.

Sometimes social time can resemble the share circle model, which we explored in chapter two. There is power in numbers when trust groups are formed to improve their company culture, voiced through amplifying the good and exposing the bad. In the 1990s, a few women from Bear Stearns (later sold to JPMorgan Chase), who called themselves the Glass Ceiling Club, met quietly every month or two outside the office to discuss how to make the company more female-friendly. These discussions included naming men whom the others should watch out for because they were sexual predators.[6]

Groups like the Glass Ceiling Club are a more forceful voice in exposing a hostile workplace, but informal groups are also powerful support systems. In another anonymous submission, one survey respondent told me that there were five minority women at the executive level who had all started with her company at the same time. "We immediately formed a connection and for the last year we have supported one another through prayer, bible studies, acting as a sounding board when workplace challenges arise, and being brutally honest with one another. These women have been a godsend."

The thing is, many of us regard this socializing as an extension of the workday, not a welcome addition to our personal lives. And not all of us are young and single with time to spare. But if a team or an office uses socializing as a tool for bringing people together, it's worth knowing, especially if you're thinking of joining the company. It might be a strong thread in the company's cultural fabric, so being aware in advance is key to creating a good job fit.

## Show Respect

I once worked with someone (call him Sam) who told me another guy on the team was a "dry drunk." Whether he was or wasn't—and whatever that meant—I knew to watch my back with Sam. EQ Fit people don't bolster their ego at the expense of others. They respect their colleagues by holding their tongue, and holding confidences, in order to build a relationship of safety with another person.

I met **Darnell Smith** at an event in Florida where I was keynoting. Darnell is market president for Florida Blue, a Blue Cross Blue Shield subsidiary. We were on a panel together when my ears perked up: the very first thing he mentioned when asked a question was the need for trust. When I caught up with him later, he told me, "I'm conscious of how I interact with others. I never talk about others behind their backs. It's villainy to do."

Our language matters. "I prefer to say we work together, actually," explained **Mary E. Talbott**, vice president and assistant general counsel at General Cable Corporation, about a woman who works for her. That equalizing was crucial when it came to fixing a crisis—together— when Mary's report came to her in tears about a mistake she'd made. "First, her willingness to come to me immediately demonstrated to me that the trust I had cultivated with her was guiding her actions," Mary said. "She was not motivated by fear from repercussions from me but by concern of letting me down through her mistake. She knew that I would work with her to find a solution rather than point fingers or blame." Saying "I trust you to do this" gives someone a boost. Saying "You don't work for me; we work together" allows for a spirit of collaboration, and creates a safe space to admit mistakes, be reassured that you have one another's backs, and find solutions together.

There might be no better sign of respect than in how you compensate your team. In June 2016, **Sherry Stewart Deutschmann** won the White House Champion of Change Award for her compensation policies at Letter Logic, a Nashville-based patient billing company that she founded. When she was running the company, everyone shared in 10 percent of the profits, split evenly. In addition, she instituted an hourly pay rate of sixteen dollars for her workers, twice the federal minimum wage. "I went to a conference early on, and the speaker said to look at those who you paid the least," she told me. "Could they live on that? How about if they had a family? The next day I upped our hourly wage earners from twelve dollars per hour to sixteen dollars per hour."

When you practice willingness and trust building, you let go of self-centeredness and get a new view of your workplace. You begin to see how many around you are worthy of your respect. With real listening, you can learn that their challenges don't stop them from showing up every day and doing their best. Respect is a close first cousin to trust. It's hard to imagine trusting someone you don't respect. Those worthy of your respect are those you want to stick with, those you want as part of your trust network.

## Take the Time You Need

Snap judgments are the worst kind of trust killers. For the start-up team at HGTV, I hired Channing Dawson to run marketing. He had no television background, but his experience working at home and garden magazines was intriguing. He didn't easily fit into any position, not even in marketing. He knew content, but wasn't a programmer; he understood our consumers, but marketing alone seemed too limiting. We moved him into many different roles over the course of his career—digital media, new ventures, and others, each successful in its own right. He had a long and prosperous career at SNI. But if I had dismissed his résumé out of hand, we would have missed out on the ingenuity he brought to every project.

Maybe the hardest thing to do in work, and life, is to have an open mind. Arriving into adulthood with open-mindedness is in conflict with how many of us have been conditioned. The tools of meditation and mindfulness we learned about in chapter three can certainly help. Having an open mind about people who don't look like you or act like you, or for whom you have no prior frame of reference, is called "inclusion" in HR circles, which I mention because inclusion is about a whole lot more than gender or skin color. Channing didn't fit any box I could put him in, but an inner instinct was guiding me to be patient and to let this person "marinate" in the organization, something that we were lucky to have the space and wherewithal to do at our start-up.

With the tools in chapter three we can make more space, create more openings. We're more emotionally agile. The actions of willingness and the vulnerability of trust building can be called on when it's time to practice inclusion. If you're willing to take the time to get to know someone, they'll always teach you something, and your organization will surely benefit from their unique perspective and skills.

Always take a moment to look a little deeper. Someone who seems standoffish might just be shy, with a wealth of knowledge and insight, if you'll just take the time to let it unfold. Angela Teague said, "Extroverts are masters at building trust through verbal expression. That's not my strength. As an introvert, I'm less verbal. And while I'm now comfortable being open about myself, I probably build trust more slowly."

Since it takes time to get to know someone and trust them, it helps to start as early as the interview. Sheli Cordero said of interviewing candidates, "First impressions are a two-way street. Beyond the standard position and qualification discussions, I tell them about the team and my management style; letting them get to know me on a personal-professional level and the team by proxy. We have families, hobbies, aspirations for the future, and I want the whole team behind welcoming a new member."

## Draw on a Larger Purpose

**Sara Rose** is a VP at Bush Beans, a 110-year-old family-held food manufacturer and marketer that enjoys a more than 40 percent share of the US canned bean market—and the company has done smart things to hold that dominant position. When she was a director, her CEO, Jim Ethier, established monthly meetings with all the directors, the functional leaders of the company's various departments, and gave them the goal of creating and overseeing the organization's culture. "Initially, many of us were reluctant to attend, because we had our 'real work' to do," she told me. "But Jim challenged us, saying, 'Everyone in the company reports in to a director. Do you want the senior VPs to manage the culture of the place, or do you directors want to do it?' So, creating the culture that we thought was best for the company became our shared purpose, one that was bigger than our own day-to-day work." Working closely with her peers, she got to know and came to trust them.

HGTV was the first job where "purpose" mattered to me. Building a business around *home* seemed like important work. Home was a place of sanctuary, safety, belonging. I'd experienced this (off and on) growing up with my family and especially larger clan of cousins and aunts and uncles. Creating a business that could honor those ideals appealed to me deeply. With a new set of teammates who showed me trust was possible in the workplace, and later armed with the tools of EQ Fitness, especially willingness, I realized that I could help build a culture of trust with my colleagues.

The five actions we've explored above will help you build trust in your organization. Combine them with the five quick tips below for a brawny list of tools that pack a wallop to your EQ Fitness practice.

## SUSAN'S FIVE FAST TIPS FOR TRUST

These two trust words matter most to me, "**honesty**" and "**integrity**," and the tips below, in pursuit of them, have been greatly helpful to this business of trust building.

1. **Become self-aware.** We did a lot of this work in part one. EQ starts with *self-honesty*. Step up to do things you have the ability to do, but don't take on too much, especially if you might let someone down. Make a habit of checking in with yourself regularly. *What am I good at? What am I not?* Say "I don't know" when that's the case. Allow yourself to be imperfect, even in a lead role. When I ran our digital assets for HGTV, I was at a meeting when our engineer began talking metadata with our software

person. "Hold it," I said. "What's metadata?" I had a lot to learn, and I wasn't ashamed to let them know it.

2. **Be honest with others.** It's the small betrayals that will wear down a relationship. Someone I trusted asked me to speak at his conference but couldn't afford a speaker fee, so I asked if he'd put my book in the swag bag. He couldn't do that either, he said, because attendees had previously complained about carrying around books. When I got to the conference, I was handed a swag bag—with someone else's book inside. Small betrayal, large impact. These actions can shred a relationship into tatters, making trust impossible.

3. **Be steady.** Steadiness is a sterling quality of EQF leaders. I call this the "no-drama rule." Running hot and cold are trust killers. Sure, once in a while things happen to throw you off your game, but unless someone is a share partner, check your soap operas at the door. If your peers are consistently moody or acting out, your job is not to fix them or save them.

When I worked with Mark Hale at SNI, he was responsible for lots of things, including our facilities. I called Mark the "patron saint of perpetual patience," because I would change my mind a million times about where I wanted people to sit (I *hated* making process decisions), and Mark would hang with me. He never once lost his temper, but I knew that when he started shaking his head in a certain way, time was up. I had to commit.

EQ Fit leaders are also conscious of how things can impact their mood. Remember: we bring our bodies to work too, and if we don't take care of the only one we've got, we might easily run up against frayed nerves and quick-trigger tempers. There was a senior executive at

SNI whom no one wanted to be around after 3:00 p.m. Turns out he had this huge jar of M&Ms that were often his lunch. His supervisor called it out, and he began eating food, not sugar, during the day. His hangry behavior quickly dissipated.

4.  **Be dependable.** Do what you say you'll do. Dependability is a reflection of one's *integrity*. Once, I was working in Canada for HGTV, pursuing a license to operate a network there. I had to testify before a tribunal in Ottawa, and Ken said he'd be there to support me. There was a whiteout snowstorm, and flights were grounded. The next morning, as I waited to address the commissioners, in walked Ken, rumpled and needing a shave. He'd ridden in a van overnight all the way from Philly. "I told you I'd show," he leaned over and whispered. Part of the hole inside me was just wanting people who'd stick, and I never forgot that moment. I tried my best to honor his trust in return.

5.  **Be proactive.** It's remarkable how helping another person can be an enormous trust builder. Take the initiative to be a problem-solver if a colleague reaches out, or with your team or department. Not a know-it-all, just someone who can add their input to the rest.

    Being proactive also means being accountable. If you think you violated someone's trust, hopefully it was not intended. (In other words, you're not an asshole.) Claim it. Apologize right away. Relationships aren't static, and neither is trust. You're always in a position to build—or damage—trust by your words or actions. Also be proactive by depositing goodwill into a bank account of trust, like Bobby Hood did at Cherokee Distributing. A kind gesture will release something splendid in another person. When you gift me with your trust, you signal that you believe in me, and that stirs the powerful emotion of hope—hope of real human connection.

Jim Clayton's extending himself to help me fix my budget mistake is my first memory of a colleague I barely knew doing something out of kindness—his only agenda was the same as mine: to help the company thrive. In that moment, he gave me hope that if others on our leadership team were like him, I could succeed there. He gave me hope that the culture we had talked about could be built, a culture of integrity and laughter, a welcoming place where people could just be who they were. Over time, with a set of teammates who showed me trust was possible, and later armed with the tools of EQ Fitness, I realized that I had what I needed to help build that culture. After Jim extended a hand in those first few critical months, I slowly began extending a hand back.

# CHAPTER SIX

# BECOMING CHIEF TRUST AMBASSADORS

*I am because we are; we are because I am.*

—AFRICAN PROVERB

**"Trust is a high comfort level** with someone's honesty," **Greg Jordan** told me. Greg is chief administrative officer and general counsel of PNC Financial Services Group, the sixth-largest commercial bank in America. The Regional Presidents Organization, which includes all thirty-five of PNC's regional bank presidents, reports to him.

In 2015, it was revealed that Wells Fargo, a financial institution in the same sector as PNC, scammed its customers by directing its employees to create over three million fake bank accounts. The scandal knows no modern comparison of blatant customer deceit. I wondered what another bank leader thought about the whole mess. **Diana Reid**, a PNC executive vice president, was kind enough to allow me access to many PNC employees, at both the corporate and regional levels.

I visited PNC's headquarters in Pittsburgh, where PNC is the largest employer. Greg is a lawyer, and—full disclosure—I came into our interview with a whole lot of bias against his trade. (All lawyers have ever done for me is say no!) But Greg surprised me. He had a demeanor of openness and candor, especially given the current reputation of his industry.

"It's beyond creepy when you think someone's opening a customer account without their consent. In banking, 'trust' is actually a business, and that's the underpinning of that business. We have ten million customers and can't be perfect, but the customer's watching. And while they may not move their business if you get something wrong, they will move their business if you've lied to them. You could make a lot of bad loans and still not do harm and damage to the company, compared to us breaching trust."

At PNC, leaders and employees communicate and build trust together, always steering toward transparency for themselves and for the consumer. The hundreds of people I've met in their regional offices and at headquarters seemed generally content and motivated. Their CEO, Bill Demchak, writes a regular blog to his employees, and he pulls no punches. After the 2016 election, some employees wanted to know if PNC's diversity policies would take a step back. Greg recalled, "And Bill said, 'We didn't have an inclusion program because we had an African American president; we did it because it's good for the company. If the new president tells us not to have one, we'll tell him to butt out.'"

The executives make a point of traveling to their markets regularly to hold forums with employees. At one of these meetings, Greg was asked why their CEO made so much money. "I answered, 'Yep, bank CEOs make a lot of money, but Bill took a pay cut this year because our performance wasn't good enough. We all took one. I know no one should feel sorry for us, but Bill took the biggest.' It's all in the proxy, but most of our folks don't read that.

"We have fifty-three thousand employees all over the country, so we try to reinforce in those meetings that we all carry around the bank's reputation. You can't police your people; you can't ever get there by policing them. You have to get there by getting into their heads and hearts."

EQ Fit leaders run companies with a sense of purpose. These qualities trickle down. Leaders who are secure and self-aware—prime qualities of EQ Fitness—help their people feel secure too. They feel safe. One of our advisors at HGTV, Dr. Steve Martin, often described how when he walked into our building, the feeling of common purpose and enthusiasm was palpable. It's what I felt at different PNC branches. This is why leaders and managers need to be advocates for trust building, because when those connections are forged, it leads to content and productive colleagues.

## EQ FITNESS AND TRUST AS A LEADER

Here's what it takes to earn trust as an EQ Fit leader and how to keep it, even while debating and disagreeing with others and making hard calls.

### "INSPIRED" COOPERATION

Every leader wants their people to perform at a top-notch level, so lowering the emotional barriers to achieve that high bar is critical. Look, you can mandate cooperation or you can inspire it. Inspired cooperation is more durable because employees become invested, not just fearful of punishment for noncompliance. EQ Fit leaders build *durable trust*. Trust helps the bottom line too:

> High trust = High speed, lower costs
> Low trust = Low speed, higher costs

The cost of distrust is high, both financially and in the emotional toll it takes on anyone in that relationship. We looked at personal examples in part one, like when someone you love consistently lets you down, or is hot and cold with their affections. When you arrive at work as an adult in emotional confusion, trusting another person is a treacherous mountain to climb. Leaders can rely on the willingness tools to clear away that wreckage so trust building can work its magic. When you're in a trustful relationship, you don't second-guess the motives of your teammates. This makes work more fluid, focused, and unencumbered by the drama our minds can drum up when we're unsure of another's sincerity.

## THE CYCLE OF TRUST

As a senior leader of any organization, you have two "trust" jobs: instilling trust in you personally and instilling trust in the organization. If you've earned both types, employees will feel they're on secure ground with a worthy guide. They will see that the company is run congruent with a value set that its leaders model consistently and that the rules applied to them individually are fair relative to how they're applied to others.

At the best—and, dare I say, EQ Fit!—companies, trust in the leader and trust in the company flow together seamlessly. An employee doesn't much think about it; he trusts the place, period. He feels *safe* enough to do his best work, without drama or conflict.

The cycle of trust should work like this:

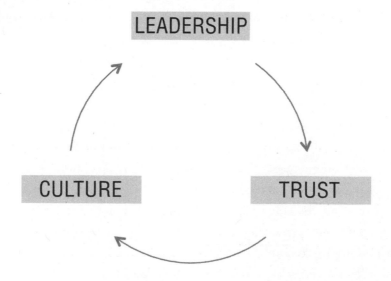

LEADERSHIP

CULTURE

TRUST

The problem is that too many of us work for jerk bosses, which feeds distrust of the whole place. If you're a leader, consider: Are you a jerk boss? Even sometimes? You try your best, but maybe sometimes you let your ego get the best of you, like when you want to take most of the credit as supervisor for a job well done by the whole team. Brainpower is only the first criterion for moving up the power ladder; usually—not always, but *usually*—people who operate from ego can *talk* a good game for a while, but they can't advance past middle management.

Even at the top, emotional immaturity and ego will be exposed. Case in point: In 2017, Uber went through a management overhaul, starting with the board forcing out its founder Travis Kalanick. Leaked video of a tirade against an Uber driver had just hit YouTube, and was soon followed by reports of sexual harassment, discriminatory behavior, and an unreported data breach. In a memo posted to the company's website, Kalanick said the criticism of the video "is a stark reminder that I must fundamentally change as a leader, and grow up."[1] Uber still has a long way to go in improving conditions and its image, but under its new leadership, it appears to be responding to sexual assault cases with more empathy and transparency.[2]

It also turns out jerk bosses impact both the emotional *and* physical health of their people. A study of over three thousand employees found that there was a strong link between bad leadership behavior and employee heart disease.[3] Remember that EQ Fitness is a program that brings the *whole* of us to our jobs, and that includes physical well-being. Poor health keeps you in "self" mode. Your self-talk might sound something like this: "I feel worse just being here. The last thing I want to do right now is play nice with all *these people*! Why do they have the air-conditioning blasting so high? I wonder if I've got Ebola?" At least, this is what mine would sound like. We build bridges of trust only when we're able to detach from our most egocentric instincts, and if we feel uncomfortable in our skin, we're too distracted to make that possible.

# FOUR LEADERSHIP TRAITS THAT EARN TRUST

Scottish author and theologian John Watson, who also wrote under the alias Ian MacLaren, said "This man beside us also has a hard fight with an unfavouring world, with strong temptations, with doubts and fears, with wounds of the past which have skinned over, but which smart when they are touched."[4] Successful leaders have fought inner battles grown in self-awareness, and found peace. That's the work of willingness in Step One, and that's where leadership also begins. EQF leaders are not looking for more power; they're finding ways to judiciously give it to others. They work hard to bring their teams along with them, rather than just assuming they'll follow because of their big-shot title. But too many haven't done the Step One willingness work, and they remain emotionally adolescent. You won't earn someone's trust if you're still acting like a child.

EQ Fit leaders understand their staff is always wondering, "How can I be successful here?" One of your jobs is to keep chaos out of the ecosystem, which helps teams relax, work with less stress, and evolve their relationships with teammates who can better help them perform. Strong relationships start with your EQ Fitness toolbox: willingness, building healthy work communities, and leading with an open heart as well as a strong brain. Then you will be someone your teams can relate to, connect with, and respect.

There are four key qualities that enable trust.

## 1. LIVE A LIFE OF WILLINGNESS

When I was in middle management before HGTV, I had zero willingness, ergo zero self-awareness, because I didn't want to deal with what I'd stuffed down inside. Something began to shift just before I joined HGTV, and I was ready to become willing. After a decade of bobbing and weaving around the inner tumult, I was tuckered out. It's exhausting to constantly hide from yourself. I didn't know any willingness tools yet except for prayer, and I just kept asking for some peace and quiet. Coming to self-understanding was a long and tough stretch of road. I began, bit by bit, moving away from things like maniacal workouts, too many cocktails, and workaholism—none of which had filled that hole in my soul. I was finally willing, as M. Scott Peck put it, to begin drawing a new map.

It helped significantly that at HGTV I was working with six grownups, men who were content with themselves and their marriages, who knew and practiced laughter, and who wanted to create a business with purpose. They were easy to trust because they offered their support when they said they would, and weren't into playing games. My story is one where Steps One and Two of EQF can run on parallel yet interdependent paths, one making the other so much easier. Willingness always starts the journey, but close behind is trust. The more trust I gain, the more willingness I have. Each gets richer as we practice both.

Willingness can take many forms, but it always starts with having an honest understanding of self, of how vacant or rich our inner life is, and of our talents and liabilities. The leaders below have done that. They lead with profound self-awareness, playing to their strengths and naming and claiming their limitations. They are running, or have run, massive, complex companies or ones that are constantly in the public eye, and they understand the commitment needed to keep their employees'—and customers'—trust every day.

**Paul Polman** is CEO of Unilever, a Fortune Global 500, €52 billion company that produces everything from Dove soap to Ben & Jerry's ice cream. When we spoke, Paul explained, "You cannot create the trust needed if you yourself are not trustworthy. That means discussing your own failures as well as your successes." The company systematically reviews failures, with an emphasis on learning from them.

**Ellen Kullman** was CEO of DuPont, a Fortune 500 company with a $73 billion market capitalization, from 2009 until 2016. (It became DowDuPont in 2017.) The company, founded in 1802, is known for its scientific breakthroughs, like nylon, Corian, and Kevlar. Ellen values self-awareness as a particularly important leadership quality. "I had to learn, and relearn, how to lead throughout my career with self-awareness. Being aware of my environment, being aware of others in that environment, their situations, their egos, and what my role was there."

She also admitted, "I've been known to have a very strong personality, and self-awareness is understanding the impact it has. Sometimes it was helpful to me, sometimes not. I know this, but I forget it a lot and have to remind myself: you can flex your style. This doesn't mean not being true to yourself. But you can flex your style and be much more effective. You need to know the book on you. There's a book on all of us. It's imperative as a CEO to know your book if you want to bring your people with you. Some CEOs really don't care about their people. They're unfortunately still out there."

In chapter one you learned the painful childhood story of **Jarl Mohn**, now the CEO of National Public Radio. When I was starting out in the media business, I watched him smartly navigate his leadership and lieutenant roles at E! Entertainment Television, MTV, and VH1 with deftness and high EQF—especially necessary in our field, the land of big and fragile egos. Jarl has worked for some of the most demanding, and many would say "difficult," bosses in the country, including media titans Brian Roberts, CEO of Comcast; John Malone, former CEO of cable giant TCI; and Bob Pittman, former CEO of MTV.

Jarl also has deep self-awareness. "I'm a terrible interviewer when I'm recruiting," he admitted. "I want to hire them all. Knowing this, I created an interview panel years ago to overcome my weakness there. I never look for group consensus—quite the contrary. If I have six people on the panel, I'm looking for six different assessments of the candidate. Each will see things I did not. There's no vote on the people. I use the observations I hear to help better inform my decisions." By bringing in staff to augment his recruiting, Jarl acknowledged a personal limitation but remained "boss"—the final decision was his to make. We learn, through working with willingness, that self-awareness gives you a stronger, more rooted sense of self to call upon in decisive moments.

Alas, no system is foolproof, and often our job as leader needs to quickly morph into that of fixer. As sexual harassment claims hit NPR in 2017, Jarl moved into fixer role to deal with its failures in the hiring processes and lack of speed in addressing harassment complaints. He also submitted to an on-air grilling by one of his own reporters. NPR now has extensive practices in place that Jarl has made public to all, unlike other media companies that have used hush money and tried to bury these travesties from public view.

Many weaknesses can quickly become assets if we're simply honest about who we are and transparent in our processes. When leaders claim both their strengths and limitations—their full humanity—they open channels of trust. Leroy Ball, our introvert leader from chapter one, not only acknowledges publicly that he's an introvert, but speaks extensively about how to manage as an introverted CEO, including his preference for one-on-one meetings versus large gatherings that all CEOs need to be in and often lead.

## 2. BRING PEOPLE PHYSICALLY TOGETHER

One of the things that drove us crazy when we were building HGTV was the meeting schedule. Our CEO, Ken Lowe, would call meetings almost daily because he always wanted a group decision. Sometimes I'd feel like saying, "*You* decide!" because I had so much else to do. But I came to understand that those meetings allowed us to have ample in-person time, which helped us learn how everyone else ticked. (They also kept things light, because we did a lot of laughing in those meetings.) I may sound like a real Luddite to argue for *physical, in-person* meetings, but if you don't encourage them as the leader, they won't happen, and your people will be handicapped from building relationships of trust. There's no substitute for sitting in a room with someone, communicating eyeball to eyeball.

There's also a weightier, societal reason for meetings. With all this reliance on technology to communicate, we risk losing what human interaction offers—namely, community. We need that sense of belonging. If we're not careful, our emerging workforce will miss the opportunities to grow emotionally fit at work, the place where we spend the lion's share of our time. They'll miss practice in how to become fully human. They'll look like me at thirty-nine, before I started on this journey—or maybe worse.

Even folks on the cutting edge of technology advocate for in-person interactions. **Dr. Andrew Moore** works in artificial intelligence. We've all read and heard the debates about how many jobs will be replaced by robots and which skills will be rendered obsolete. What's interesting is that jobs requiring high emotional fitness, such as in health care, caretaking, teaching, and the like, are the least vulnerable. You can't replace the human touch with any facsimile.

Before Dr. Moore took on his role as dean of the School of Computer Science at Carnegie Mellon University, he worked at Google for twelve years. "We did a lot by videoconference, but it can only go so far. I noticed if I wasn't physically with my team for a while, working only by videoconference, then the email chains became us versus them. Trust broke down after two months." He frequently has his first-year students work in teams to get comfortable together, side by side. Science, technology, engineering, and math (STEM) jobs rely heavily on teamwork.

When **Jim Ethier** was taking Bush Beans from a regional vegetable canner into the national market leader it is today, he instituted the monthly meetings with the departmental directors that Sara Rose described in chapter five, despite knowing that his directors were concerned about their assignment to create a cohesive culture. Jim told me that one reason he did that was to grease the wheels of collaboration among his future leadership. His relentless focus on trust building and relationship building also led him to institute a "ninety-day coffee break" for new employees. For the first three months at Bush

Brothers, a new hire's main task is to meet other employees face-to-face and learn about their skills and experiences.

Wouldn't it be lovely if all companies offered such on-ramping, even if only for a week? Or a day?

Ellen told me that at DuPont there was a "back door," which she nailed shut when she took over. "I didn't understand 'back doors' until I got to DuPont. You'd sit in a meeting and make a decision, and a day or two later the boss would come in and say, 'I understand this and that,' and he'd change the decision we made. What happened was someone in the meeting wasn't happy with our decision, so they'd take a backdoor route, meet one-on-one with the boss to change his mind.

"When someone would try that with me, I'd say, 'OK,' and I'd call another meeting. I wouldn't rat out the person, I'd just say there were some concerns about our decision. I was very respectful. I'd say, 'Let's make a decision we're all good with, that we've covered this enough and we're not fooling ourselves with the wrong decision.'" Ellen changed the unproductive backdoor practice not by edict or email but by bringing her team together again.

I've run many regional offices in my day, and while autonomy is appreciated, there can be feelings of isolation too. In looking for ways to build team cohesion, Anisa Telwar decided to bring her people from all over the country together once a month to exchange best practices. The additional travel expenses aren't cheap, but her employees feel more connected to her, to one another, and to what's going on at Anisa International's corporate headquarters in Atlanta. That investment is reaping dividends in the EQ Fitness of the team.

## 3. TREAT PEOPLE AS HUMAN BEINGS INSTEAD OF COMMODITIES

In 2015, overworked, exhausted, and desolate, twenty-four-year-old Matsuri Takahashi jumped to her death. Before she took her life, she wrote in a Twitter post that her employer, Japanese advertising agency

Dentsu, was making her work Saturday and Sunday again, and she was just so tired she wanted to die. She was putting in one hundred hours of overtime a month, which was—incredibly—not unusual at her company. (The CEO of Dentsu subsequently resigned.)[5]

"Too many companies put shareholder primacy at their core," Unilever's Paul Polman told me. "That's one of the reasons we have a significant drop in the average lifetime of a publicly traded company. At Unilever, we squarely put our people, and serving the world's citizens, at the heart of all we do [through its Sustainable Living Plan] so we can be a net contributor to society, not a taker. Business cannot succeed in societies that fail. How we treat our people and consumers is one of the reasons we get 1.8 million job applications in every year from LinkedIn. They are looking for meaning in their work."

When researchers at Google data-mined employee performance reviews, feedback surveys, and managerial award nominations to find the company's best managers, they predicted that those with the top technical skills would be seen as the best. Instead, they learned that making time for one-on-one meetings and helping employees with problems were the criteria mentioned as the most critical.[6]

"The single most important thing I feel I can do for our execs is to meet with each of them and ask, 'What can I do for you this week?'" said Jarl Mohn. "It helps me to find out, quickly, what is important to them, and it reinforces that I am there to make them more successful. Not one of them ever asks me to do their jobs for them. Every single time it's a request for something I can pretty easily do that helps them and their team succeed. Every time I complete one of those asks, trust builds."

· · ·

At DuPont, as the newly elevated CEO, Ellen Kullman recognized that human touch meant respecting the culture, which in turn meant respecting the scientists and other employees. Ellen, a mechanical engineer by training, honored the over two-hundred-year-old scientific history of the company, and people trusted her to lead. She helped foster tremendous pride in the products and innovations that came along. "But many things needed updating. So if I honored what we did well, my people would come along with me on what needed to change."

Over the years, I've asked my old SNI colleagues for some of the most powerful memories they have of building the business. The million-dollar giveaway comes to many minds. It was about four years into the start-up. We'd begun making a little money and were project-ing getting to one million in profit soon. We came up with a plan to pay our first million out to our employees, weighted only on how long they'd been there; an assistant could earn more than her boss (and that happened in many areas). We removed ourselves from the payout. When we called a company-wide meeting to announce it, there wasn't a dry eye in the house.

But here's the other thing people will say: "You went to my father's funeral." Or a wife's, or, God forbid, a child's. We tried to make all of these.

We did many things to create community and foster trust. This took the form of nonstop, open communication with our employees. We were almost fanatical about keeping them in the loop. Among the things we did:

- laminated cards with our core values for every employee;
- held quarterly brown-bag lunches where a division head up-dated the rest of the company on what new and fun things were going on in their department;
- started a monthly newsletter for company news, like work anniversaries and birth announcements;
- created a yearbook with everyone's pictures and titles; and
- hosted annual Thanksgiving lunches for every employee in town on the Wednesday before the holiday, where we'd pass around a microphone and ask people to share something they were grateful for that year.

We didn't realize it at the time, but we were taking those pesky instincts I wrote about in chapter one—safety, acceptance, and belonging—and incorporating them into a safe, nurturing culture. A culture like home. A place where trust could be readily built.

If you can pull this off, you free your people up to take what they're made of—their temperaments—and express them comfortably and respectfully, without a whole lot of drama. When you believe fundamentally that your workforce is your lifeline to success, your employees give that back to you in spades. They trust you to do right by them. A simple thing, but not an easy one.

## 4. ACT LIKE A LEADER

When my sisters and I were growing up, my mother often had a "one-time" policy—in other words, inconsistent. It was like a carve-out in contracts—except we were in grade school. For example, when we got to eighth grade, we could go to *one* mixed dance. (What, like we couldn't get any action there because we had only one night to do it?) There wasn't a lot of logic behind this rule, and it made us shake our heads trying to understand it. Any parent knows that consistency matters.

Acting like a leader first means *you are balanced and consistent* in both your temperament (hello, EQ Fitness!) and your policies. You're reliable. You don't play games. Sleight-of-hand practices, like the back-door one that Ellen nailed shut, breed distrust. You tell people the truth, consistently.

Next, it means *being the boss*. When tough things require a strong hand, you handle them—with civility, but you handle them nonetheless. You act like the leader you were hired to be and have trained yourself to become through EQ Fit practices.

**Joyce Russell** has the gift of holding power and kindness in equal measure. Joyce is president of Adecco Staffing USA, part of Adecco Group, a multibillion-dollar staffing business. In any week, Adecco

Group puts 700,000 to 900,000 people to work, making it one of the largest employers in the world.

She shared a trust story with me that reflects magnificently how having strong, candid conversations don't erode trust—they build it. At the time, she had a team member who was talented, smart, and driven, but who had a harsh communication style that was damaging her reputation. "I had a difficult conversation with Ann," Joyce said. "I told her I wanted to invest in her and hire a personal coach, and explained why. At first she was defensive, but we talked more, she trusted that I had her best interest at heart, and she has been on my team now for several years."

Trust building isn't like making Minute Rice. It takes time and patience. You should bear in mind that most employees *want* to trust you, but you have to prove you're worth that trust, especially for the many of us who have experienced betrayal or conditional affections. This takes time. Joyce knew she couldn't have these tough conversations until she and her reports were on a common ground of trust. Because they'd worked together for a while, Ann was the beneficiary of Joyce's time and financial investment in her.

Finally, acting like a leader means *fostering debate* so that the best thinking and outcomes can be attained. This is one of your most important jobs, and the trick is to do it safely, without combat. This also includes debate and disagreement with *you*. EQF leaders, highly self-aware and wanting honesty over platitudes, are comfortable with reports disagreeing with them. They don't react defensively (as long as the communication is respectful). Remember, you're paid to be the adult in the room.

With EQF, you can also settle conflicts without combative conversations that put everyone's backs up. It might sound something like this:

> *I'm not here to argue. I'm here to understand, and I hope all of you are too. We don't all share a common position on this, and*

*that's OK. I hope you still are open enough to have a few ques-*
*tions left on both points of view. Let's focus on solutions, not a*
*rehash of the problem. Let's keep asking, "What's in the best*
*interest of the company?" since we all share that goal.*

I tell the leaders I coach that we don't have to be right to feel secure. EQF leaders bring open-mindedness into every room.

I asked Paul Polman how people at Unilever disagreed. "People voice their disagreements when issues are discussed, but we expect a clear understanding of where the decision-making criteria are vested, and an 'agree/disagree, but commit' behavior in public. Debate is fine, but not after decisions are made."

Ellen Kullman always told her reports at DuPont, "If you don't tell me when I'm wrong, you're not that helpful to me." She was careful to never take their heads off—she really wanted their feedback and knew they'd never give it to her again if they were worried about reprisal.

Ellen and I have both worked at GE, so we went through its "Work-Out" process, where, if there was team dysfunction, everyone went into a room until the problem got ironed out. It wasn't pleasant, but it worked. Looking back, Work-Out feels like a rather combative practice, but it was successful at GE because the culture was so direct and hard-shelled. I just wonder: How much *more* successful might they be with a more diplomatic version of Work-Out?

PNC's Diana Reid shared a story that I really love because it's rich with a leader's self-awareness, and a picture of how openness, vulnerability, and trust building can work when styles don't line up neatly between two people.

"When I joined PNC, one of my direct reports and I struggled to communicate effectively. But I knew he was very talented, and he was likely the one person I needed to train and prepare for bigger roles. We were both frustrated with ineffective communication, and it bothered both of us. We decided to get an executive coach to help us, and we scoped in three of our colleagues to participate. It took time and effort, but the breakthrough moment was going through MBTI [Myers-Briggs Type Indicator] assessments and we saw our approach to every issue was completely different. He is an extreme extrovert, and approaches every situation confident he is the 'smartest person in the room.' I am an extreme introvert and approach everything as an opportunity to learn and improve. Once we were aware of our natural approaches, we were able to moderate them."

Barron Patterson, the Vanderbilt University pediatric doctor you met in chapter one, is also vice chair for ambulatory services. As a leader, he's often charged with running meetings and mediating disputes. As an introvert, he's very conscious of pulling others' opinions out, especially those he sees as quiet or shy. Maybe they're introverts, or maybe the topic is unpopular, or perhaps it's because of who is sitting across from them.

"The power differential in the room matters," he said. "If the COO is present, a PSR [patient service representative] might say nothing. If it's a large initiative, we might create a website so they can text their thoughts either anonymously or put their name on their feedback if they'd like. It's important to hear from everyone if possible."

If you're an extrovert, flexing your style when working with an introvert might mean not dominating the discussion or always jumping in to fill silence, since that silence might mean the person is processing. As an introvert, while you might listen and process well, you should try to add your voice and value to the conversation, or respond through feedback portals set up for that purpose.

## 4 ½. ISN'T TRANSPARENCY A TRUST EARNER TOO?

### Policies and Practices

Transparency is of course important, but above all, your company's policies and practices have to be executed with fairness. You, as leader, may think they are, but is that an opinion shared by the rank and file?

EQ Fit leaders pause to ask this question of themselves and their management team.

In 2017, the *New York Times* was sent salary and bonus information compiled by twelve hundred Google employees. A former employee had wanted to help coworkers negotiate fair salaries, and her research examined pay parity between women and men. Google has long prided itself on its culture of openness and transparency: employees share information on one of several internal forums, like Memegen, and can challenge executives with questions selected by their peers at their weekly company-wide meetings.[7]

The pay research covered six of the nine jobs levels there, from entry-level positions to senior engineers (the top three were not included, which would have likely made the disparities even worse), and revealed that women were paid less than men across the board.[8] This wasn't a scientific study, but it nonetheless contradicted what Google had claimed, which is that their female employees made 99.7 percent of what their male ones did. The company defended itself by saying that this wasn't the full picture: one needs to take into account factors like tenure, job role, level, and location. So if you work there, what do you believe? Who do you trust?

In my experience and with the executives I interviewed for this book, yes, transparency is necessary in trustworthy organizations, but it is not sufficient to earn trust. It must be backed by the facts showing that fairness thrives there.

## HARD WORK: LEADERSHIP AND FORGIVENESS

Cherokee Distributing's Mary Ellen Brewington and I were talking one day about how she handles conflict in emotionally healthy ways, and she got me thinking about forgiveness. Forgiveness is an emotion we rarely talk about at work. We don't imagine we could ever go deep enough in a work relationship to need to forgive someone or, for that matter, to be forgiven. That's ego talking. We're not made of steel, and as we work more with willingness and trust building in our EQ Fitness program, we keep making space to let others in.

Maybe you're disappointed because someone you handpicked has thrown away an opportunity to grow into the role you put them in. Some may hurt your pride by telling you the truth, even though you asked for it. Some may break your heart. You might work for parents in a family business, and whatever you do, you fall short in their eyes. Or you come to care for a colleague who one day announces they're going to your competitor. That could be best for them—only they can know that—but it still stings, at least for someone like me who carries that super-sensitivity gene.

Your disappointments can morph over time into resentments, which keep us sick and emotionally adolescent. Forgiveness is like a spiritual car wash. Surrender the "mad" and feel cleansed, lighter.

Mary Ellen is a big believer that in any conflict, you must practice the tools of chapter two: name it, claim it, and let it go. It helps, too, to know that "truth" can be subject to interpretation. She starts those difficult conversations like this: "My intention for this meeting is to get this off my chest, and to hear what you have to say too, because we all see and hear and understand things differently." "That seems like a good way to begin," I told her.

"Yes, but the other party might not be emotionally ready to put the hurt or resentment to bed. So you have to walk away knowing you've done your part," she said. "And then it helps to forgive."

. . .

It would have been hard to screw up HGTV. My friends who started it with me would probably disagree, given our long hours, setbacks, and talent issues along the way. But I still think it's true for two reasons. One, HGTV is experiential, meaning that people relate to it in a personal and emotional way that reflects their love of their homes. We were sitting on a powder keg of passions, which makes it easier to succeed than, say, if you're selling bolts and screws. Two, many of my colleagues (although not me, not at first) were EQ Fit enough to create an open and honest culture bonded by teamwork and trust, the intangibles that animate so many thriving workplaces.

As a leader, you're given power, and through willingness, you're given grace. How lucky we are! We can deploy these gifts to build cultures that are honorable, where your teams feel safe to do their very best work. Where they feel a sense of belonging to something that's bigger than their own self-interest. Where their work has meaning. All these things are possible! I know because I've seen it. It starts with self-understanding, and then walking out into the world and building relationships worthy of others' trust.

# CHAPTER SEVEN

# MY CAREER STORY
## Consumers, Cultures, & the Value of Trust

*I also find it fascinating that baseball, alone in sport, considers
errors to be part of the game, part of its rigorous truth.*

—FRANCIS T. VINCENT JR.[1]

In reflecting on my career for the writing of this book, it's now clear
to me how helpful various people in my life were in modeling emotional maturity, from my earliest job working for my dad to the latter
years as a seasoned executive. I always had the mental and physical
firepower to advance—just not the emotional fitness and spiritual insight that rounds out a leader. Those came later, with help from many
others.

While my story is my own, what's common to all of us is that it's
never too late to grow up, and to find some inner ground of meaning
in your work and your life.

## WATCHING SOMEONE WILLING:
## EARLY CAREER

I moved through college in staccato fashion—I was all in, then pulled
out, then dove back in. When I finally had enough credits to graduate,
I thought, why not just keep going? I realized I could "do" school, and
I'd even come to enjoy it. So I went for a master's in advertising. What

I enjoyed most of all was not having to confront real life. Like getting a job.

But contrary to popular belief, school does teach you important truths about the "real world." My most memorable experience in graduate school was working on the Marathon Oil project. Marathon had approached Michigan State with a competition in which students would concoct new ways to attract customers to their gas stations. I joined up with a team of classmates. I had this idea—what if they laid red carpets next to their pumps? It would say, "You're our privileged customer." I went to ad agencies in downtown Lansing and cajoled one to create a slide for us gratis of a red carpet superimposed on a Marathon Oil station. It was fantastic! We were sure to win!

We lost. This would be my first "career" experience with a bruised ego. The Marathon executive said our idea wasn't practical. Well, who said *that* mattered?

Every weekday of every summer from the ages of fourteen to twenty, I worked with my dad at a small direct mail company called Ad-Mail Services. My dad was a salesperson serving local Detroit advertising agencies and auto suppliers. I collated print pieces into direct mail packages in a factory building that was stifling hot, with no air-conditioning or windows. Later, I was hired to my first white-collar job as my dad's secretary, promoted from the factory floor to a nice cool office. My hourly wage increased only a tiny amount, but I knew I was running with the big dogs now.

Unlike the big-cheese owner (his boss), Dad never closed his door, even if a customer was railing at him, and I could hear as he gently talked the client down. Then he'd walk out of his office and talk with everyone, maintaining the same patience and kindness he'd used with that self-righteous customer. We were never on the firing line because Dad's day had turned bad. He was steady, like all EQ Fit leaders.

Sitting just outside his office, sponging up all that my father said, I learned to have respect for every customer, even the difficult ones. I learned to work hard. My father was an open guy, and openness is a key quality of EQ Fitness. Maybe some of that came from his service in World War II, when he'd been shot and left for dead during the Battle of the Bulge. (I didn't know much about that story until he shared it with my son when he was six or seven years old. For whatever reason, he was finally ready to tell it.) For staring death in the face and finding the grit to live, he earned a Purple Heart. Perhaps that taught him not to sweat the small stuff. He has always been one of my heroes.

A few years after my dad passed away, we found a diary he wrote while in boot camp, getting ready to deploy overseas. He shared many personal things in those pages, like missing his future wife, my mom, and his pride in having "best bed made" and "cleanest equipment." It made me think, *What willingness this man had!* Dad was first-generation Italian American, and all the men in his family were stoic. They valued family, Catholicism, and a strong work ethic. And yet here was this small weathered book, clearly the share partner of his day.

It's not lost on me that as I write this, I'm practicing Dad's brand of willingness. "*Write it down,*" I can hear him whisper to me now.

# WATCHING HOW TRUST WORKS. OR NOT.

## BUILDING TRUST WITH CUSTOMERS AND TEAMS: HBO

In the programming business, where I've worked since I was twenty-five, there are key distinctions between consumers and customers. *Consumers* are our viewers—those who "consume" or view a show on our network. *Customers*, on the other hand, are business-to-business (B-to-B) relationships, like distributors that carry our signal into homes and advertisers that buy spots on our channel. We work through our customers to reach our consumers, the viewers themselves.

After those summers and out of graduate school, I got my first media job, at HBO. HBO was great fun. In *New Rules of the Game,* I wrote about doing crazy, risky things there, like climbing poles with cable operators (one of our customers) in order to better understand their business. I didn't *have* to climb those poles. I didn't have to do many of the things I did, in fact, like standing in freezing cold equipment rooms trying to learn the difference between a modulator and a receiver. I didn't *have* to because our customers' subscribers were already asking for HBO; it was an almost certain sale if I just showed up. But even if I couldn't put it into words at the time, I was demonstrating that I re-spected what they did and I cared enough to understand it a little more. I was working to build their trust. In short, basic EQ etiquette.

HBO's leadership was playing the long game with our customers. They gave us generous budgets to travel all the time if we so chose. As a first or second job out of school, who didn't want to see the world, even if it was only Peoria, Illinois? I was based in Chicago, running the surrounding region, so my hot spots ran from Skokie to Terre Haute. Management underwrote events we'd hold to say thank you for the business. And when I asked, the HBO big brass would leave their New York headquarters and come out to thank our customers personally. They recognized we'd need these partnerships on the next network rollout or marketing program we'd want them to promote. They taught me that no matter what level you rise to, your customers are your lifeblood.

HBO's leaders also knew that trust *within* the company was import-ant. They encouraged us to build camaraderie with others in the field and those who supported us in back-office jobs. We were allowed to use our expense accounts to buy our colleagues lunch or after-work drinks. Once, when I worked in the Los Angeles office, I asked an au-dit manager down the hallway to lunch. It was, let's just say, a memo-rable meal; reader, I ended up marrying him.

The moment we were hired, we were allocated four weeks of vaca-tion. It was a signal to us, the entry-level hires in our twenties, that management trusted us to do our jobs without a hammer over our heads. We were adults and should be treated as such. They invested in us out of the gate, too, with training programs that helped us to sell more thoughtfully and build trust with our customers. Like any big organization, HBO had its share of bad actors in management, people who were self-aggrandizing egomaniacs. But I'm eternally grateful to have started out at a place where the leadership modeled trust with its employees and its customers.

Regrettably, life invaded with some really tough stuff. As I mentioned, I was assaulted in my hotel room while traveling for business, and as a result, I came to feel detached, restless, and impatient at HBO. Two years later, while traveling internationally to see my sister, I was pulled out of the security line, brought to a private room, and strip-searched. It was another experience of feeling violated and completely powerless. All that budding willingness (Step One) to build trust (Step Two) with others disappeared. I was now in the sloshy place of questioning, all the time, my safety. As we learned from chapter one, safety is the most basic of our instincts, and you need it to be balanced and to engage well with others. My reaction was to put my feelings on lockdown. It wasn't visible to friends and clients, because I could still play the part well of an engaged and engaging person.

What does any twentysomething know of working through this kind of trauma? My new husband, Bill, a wonderful, gentle man, was fully in step with me, and he helped immensely by doing simple things like listening when I needed him to. He also understood when I needed to be with him without words. But at work I still felt detached, uninspired, and restless, so I quit. Some might say I ran.

## LACK OF TRUST WITH CONSUMERS: Z CHANNEL

In my next job, I was hired to turn around a potential gem of a business. It was called Z Channel, a subscription-based movie channel based in Los Angeles. It was a Hollywood darling because it showed all movies all the time, from mainstream hits to foreign films to uncut black-and-white classics. The business problem was that its distribution was too limited for it to make money. It was my job to get us into more homes so we could turn a profit. I reported to the owners, as did my new partner, Jerry Harvey, a Z Channel veteran. Jerry had done the programming there since its earliest days. He had an awe-inspiring knowledge of movies and knew exactly how to schedule them.

The new owners had access to first-run sports rights. They thought that if we added programming like Dodgers and Clippers games (the Lakers' rights were tied up), we could broaden our reach. Any ammo I could use to pitch to distributors was welcome, so I was gung-ho. I could tell that Jerry disagreed with the strategy, but he held back from direct confrontation. Without the tools of self-awareness and emotional fitness, I didn't know how to move from "hearing" his silence (what are you *not* saying?) to encouraging a dialogue within the team. Z Channel leaders were singularly focused on making our audience bigger, rather than more loyal and satisfied, which are two fundamentally different strategies. The strategies can be compatible with the right leadership in place, but we were missing that critical piece of the puzzle, and we stayed small in modeling Z Channel's potential, and because of it, our thinking was flawed.

I never imagined the degree to which Jerry objected to our direction, or all the other things that were going on in his life at that time. I knew little about his personal life, so I was completely blindsided when, one sunny Los Angeles afternoon, he shot and killed his wife and then himself.

You may not be able to relate to a colleague doing such an extreme, terrible thing, but most of us have experienced trauma, which, in the moment, takes your breath away. It remains with you unless you become willing to get past it. For me, having been blindsided three times in rapid succession, my response was to show up at work fully rehearsed. Like an automaton. I knew logically that the leadership team wasn't responsible for Jerry's tragedy, but I'd be a liar if I didn't say I felt some of that right afterward. We never tried to hear him, not really—which is basic to EQF—because he was this eccentric genius who, half the time, I didn't understand. We certainly didn't hear what he *wasn't* saying. When I rehashed this story in my first book, I still felt angry (after more than twenty years!) at Jerry. Now all I feel is deep sadness for him, and for his poor wife, a victim in his path of violence. Now I can look back at that time with the eyes of emotional fitness. Sometimes we wish the worst moments had never happened, but these are the very ones that push our emotional growth upward.

I've gained more "aha"s since then, wisdom for which I've worked as hard as if my life depended on it.

First, people like Jerry need to develop their emotional fitness like their life depends on it too, because for them it truly does. Second, Jerry's whole persona was wrapped up in the movies he brought to air. His life was his work, and his work was to live in the fabricated world of film. I don't think he stood a chance as long as he remained in that psychological and emotional place. In many ways, his story was my own. I could function in "work as life," not so much in "life as life," because at work I didn't need to confront my own fabricated world of denial. Emotional fitness has helped me to see that, and the many shades and blends of the real world that Jerry never had a chance to see. I've come to understand that Jerry and I shared a disease, which can manifest as substance abuse, but it goes much deeper. Tragically, Jerry never found the treatment and help that's out there. Parker Palmer's words resonate: "Violence is what happens when we don't know what else to do with our suffering."

As for his business instincts, Jerry was right about the network. Our viewers hated the sports programming. Sure, a few die-hard fans signed on, but our core viewing audience had no interest. They wanted their movies back. We ended up with two separate audiences, neither of which liked the interruption of unwelcome content. We'd failed to do the most important thing: to first ask our existing consumers if they wanted sports programming. Perhaps if we had scheduled sports in a certain way, we could have retained our core viewers *and* brought in some new ones. But we instead acted with naïveté, and arrogance too—hey, we're giving you something that you're sure to love, even though you never requested it! This was an enormous lesson: You can never, ever take your consumers for granted or assume you know what's in their best interest. *You need to build trust and then work each day to keep it.* A great idea doesn't mean squat if it's not road tested, and if it's not in a sweet spot for your customers. Some of our most important lessons can come from the mistakes we make.

Not too long after, Z Channel folded.

I didn't take a break to deal with the assault, the strip search, or Jerry's breakdown and death. Bill was always there for support, thank heavens, but I reverted back to my MO—I marched on, as we fanatically self-reliant workaholics do. I wasn't close to any kind of emotional fitness or spiritual insight. Besides, even if someone had laid all the tools at my feet, I wasn't ready. I now see with compassion that young woman, so brave and so lost. Self-compassion is one of the exceptional gifts that willingness has given me.

## LACK OF TRUST BUILDING WITH CONSUMERS *AND* CUSTOMERS: NBC

What I lacked in EQ Fitness I made up for in mental and physical resilience. I had survival skills and a respectable brain, so my career continued to flourish. While we were trying to reformulate Z Channel, NBC reached out and offered me a job to launch a new cable programming division, and I jumped aboard. First up on the priority list was a financial news channel. NBC had an enormous newsgathering operation that fed all its stations, so it figured it could tap those resources to get a channel off the ground. I ran the Midwest sales office that was responsible for distribution in a large swath of the country, and I also oversaw some key national accounts. A couple of years in, I added Canadian distribution to my responsibilities.

## Consumers

Our competition—if you want to call it that—was a rickety cable programming network called Financial News Network (FNN). It was going broke. NBC decided to swoop in and buy its assets so we could get a head start on airing FNN's programming (of little value) and leveraging its distributor contracts for access to significant viewership (of enormous value).

To add a little personal drama, as the FNN deal was being finalized, my husband, Bill, and I went overseas to adopt a baby. Bill had a small, struggling retail business, so we relied on my income to pay the bills, and depending on the way the deal winds blew, I might not have a job afterward. Who knew? But we didn't want to hold off on the adoption. While abroad, I tried to call my boss to check on the deal. I couldn't get through, so I had no idea if I'd be unemployed or a working mom when I came back.

I was terrified of both outcomes. I knew nothing of taking care of an innocent life. But I was always up for a challenge and knew I'd do the best I could. Thankfully, there was still a job to return to when we touched down back in the States.

## EQF Means Learning Your Lessons

When I pass into the great beyond, I hope people will say, "Ah, yes, Susan Packard. She always learned her lessons." I knew all too well from the Z Channel debacle that for CNBC to deliver, we needed to know what the current FNN viewers liked about their programming. But the programming folks at our headquarters in Fort Lee, New Jersey, didn't think much of the existing content. They said it was boring and unimaginative. Yet the fact remained that we *had* inherited a viewer base, and these viewers must have been loyal to *something*.

I feared another failure, and I could see one in the making. Even though I didn't work in programming, I thought I could lend a voice on behalf of the viewers if I figured out how to connect with them. I camped out with a few colleagues at some of our cable distributor offices as we switched the FNN signal to CNBC and answered calls from subscribers about the changeover. I was there to listen—a key EQF skill. Most people just want to be heard.

For the most part, the conversions were smooth, except for the matter of the ticker. FNN viewers loved the FNN ticker, which our CNBC programmers had decided to replace. Viewers told me, "It's too blue!" or "It's too fast!" or "The symbols are too small!" I don't know how many times I asked my leadership to talk to programming about resurrecting the original ticker.

You know the old saying "If it ain't broke, don't fix it"? Once again, I learned how arrogance—the worst form of unwillingness—is usually accompanied by enablers who'll say everything you want to hear. Arrogance will sink a business—and I was getting a bad sense of déjà vu. I might not have known willingness, but I still had some valuable practices that sprang from bare-bones emotional intelligence. I knew to listen, and I knew to share what I was hearing, and boy, did I pull out all my persuasion skills to get our programmers to hear our customers too. Finally, after lost time and capital, we went back to FNN's ticker.

## Customers

We also made a couple of bonehead moves—rooted in that same arrogance—with our customers, the distributors. The first resulted from offering them financial incentives to carry us on their cable systems. The reward was based on rolling out CNBC to a certain number of their subscribers. Many of our customers signed up for the program and launched CNBC. They were all in, but then NBC pulled the deal, saying they wanted more subscribers than what the sales team had secured. This change of heart meant that no one got paid, not even the distributors who had launched CNBC. It was a mess. That sort of behavior might fly if we were *never* going to work with those customers again.

But you're always going back to your customers with a new product, service, or marketing idea. You're always asking for something. When trust is broken, they have no reason to jump on board the next time.

I was at NBC for six years, enough time to gauge job fit, especially culture fit. It was a "winner take all" business, which seemed to work for the folks who stayed long-term, but I needed a place with more humanity. I needed a place where a customer wouldn't come up to me at a black-tie event, as one did, poke me in the chest, and say, "Your people are pigs!" That moment cemented that I didn't fit in there. (The final straw came when I lost out on a promotion to another guy.) EQ Fitness offers discernment, in this case choosing what's *not* for you as well as what is. This perspective is also called wisdom, and it grows as your emotional fitness does.

My NBC experience taught me that corporate arrogance trumps anything I might do to counteract it in the field with my customer relationships. I needed to *be* part of a corporate team with the authority to impact key decisions if I was to steer my own career into something that would be fulfilling.

It's fascinating that a person (me) can keep reaching for the brass ring while living with so much fear. It goes to the human spirit, I guess, in not allowing your fear and pain to sink you. My girlfriend Macy says, "When in fear, when in doubt, run in circles, scream and shout!" I did a lot of screaming and shouting in those days, at least on the inside, as I edged closer to willingness.

## THE EQF DREAM TEAM: HGTV

Here's the beauty of EQ Fitness: it makes your world so much bigger. You can be "successful" without it, as I was by many measures. But the important question is, Are you happy? Many of us are Oscar-worthy actors. We look the part, but we're suffocating inside, like a house with the windows permanently shut.

A window cracked open when I joined Home and Garden Television (HGTV) as its second employee. If I could have asked the cosmos to bring me an EQF dream team—if I had even known how to ask such a question—it would have looked like my colleagues at HGTV. They had a whole lot more emotional maturity than I did. They supported me openly and good-naturedly, like Jim with my first budget, and like Ken with my tribunal testimony in Canada. Given all the hostile workplace issues currently in the spotlight, particularly around sexual harassment, I'll add that I never experienced any disrespect or innuendo the entire time I was there. I knew I needed a fresh perspective to stop seeing the men I worked with as unsafe. I was ready to draw a new map, and this dream team made it that much easier. They helped me see that your past doesn't own you.

It also helped that I was an equal around the table. I'd earned that spot, which I was proud of and didn't take lightly. I felt a great responsibility for the many people who'd come to work there.

## Consumers

In chapter four, I covered the importance of job fit. I felt that belonging instantly at HGTV because, as I've said, I had a real passion for building a brand around the concept of "home." Home was about rootedness, grounding, things I longed for more of in my life.

Our start-up team envisioned the business as a stool with three legs: viewers (consumers), advertisers (customers, and where the lion's share of our revenue would come from), and cable and satellite distributors (also customers). But if there was one leg that we leaned on more than the others—that held up all the rest—it was our viewers. What difference did it make if we got homes that carried HGTV and advertisers to pay if no one tuned in? In every decision, we started with the consumers and how we could earn their valued trust. Our head programmer, Ed Spray, and his team worked from the three Is: every show would contain **ideas**, **information**, and **inspiration**.

Those benefits and the consistency with which we provided them were a big part of our appeal.

## A Quandary!

Here's where things got tricky. We didn't have direct access to our viewers because that relationship was controlled through the cable operator. Even today, less than 5 percent of national viewing comes from alternatives to the cable companies, like Netflix and Amazon Prime streaming services (although that market share continues to increase). We wanted ongoing access to our viewers, not just onetime communication. With ratings as our scorecard, we needed their input as the network unfolded.

We looked around at ESPN, CNN, Discovery, and all the big companies that had been around a lot longer, but no one had bothered to figure this out. Channing Dawson, the guy I'd hired who didn't fit into any easy box, suggested setting up a call center. What an inventive idea! So we did. We included a toll-free phone number at the end of our shows so people could call in with questions and feedback. Competitive networks thought we were loco. What they didn't know was that we could run this on a shoestring and still do the one thing vital to success: build trust with our consumers.

Viewers told us—in no uncertain terms—what they liked and what they hated. They loved how-tos; they hated shows like *Star Gardens*. *Star Gardens* featured B-list actors (because that's all we could afford), like Eva Gabor of *Green Acres* fame walking around her manicured estate and talking about how much she loved tending her gardens. It didn't take long for our viewers to call foul; they knew these people didn't pull one weed, and they couldn't care less about "star" value. They wanted information from experts. "Keep it true," they guided us. And because we listened, as EQ Fitness teaches us, they felt some ownership in the building of this network. That's a powerful thing, a real trust builder, and a critical lesson for anyone in business today.

One of the reasons we were able listen was because our programmers weren't defensive when they got bad news. It was my first experience with programmers without a huge dose of ego, who didn't think *they* were talent; they genuinely wanted what was best for the person at home. Ed Spray had been a longtime CBS broadcaster who'd retired early to teach media at Syracuse University, in New York. The tone he set for his team, and all of us, was to heed our viewers first and foremost. When Ed later ran SNI, he did a fabulous job managing the place with a steady and respectful hand.

Over years of talking to our viewers, we learned what was most important to them. The Rose Parade had been on the air for a long time before we decided to do it our way—the way our viewers wanted. They loved seeing the floats and the inventive arrangements of roses and other flora. They hated missing out on seeing a friend or relative's child in a marching band, because the commercials cut those parts out. Could we possibly air the Rose Parade commercial-free, they asked? We figured out the economics and did just that. It was an instant home run, and secured trust and loyalty from many viewers. HGTV still airs it that way today.

But trust is a fragile thing. We knew we had to keep working at it. With feedback from the call center, focus groups, and consumer panels, we came to build a brand that inspired and informed our viewers. In another effort to honor them, and our country, we pulled all programming on 9/11 and displayed a simple message of shared grief and sadness. We felt it wasn't appropriate to show lighthearted ("relentlessly pleasant," one review called it) fare in the midst of such tragedy. After a few days, our call center lit up with requests to resume our regular programming. People needed to watch something uplifting, something that reminded them of where they felt safe—their homes.

HGTV has that call center today, with six customer service representatives who still get a few phone calls but mostly respond to emails. Our viewers feel respected and taken care of, and in return they offer the network their time and allegiance. It's win-win.

The worst thing you can do with your consumers is to take them for granted, and that's true of emotional fitness too. Don't let up on either one. Make time for willingness tools, like listening, sharing, prayer, meditation, and building a community of trust-filled relationships. Your business will keep growing, as ours did.

## Customers

At HGTV, I worked hard to build trust with our customers too. My job was to get our network into homes, over cable lines, and through satellite providers like DIRECTV. These clients were beginning to feel abused by programmers (like my former employer NBC), which kept raising their rates every year. So we went in with reasonable rates *and* we made them true partners, offering to split advertising revenues with them for the first few years. They would share in our wins and celebrate the milestones together.

I was also responsible for starting up our international operations. I studied what had been done right and wrong by other programmers that were trying to export their brands. So many of the failures were based in—you guessed it—arrogance! I spent time wooing Canadian partners to work with us on launching a Canadian version of HGTV, but they were leery. One terrific group called Alliance Atlantis seemed open, so Ken and I spent time with them on their soil. This EQ Fit practice really mattered to our friends up north, who had experienced some strained relationships with American corporations that would meet only in the United States because, after all, we're all so busy here. The twin trust builders of face-to-face time and respect for them and their place of origin allowed our partnership to flourish, and shows like *Property Brothers* and *Holmes on Homes* can now be enjoyed by both US and Canadian audiences. These are still some of HGTV's most popular shows on the air today.

I've done a lot of negotiating over the years, and I now see that trust was a critical component every single time. When I wrote *New Rules of the Game*, I shared a story about negotiating with a man who was really short. He seemed uncomfortable when I'd wear heels and become taller than him, so the next time I saw him, I wore flats. I wrote that passage just a few years ago, but today I see the interaction, which I had described in terms of power and money, in a whole new light. When negotiating, you must always keep the other party from seeing your win as their personal defeat. Sure, I wanted a W for my company—that was my job. But I also wanted this guy to feel comfortable in the process. By starting on even ground—literally—we both left the table feeling like our companies had come out OK.

## FROM EQ TO TRUST TO EMOTIONAL FITNESS

You might remember when I asked Joe Zarantonello what makes a great leader, he said that great leaders are "fully human." That means that after everything falls apart, as it does for many of us at some point or another, you can choose escape or push through the muck and emerge more fully formed.

My life fell apart again during my time at HGTV. I lost my dad, mom, and sister in the span of just a few years. I knew enough not to run from that pain this time. When my sister died, the last of the three, I took a leave, and as hard as it was, I sat with all that loss. New insight came in that time, and a few years later I left the company.

My sixteen years at HGTV began that work toward becoming fully human. I'd practiced good EQ before, managing my emotions at work, reading others, and responding thoughtfully to them. These are only surface behaviors, however. They make work more efficient and let you get your way more often, but they're only ankle-deep. We need more. Maybe it's no coincidence that "Home" is the first word in both HBO and HGTV, jobs that were bookends to a media career I'm grateful for. Home is that place of rootedness we all seek, and home is where you grow up too.

# TRUST

## Mapping Your Career and Building Teams of the Future

### PRACTICE:
### Do a Career Trajectory

Map out how you got to where you are in your career today, whether it's your first job, you're in middle management, or you've been promoted to senior executive. Then write down moments of EQF along the way. Was the moment one of willingness or trust, or both? Did someone help you take a more expansive view, or did you arrive there on your own? What other factors played into these moments—office politics, organizational culture? What actions, solutions, or wisdom did you arrive at?

### PRACTICE:
### How to Design a High-EQ Team

You want to put people on teams who will work together fluidly, quickly, and well. Thinking analytically about team composition is especially key today, because in large and midsize companies, you may need to bring people together from different departments, divisions, and even countries. It can be a cost-saver too, since you're not staffing all new employees for a given project, especially if it's short-term.

Look for a team high in "collective intelligence." This is a group's ability to work together. Social perceptiveness, a component of high EQ, is the most powerful factor for collective intelligence. Those high in social perceptiveness pick up cues from others and are talented at getting everyone on the same page. Women are higher on social perceptiveness than men, so consider that in the balance. Avoid domineering personalities. Since trust improves when everyone thrives, getting teammates who know how to build small wins will foster trust more quickly.

When I ran SNI New Ventures, our goals were to create brands, develop video-on-demand capabilities, and dream about what the future might look like for television. To staff this team with me, I chose two women and two men. Both women already had full-time jobs: Kristen Jordan, who was running our international group, and Ruth Tatom, who handled the large accounts of our cable operators. These women had done fine work for me in the past, and I knew that building new businesses excited them. I added one full-time employee, an engineer, and transferred Channing Dawson, our big-vision guy, over full-time. I tried to be considerate of the women's day jobs and checked in frequently about their workload. We set up bonus goals so that everyone would be financially rewarded if we met our goals, in addition to the incentives they'd earn from their primary jobs.

## TIPS

- Start with a pool of high-EQ talent. Get to know people in your organization, and/or screen for EQ with a test like the emotional and social competency inventory (ESCI) at www .eiconsortium.org.
- Consider co-captains or co-leaders for the team if you're staff-

ing from existing employees, so that you have backup leadership if one person's day job pulls them away for a time.

- Keep teams small and nimble—from three to eight people.
- Establish an end date to your assignment, say six months or less.
- Staff at least 50 percent women.
- Have a kickoff meeting at which the leaders ask each member about their other job duties and what they're working on. This will add perspective if a member can't show up for every meeting.
- Create norms of behavior, like "email communication needs to copy all." Establish emotional norms too, like respectful debate and "let's have fun with this project."

*Thanks to **Dr. Anita Williams Woolley** at Carnegie Mellon University for her work in collective intelligence.*

# PRACTICE:
## Trust in Future Work Teams

## TRUST U.

In April 2017, I had the privilege of spending the day with Carnegie Mellon Tepper School of Business faculty and students. I met over lunch with **Dean Bob Dammon**, Dr. Robert Kelley, Distinguished Service Professor of Management, and **Dr. Laurie Weingart**, interim provost and Richard M. and Margaret S. Cyert Professor of Organizational Theory and Behavior. We centered our discussion on trust—specifically, what academics are noticing about their "consumers" (students) who have grown up communicating through technology. What are their interactions like with one another and faculty? How do their teams work together to solve problems, or not? Are their devices facilitators or inhibitors to team building?

This is an edited representation of our dialogue and includes thoughts from a follow-up conversation with Dr. Kelley. Use it as a study guide to exploring trust, and how it impacts our current and future workplaces, from these forward thinkers.

Dr. Weingart noted that as faculty of a business school, "from the behavioral side of it, we're very concerned about ways to grow trust. Where is technology getting in the way of human interaction? Where can it be used to improve it? That's the constant battle. In the classroom we struggle with this. We keep pushing students to close their laptops, for example. We're looking at how technology interferes, and how it can be leveraged."

That's an important point: it's really about the sweet spot of what technology can facilitate and where it holds us back. "This is a big deal for CMU," Dean Dammon said. "Beyond the interaction issues, more broadly, this is a university that's at the hub of creating many uses of new technologies."

"My concern is where technology holds us back from human connection," I said.

Dr. Weingart nodded. "You hit the nail on the head. Connecting with people is really about looking at them in the eye." She asked me to define "trust."

"I see it as the feeling of safety with someone or a group that allows you to be willing to take chances or take on risk."

It turns out that's pretty much in line with "the academic definition of 'trust,' which is the willingness to be vulnerable to another person, and to rely on them in the absence of monitoring them," Weingart explained. "This is a really interesting piece of human connection, the willingness to make yourself vulnerable. The ways parents are controlling kids' interactions today, children never have to be vulnerable. We put too much protection around them."

Dr. Kelley took on a more pessimistic tone: "Because kids are growing up so tethered to their devices, they're not able to read other people. When you show them a face with an emotion, they don't know what to make of it, and as a result they don't know how to respond or close themselves off.

"If you google 'children reading emotions,' you'll see increasingly, as kids can't read emotions from other people, we're going to be in bad shape. Tune in to the video from Sandy Hook Promise, and you'll see that people aren't reading other people, not because they don't want a relationship, but because they're not *scanning* their environment to look at others and see if someone's sad, or upset, looking at those around you. This is about being a citizen, being part of a community. Some people are trying to intervene, to help. They're working with kids that are ten years old, and they take their devices away and teach them about empathy and reading others. They've found it takes six to eight weeks before the kids make progress."

. . .

As we develop our individual EQ Fitness, we also have the opportunity to shape the EQ Fitness of our future colleagues. Share this passage (available on my website, www.susanpackard.com/carnegiemellonu) with a colleague, mentor, or friend and discuss the questions below.

1. How do you define "trust"?
2. Do you find that your use of technology—as my friend Lynn describes on page 110—is affecting how you communicate?
3. If you are a parent or work with children or young adults, have you noticed how children read or adapt to emotions? In what ways?

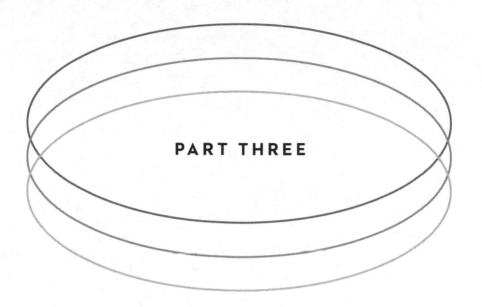

# PART THREE

# EMBRACING "WE" PRINCIPLES

*Close both eyes*
*and see with the other eye.*

—Rumi[1]

The Sufis sometimes speak of the Great Ocean. Not five oceans, but the single connected water mass that comprises over 70 percent of Earth. In that Great Ocean, also called Spirit, there are waves. Each wave looks separate to the human eye from the beach, but they ebb and flow and blend together as one. The Great Ocean does not recognize the word "only."

Meditate on that a little bit. It will help as we embark on Step Three. Until now, you've been enhancing your EQ so you can arrive at work and build relationships of trust. You're deep in your EQ Fitness practice, but this is just the beginning of leadership, which includes being the leader of your own life. Now, we become people who can put our own interests aside when needed to see more expansively.

We have gone from "me" to "we." We are united in the Great Ocean.

## THE "WE" PRINCIPLES

Step Three brings us spiritual insight, as lived through We Principles. We find connectedness through hope, generosity of spirit, and moral courage. Values like these bind and sustain us when we celebrate euphoric moments, like turning a profit, and they undergird the most challenging times all organizations face, like encroaching competitors or economic crises.

Spiritual insight is a dimension of self—of an inner life—that is like light entering a room. Or like one day, you feel all your jagged edges have been smoothed out and the picture of you is now complete. Developing an inner life brings an awareness that you're connected to something larger, that there is a higher order of things. This higher order is not any particular religion, because it has more breadth than any one idea. What trips us up is when we imagine too tiny a God.

Spiritual insight provides emotional balance, deeper discernment, and inner strength, and galvanizes you to build relationships that will endure. You can cultivate spiritual insight, but not demand it. Like all wisdom, it comes upon you quietly. We Principles are more than qualities—they express as a powerful set of actions that help fuel wisdom. In *The Road Less Traveled*, M. Scott Peck calls spiritual growth a "promotion, a call to higher responsibility and power. A transcendent call to grace."[2] I admit not understanding how all this works; I just know that when I lead others and live my life from a place of We Principles, I feel a sense of well-being. I believe that outcomes will be as they should—which is *trust* too. That peace of mind is a gift, I think, for simply trying to create a welcoming place for grace.

## WHAT MASLOW KNEW

Psychologist Abraham Maslow, like me, was well into his career when he arrived at the importance of spiritual insight. His renowned Hierarchy of Needs (figure I), which is still taught in psychology and business management courses today, lays out our order of needs, from the most basic—physiological—to the most meaningful, which he called self-actualization. Later, Maslow discovered that we don't stop at the actualizing phase, that we grow spiritually too, and he called it self-transcendence (figure J). This is our need to find purpose outside ourselves.

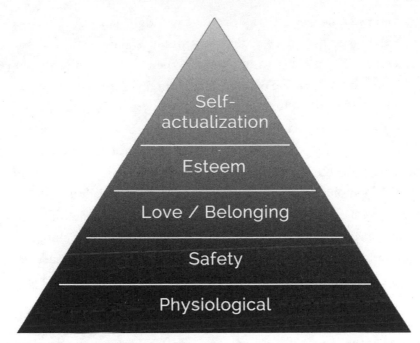

**FIGURE I:** Maslow's Hierarchy of Needs

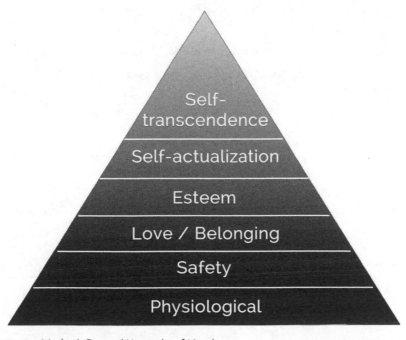

**FIGURE J:** Maslow's Revised Hierarchy of Needs

We Principles embody right actions *and* right motives. Everyone will find his or her own way to them through the tools of emotional fitness; getting there is an inside job. When we do, and we deploy them in the workplace to build relationships of trust, they help create titanium-strength cultures, like the culture we built at HGTV that sparked our team toward remarkable success.

Here's the thing—we're not always in a place of selfless motives, because we're human. This is a program of progress, not perfection. It's the right *actions* that matter most in the final analysis, and We Principles are your measuring stick. The good news is that the more you practice picking up the tools and *doing* the next right thing, the more your motives will become we-centered too. It's like a dancer who rehearses a certain step over and over until one day she does it fluidly, with complete ease. It's become second nature.

It's time to step up to the values that underpin our finest emotions and to evolve spiritually. The world is constantly shifting and unfolding too. To paraphrase a Parker Palmer line: What are we sending from within ourselves out into the world? Start where you work and where you call home.

Here's a promise: when you carry We Principles into your workplace, home, and community, your life gets a whole lot better.

# CHAPTER EIGHT

# MANAGING PRIDE & EGO

*The fundamental cause of the trouble is that in the
modern world the stupid are cocksure while the
intelligent are full of doubt.*

—BERTRAND RUSSELL[1]

**read a story years ago about** a woman who thought she was more powerful than death. Her name was Sarah Winchester, wife of the inventor of Winchester rifles. After the deaths of her husband and child, she began building an enormous, bizarre home in San Jose, California. The construction kept sixteen carpenters employed full-time for thirty-eight years. Before some of it was destroyed by fire, it contained two thousand doors and ten thousand windows. There are twists and turns and mazes galore; today it's a mystery fun house that's open to the public. Mrs. Winchester kept building and building, convinced that if she just kept on adding on, she could trump death. But it came for her just the same.

You might think, well, she was just wacky. When I scroll through the news, however, I see a parade of executives who think they're immortal too. As I wrote this book, CEOs from Wells Fargo, Volkswagen, Mylan, Turing Pharmaceuticals, Peanut Corporation of America, Massey Energy, and many others have made national news with stories of consumer cover-ups, price gouging, and deaths of their employees due to unsafe practices. Brian Williams was demoted from lead anchor of *NBC Nightly News* for fabricating his reporting. The #MeToo social media hashtag, which resurfaced in the fall of 2017 for women to share their stories of harassment and assault, has led to a mainstream conversation about power, assault, and complicity—with real consequences for many abusers. We've seen male leaders from Netflix, Uber, Fox News, Amazon Studios, the Weinstein Company, and countless others yanked from their positions in the aftermath. In fact, from 2010 to 2017, US companies paid more than $295 million in penalties over sexual harassment claims.[2] (The number is likely much larger; those penalties were revealed in disclosures by public companies and don't include private company settlements.)

Arrogance and greed lead to the corrosive use of power—executives on ego trips. They can infect an organization until its stock prices take a dive and the company culture craters. From 2000 to 2013, about 25 percent of the CEO departures in Fortune 500 companies were involuntary, according to research association Conference Board.[3] The fallout in shareholder cost is astronomical. On the flipside, leaders who get high marks on qualities such as compassion and integrity run companies with an average return on assets of 9.35 percent over two years—five times those who got low marks, whose companies average 1.93 percent.[4] If it's not clear yet: pride and ego are culture corrupters. As a leader, you can't stand with your people if you're standing above them.

This chapter explores different kinds of dysfunctional and adolescent behaviors that are on the opposite end of the spectrum from the factors we looked at in chapter one, where fear and insecurities can keep us immature. Here we focus on excessive pride because it breeds employees' distrust and is one of the easiest ways to destroy the emotional fitness of an organization. It creeps in when you get a taste of power or control, and it's a very emotionally unstable place to be, because one's happiness depends on external factors, not a core of inner peace. These kinds of callow leaders cannot defer their own needs for the greater good. They're in dire need of We Principles.

# EQ AND "WE" MOTIVES

In the bestseller *Emotional Intelligence 2.0*, the authors reveal that CEOs, on average, have the lowest EQ scores in a given workplace, while middle managers have the highest.[5] That midlevel talent, in the thick of projects and deadlines with people above and below, wouldn't stand a chance without prime EQ. What happens with CEOs, however, is that they increasingly remove themselves from their people. They interact less and less with the rest of the organization. Their most important job—working through their teams to drive the company's success—becomes a low item on their to-do list. They transform into the big shots, "the execs on the forty-first floor." EQ behaviors, which may have gotten that manager promoted to an executive in the first place, start to take a back seat to egoistic behaviors. It's all too easy to move from "we" to "me" if you're not vigilant.

A joke sums it up best: We all know the executive who, despite an arrogant exterior, is very much capable of love, affection, intimacy, and caring. However, these feelings don't usually involve anyone else. Too bad the joke is on us, since a whole lot of organizations are still run by the big shots with an exaggerated sense of their own importance. For these men and women, self-worth is solely a measurement of net worth.

I've known leaders who exhibit keen EQ by its strictest definition: they regulate their emotions well at work and can read others and respond in ways that draw them in. This looks like EQ but doesn't take into account *motives*, a key element that's been absent from the discussion around emotional intelligence. Motives can be constructive, like those stemming from practicing We Principles, or destructive, focused on one's narrow self-interest. Behaviors are easy to see, but motives reside within, so they're harder to ferret out. It needs to be done, however, whether it's in the interview process, through personality screenings, or by exhaustive reference checking. A leader may seem like a dream hire, but before you know it, they begin to dismantle the culture from within because it's all about them.

Perhaps a more useful framework is to look at what psychologists call the "dark triad" traits of personality: narcissism, Machiavellianism, and psychopathy. The story never ends well when these traits are present, according to the research. Organizational cultures always suffer. Narcissism is a 24/7 ego trip, but it can present as charisma, charm, and magnetism, which are "superhero" qualities that often inspire devotion and loyalty. Machiavellians are masters at manipulating others to further their own ends, but they can be so clever that you don't see the maneuvering going on. "Psychopathy" is an umbrella term for exploitive, antisocial behavior and other forms of mental illness. Psychopaths make up about 1 percent of the population—yet one in five CEOs is a psychopath.[6] Similar research has found that the base rate of psychopathy is three times higher among corporate boards than in the general population.[7] The dark triad qualities are all in service of the same ends: to further the leader's agenda, regardless of the damage caused to those they lead.

## PRIDE AS THE GREAT SIN

Overly prideful people have been studied and written about for millennia. The ancient Greeks called it hubris, a tragic flaw that led to a man's downfall. In the sixth century, Pope Gregory the Great said pride was the cause of all other sin. British novelist and essayist C. S. Lewis called it the "Great Sin." Being in a seat of power can bring a tremendous swell of pride, which, unchecked, can lead to feelings of entitlement and greed. Contemplative monk Thomas Merton said that to grow spiritually, we must be content to live without watching ourselves live.[8] In those few words, Merton tells us that excess pride is a soul sickness, curable only by moving away from a relentless focus on self and toward a focus on others.

One of our HGTV advisors, **Dr. Steve Martin**, was often on hand when we discussed company culture. I always thought of him as our "culture czar" because he had influenced much of our thinking with his wisdom. Sometimes, when one of us began feeling that hubris the Greeks warned about, he'd say, "Don't forget the first law of philosophy, theology, and common sense: I could be wrong." But still, as COO, I felt a few heady moments of big-shot grandeur. When we finally got around to building new office space, CEO Ken Lowe and I had a suite with a shared conference room, and moving into that space was a big-shot moment. I could have stayed in these "walls of power" and taken all my meetings there, but that would have been a disservice to the culture we were trying to build, so I tried to schedule several meetings a day outside my area. Anyone who needed meeting space was also welcome to use the conference room, so folks from different departments would regularly swing by.

If you feel a sense of belonging and are *then* given power, like I was at HGTV, you generally don't glom on to that power for your own benefit, but instead are concerned about how it will impact others in a meaningful way.[9] A year after I came to the organization as executive vice president, I was promoted to chief operating officer. The team coalesced in that year, and because of it, I don't think I acted out of pride or ego alone. Some things fell to me, decisions that only I could make, but I can honestly say the team remained equals because we started that way. We all came to work with the focus on building a business and a culture that would live on. This shared purpose was bigger than any one of us.

## TAMING PRIDE

Managing pride is the segue to Step Three, which is why it requires a whole chapter. Take all we've learned from our willingness work in Step One, which has made clearer our gifts and limitations, and given us a more objective view. With Step Two, we began to extend olive branches of trust and use other new skills, such as vulnerability, which is a pride crusher. We bring all these practices to Step Three, because ego-taming is hard work. It goes against the grain of many type A personalities and accomplished people. But it is absolutely imperative if we are to reach the final frontiers of EQ Fitness: building collaborative work cultures and rich inner lives.

Let's start examining the illusory nature of power and control.

## THE MYTH OF CONTROL

Sometimes, we act "me" rather than "we": *not* from a place of vanity but from a belief that we need to be in complete control to stay in the game. In *Recovery—The Sacred Art*, Rabbi Rami Shapiro describes ego as the part of you that feeds on and maintains the illusion of power and control.[10] But it's a fallacy, and your ego is quite the trickster. If you're willing to pay attention to the world outside yourself, you'll quickly learn that not one of us has absolute control.

Life unfolds in a zigzag. You're responsible for your choices, sure, but much of it is beyond just you. Surrendering to that understanding might seem demoralizing, but in my experience it is just a big relief. Philanthropist and author Sarah Ban Breathnach describes it as "the long sigh of the soul,"[11] and that's how it felt when I finally saw how things often unfolded with a jolt. Unexpectedly.

EQ Fit leaders accept that there's much beyond their ken, which keeps pride in check. Recognizing the limits of our own power is also an important life skill, because it gives us a more patient set of eyes to assess our conditions as they change and evolve. When you recognize your own limits, you also recognize that life deals all of us some losing hands—you didn't cause them. For example, a group layoff. Or half of your family dying before their time, like mine did. In these moments you know how small your sway over life is. Sometimes those moments bring you to your knees—a cosmic surrender.

Can you accept that you can't succeed by raw willpower alone? This one's even juicier: acknowledging that you can find lasting joy only by allowing others in. As the behavioral therapist O. Hobart Mowrer said, "You alone can do it, but you can't do it alone." The talents you have are uniquely yours, but you still need others to complement and complete them.

The work we do as leaders is to influence others, not control them. Domination and bullying may work for a time, but you'll just push people away in the long run. Coming to a place of acceptance will grant peace of mind, and, as we saw in chapter three, there are many competitive advantages of coming to work in a place of inner harmony and peace.

## SEEING WITH NEW EYES

When the pupil is ready, the teacher will appear. I was in the saddle at HGTV for a year or two when a friend of mine sent me David Whyte's *The Heart Aroused*. Whyte argues for workplaces with more heart and soul, more "poetry." He recasts the life of the middle manager, who's living a rigid but safe existence, through Dante's *La Divina Commedia*. After a lifetime of believing that success was all he needed to stay safe, his protagonist "wakes in a dark wood," not recognizing the road at all. Whyte urges the reader to "awaken," and look hard at the path she is on, and ask the most important question of all: Where does this lead?

*The Heart Aroused* shook me to the core because I was in the right place to receive its message. Working with purpose to launch HGTV, with a team I could trust, a coach I could talk to, and a book that forced me to look deeper, I had an EQ growth spurt. I began asking those questions that soul—not ego or pride or fear—presses us on to ask.

I was lucky to have it all come together, but you can set up your own fertile ground for growth too. Find the willingness to seek out work that gives you purpose, like we saw others do in chapter four. Find trustworthy partners, like those we met in Step Two. Do the share work every time there's an opportunity, as we explored in chapter two. You'll discover that when you're ready, you'll get the lesson you need, and it will come from a place far deeper than your ego can ever reach.

## ANOTHER VIEW OF EGO: SELF-MANAGER

While big egos and puffed-up pride are a common malady of "me"-centric CEOs, there's another definition of "ego" that psychologists use, and it's relevant to business leadership. Freud's model of the psyche was id, ego, and superego. Id is impulse, superego imposes social and moral value, and ego mediates between the two so you can function in society. Ego functions as a survival machine, putting armor around your most fragile parts. It sublimates traumas and other inner pain so you can live out in the world. Its mission statement is "No change. Stay safe."

My spiritual director Joe Zarantonello describes people who live in a perpetual ego state as a "head on a stick." It's a useful image of someone rigid who rarely ventures out of their comfort zone. I was a head on a stick for years, walking around expecting to be attacked. I had smoothed over the rough edges on the outside, but the anxiety was still there. There are so many ways we get to that place: insecurities, immaturity, or childhood pain manifesting with an inability to trust, so the trust work in part two is key.

If you didn't have an ego in this sense, you'd probably be balled up in a corner somewhere. Ego helps us to get up in the morning, to stand up in the world. It helps us to form an identity, however one-dimensional it might be. Our work now is to lessen the ego's prominence in our identity, whether it materializes as excessive pride, or living an anxious, boxed-in life.

## EGO AND SOUL ENERGY

A couple of years ago, I gave a TEDx talk at the University of California, Los Angeles, on emotional maturity, or as I call it here, emotional fitness.[12] I shared how you grow in emotional maturity through the right mix of ego energy and soul energy. This expansion always begins with self-awareness. Consider: What are your gifts and shortcomings? What skills do you still need to learn? Those issues require **ego energy**, a left-brained process, and from these our ego-self develops. Then you can move to the deeper questions: Who were you meant to be? What is your place in the world? That kind of **soul energy**, which comes from the right brain, explores how you are connected to the larger family of workplace and community.

Joe always reminds me to charge my "soul phone" each morning. That's his way of saying to start the day with meditation, prayer, and writing, all right-brained practices. Einstein found a similar equilibrium by listening to music before diving into his (left-brained) mathematics work. When we strive for balance, a *fully* human integration of our potential, the matter of pride falls away because we're pulled toward connection with others—"we"—and away from just "me."

## THE DANCE OF THE RIGHT AND LEFT BRAIN

I created a chart that illustrates, in one or two words, the main differences between ego energy and soul energy. Engineers and operations people work predominantly with left-brain tasks (if you need a refresher on left- and right-brain actions, return to figure D in chapter three). We need our ego brain, but in Western culture we've placed disproportionate value there. We can nourish our right brains through practices like meditation.

In short, the ego asks "what?" while the soul asks "where?" Both questions are key to navigating life. We need both soul and ego, right

| EGO ENERGY | SOUL ENERGY |
|---|---|
| Answer | Question |
| Box | Horizon |
| Intellect | Imagination |
| Word | Silence |
| Order | Influence |
| Worry | Prayer |
| Job | Purpose |
| Plan | Unfolding |
| Judgment | Experience |
| Heaviness | Lightness |
| Protection | Vulnerability |
| Conscious Mind | Heart, Gut, Sense |
| Drive toward | Drawn to |
| Attachment | Love |
| Sadness | Deep Grief |

**FIGURE K:** Ego Energy vs. Soul Energy

and left brain, to function well in our jobs. This is true in my writing today. I have to use my left brain to structure and bring order to the content, but I preface most writing sessions with meditation, so I might have openings to connect with you from a deeper place.

# WHAT SOUL ENERGY LOOKS LIKE IN ORGANIZATIONS

## IT FUELS OPENNESS

There is an attitude in the Korean Zen tradition called Don't-Know Mind. It sees each moment as offering something fresh to wrap your mind around. The willingness practices of mindfulness and meditation we discussed in chapter three help with developing Don't-Know

Mind, as they anchor you in the present moment, when you're not distracted with past or future worries and can absorb new ideas. Fully human is fully present. In that place, you are open and alert to learning and enlarging your world. This means, too, that you're open to not being perfect.

You wouldn't think a brigadier general Green Beret in the Army Special Forces would be emotionally "open." But people have ways of surprising you. It took twelve years from his first battlefield trauma for Brigadier General Donald C. Bolduc to seek care for PTSD. After three years of treatment, he shared his story with his soldiers so they would see it's OK—not weak or unmanly—to seek treatment for their own mental health issues and unseen injuries. He views PTSD like a broken bone; asking for help should be expected and encouraged, and in the long run it will bolster, not hurt, a soldier's career. Since he spoke out, other high-ranking officers have come forward. One even went on CNN to urge a sea change in our cultural approach to PTSD; otherwise its stigma will continue to keep too many soldiers from getting support. Bolduc has focused his soul energy on leading his traumatized soldiers back toward wholeness, and with that, he inspires other leaders to open up too. PTSD expert and psychotherapist Edward Ticks recounts in his book *War and Soul* how soldiers with PTSD experience reciprocal healing from working with sick and orphaned children. A virtuous cycle continues.

Centering Prayer, the form of meditative practice we examined in chapter three, is another way to open your mind. As with other EQ practices, it also helps strip away the corrosive, habitual behaviors and beliefs that build up over a lifetime.

## IT FUELS BEING RIGHT-SIZED

Soul energy directs our egos to a place of balance, toward their right size. Being right-sized means having a realistic view of yourself and your dominion. Unilever's Paul Polman said he's not a CEO with immense power; instead, he has what he calls "convening" power, which he uses to bring people together with resources and to find the right partnerships for his company. He then allows the specialists to do their work. Similarly, former DuPont CEO Ellen Kullman was brought up understanding that she could never "out-PhD a PhD chemist." "Early in my career," she admitted, "I had to lead people where I wasn't as technically proficient, so you learn to lead in different ways. It's more listening than telling."

Being right-sized can even take the form of a willingness to let go of your power. "Good CEOs become dispensable," said NPR CEO Jarl Mohn. "When I was out six weeks with open-heart surgery, the team operated spectacularly. They ran the business and occasionally let me know what was up, but generally moved ahead without me. I sense many execs fear being dispensable, because it may put their jobs at risk. I've found the opposite. The better the team performs, the more successful the overall organization, including me."

## IT FUELS "WE" OVER "ME"

Mary Ellen Brewington had a dilemma. She was one of four children who had taken over her parents' business, Cherokee Distributing. While her brother George was heir apparent after their father passed away, the siblings were all equal partners. Then two of her siblings sadly passed away too. She and her brother were left to run the business. Before it had all fit together so naturally. Now what? "Family members can be terrible about jumping in each other's lane," she told me. It can happen when siblings (like some colleagues) don't respect the other's position or authority.

After sitting with this situation for some time, she knew what she had to do, for the good of the company, for her brother's sake, and for her own. She went into her brother's office, closed the door, and said, "You have my permission and blessing. You are the boss." Their partnership today is one bred of mutual respect.

She'd be the first to admit that it wasn't easy, but it was the right choice because it provided the company with clear and consistent leadership, something that can be elusive when you have two captains. She adds that saying those words were as much for *her* as for her brother or the company. As we've seen time and again, simply saying something aloud frees us to move on: name it, claim it, and let it go.

When Hubert Joly, chairman and CEO of Best Buy, took over in 2012, the company was on life support. He put many policies in place, but one especially resonated because it told his new workforce that he saw them, heard them, and they mattered: He resurrected the employee discount. Cutting the discount had been a mere matter of crossing out a line item on an income statement—simple math that was enormously harmful to morale. Bringing it back was a soul practice, prioritizing the "we" who were working within a tumultuous environment. Joly said, "Once you've had a near death experience, arrogance, if you had it in your bones, has disappeared forever."[13] And it didn't just improve morale; it also helped sales pick up dramatically.

## IT FUELS LAUGHTER

What always helps me choose "right" over "easy," soul over ego, is laughter. Humor is a funny thing (*sorry*); what's funny to one person often isn't to another. But whatever gets you laughing releases something elemental, and not just serotonin and endorphins. Father Carl Arico, a Centering Prayer leader, says that it's only in laughter that our minds let go and our hearts open. Laughter softens us, and releases tension. It brings perspective. At HGTV, we did silly things like print bumper stickers that said COMPOST HAPPENS. Get it? See, you might not think that's funny at all. But enough of us did that this one small thing helped people to breathe—especially after working sixty-hour weeks, something not uncommon in the launch phase of a business. It made trust building so much easier, because when laughter comes easily to someone, they're just easier to warm to.

It's also cheap therapy (as in, free), so why not add it to your arsenal?

## BEFORE WE GIVE PRIDE A SEND-OFF . . .

Let me be clear: pride can be a wonderful thing. Having pride in what you do stems from self-respect, a gift of the willingness work we did in part one. A secret to employing emotionally fit leadership and We Principles is self-awareness, a healthy pride in what you accomplish, and balancing power with values of service.

Paul Polman embodies that right balance of power and generosity. He said to me, "A good leader is a good human being in the first place." Leaders who carry themselves with quiet confidence are out there, but they don't make headlines, because they don't act outrageously to get them. They see their jobs as perpetuating financial *and* emotional health in their employees. They model dignity and grace, and do what they can to leave a positive impact. They value their position as one of stewardship, which is a commitment to leaving their organizations better off after they're gone. When I asked Jarl about what he'd like his legacy to be at NPR, he said he just wanted it to be financially secure enough to live on for many decades more.

As you can see, a linchpin to EQ Fitness is *balance*. This means recognizing both your gifts and your limitations, and being open to trust but shrewd enough to identify someone who won't make it a two-way street. We Principles require balance too; through ego management, you can maintain sturdy self-respect while detecting when overblown pride creeps in. Step Three provides a solution—We Principles, which we'll see in action next.

# CHAPTER NINE

# WE PRINCIPLES IN ACTION

*The person with the power must be the person with the grace.*

—DR. STEVE MARTIN

The head emergency room doctor was training a resident when the head nurse overheard the younger doctor's performance review and retold this story. The senior doctor then turned to the resident and said, "Did you notice the man who's come and cleaned the room each time we've had a patient in?" The young doctor stared back blankly.

"His name is Carlos. He does a fantastic job! He turns our rooms around so quickly that we can see many patients. His wife's name is Maria. They have four kids." He named the four children. "How about next week you tell me something about Carlos I don't already know? Now let's see our next patient."

This true story beautifully illustrates We Principles, three actions that bind teams together with shared purpose. These are **hope, generosity of spirit**, and **moral courage**. The senior doctor offered hope to Carlos, and to the young doctor, too, because he gave him a broader understanding of the talent in his workplace. He modeled generosity of spirit, showing compassion for someone whom others may not have noticed or stood up for, and showing gratitude for that person's work. His moral courage shone through in doing what was right, reflecting a humility that's often hard to find in the US medical profession.

Emotional fitness, the transcendent state of emotional intelligence, is a program of growth. We Principles are the last step. On our path so far, we've looked at how to show up and channel our healthy emotions, as a leader or manager or employee. We are mercurial beings, but we can temper our low moments by how we *act*. Even when we feel bad or are off our game, we can always choose to do the next right thing, rather than get leveled by fear or anger. Whenever we act for the benefit of a colleague or the greater good of our organizations, and not in reaction to our self-serving, squirrelly minds, that's practicing emotional fitness. You model it for your teams and coworkers when you choose "we" over "me," gratitude over greed. You model it by the actions you take every moment you're in a leadership role.

A strong inner life, the spiritual dimension of self, helps a lot here, because it's a perpetual reminder that you're not doing this work alone. As you gain more spiritual muscle, you become more rooted in right actions. It's like a tree that begins as a seed, and with nourishment grows from sapling to maturity, and is able to carry the weight of branches and wildlife that might want to make a home there. Meditation, prayer, and serving others make emotional fitness more accessible and authentic actions of the heart.

We built HGTV around these core values:

**FIGURE L:** HGTV Core Values

These were our guiding principles. Working with these values, and subsequently with the organizational consulting and coaching I've been doing, I've arrived at three principles that have the most potent impact on engineering strong communities and strong cultures:

| WE PRINCIPLES | ACTION | MOTIVATION |
| --- | --- | --- |
| Hope | Lead with it | Aspirational, expansive |
| Generosity | Respond with it | Being of service |
| Moral courage | Model it | Being true to you and your values |

**FIGURE M:** The Three We Principles of EQ Fitness

# HOPE

Hope is an integral quality of emotionally fit leaders because it is the most contagious emotion we have. The more hopeful you are about the promise of your organization, the more hopeful your people will be.

Hope is infectious, but so is despair. Despair has given rise to a whole industry of crisis managers, ready to plot the gloom and doom of some sticky situation you're up against, unless of course you hire them. But before we call something a crisis, we should refresh our lens of hope. A willingness to begin with hope helps us discern how grave a situation really is, or is not.

## HOPE AS EDUCATION . . .

I got to know **Judy Girard** when she came to SNI after a luminary career in network programming. She ran our two biggest brands, Food Network and HGTV, and was there during key times in their growth. Then, sadly for SNI, she retired.

"I left all the corporate stuff behind, moved to a beach in Wilmington [North Carolina] with my husband, traveled, and read books. That's all I wanted to do," she told me. "I was tired! Then one thing leads to another and before I know it, I'm working to get a charter school up and running for middle school girls in Wilmington."

As is so often the case, the "before I know it" details are the ones worth hearing. Those are all the times she said yes when someone asked something of her—and when she saw a yes moment before even being asked. She took on the YMCA dues of four-year-old Tiffany,[1] so this energetic little girl would have a place to go after school and not be removed from her aging grandmother's care. This, in turn, led to her witnessing how poorly the public school system treated Tiffany and the kids of color under its care—segregated and without hope. "They haven't got a shot!" she'll say fiercely. She said yes to a rising senior at a girls' academy in Harlem and helped her get ready for college interviews. Today, Judy's charter school is modeled after the Harlem Academy. She said yes to a full-time unpaid job for two years to get paperwork and charter applications together ("I hate process!"), and she said yes to raising money for the school.

Judy's school, called GLOW (Girls Leadership Academy of Wilmington), has been up and running since 2016, with two hundred girls who qualify for free or reduced-price lunches filling its sixth- and seventh-grade classrooms. If her school replicates the achievements of others in the national Young Leadership Network of eighteen schools, 98 percent of its students will graduate from the high school they've yet to build, and 100 percent of those kids will go on to college.

"I had a three- to five-year retirement plan, like how I managed my career. None of that has happened. One day I'm walking on a beach, and GLOW takes on a life of its own. You can't plan where life will take you. You'll just be led."

## ... AND HOPE AS WORK

Father G of Homeboy Industries, the priest you met in chapter one, leads kids out of gang life through meaningful work, giving them a reason to envision a future. They get paid for making silk-screens and baked goods; doing maintenance and repair, merchandising; and staffing their café. They wear T-shirts that say NOTHING STOPS A BULLET LIKE A JOB. How's that for hope?

Father G believes that "if we were more sensible . . . we'd be somehow infusing the kids with hope when they can't imagine their future and they're planning their funerals. Or we'd heal kids who are so damaged that they can't see their way clear to transform their pain, so they continue to transmit it."[2]

As Nazi survivor Elie Wiesel reminded us, "Just as man cannot live without dreams, he cannot live without hope."[3] Hope looks like school for Judy's kids, and work for Father G's. The two things that can give all kids a shot at a promising life are education and work. With these tools, they can take their place beside others who are forging their futures. They, too, can dream.

## HOPE AS YOUR COMPANY'S MISSION

Hope has its roots in willingness, Step One of EQ Fitness. Hope is a willingness to *believe in positive outcomes*. When I left SNI, I was asked to join a consulting group that did leadership work, and I agreed. For one client, I was hired by the owners to help develop two senior leaders into C-suite executives. What I didn't know was that this was an impossible task because of their CEO, whom I would meet later. His instinctive response sounded something like this: "No." He led with a lethal absence of hope. After hearing enough "No"s, his folks retreated, and when he was finally fired, the company needed restoration.

In corporations, a leader can give hope to an individual by acknowledging good work (which makes them want to repeat that behavior) and cheering them on toward grander achievement than they ever thought possible. These are actions we can all do, regardless of our position. On an organizational level, hope is found in a company's mission, that quest that's bigger than any one person and unites everyone in shared purpose. Lots of factors determine how appealing a job will be in the long run, but those that contribute to improving other peoples' lives are ranked at the top, and those with a clear sense of purpose have better financial performance.[4]

When we launched HGTV, we were creating experiential television. We took a very one-dimensional pastime—watching TV—and injected it with the love of home so that it would jump off the screen and lodge in the hearts of our viewers. We built our culture that way too. Our staff related to the business in personal and emotional ways that reflected their own memories and passions around home. We stressed sanctuary, beauty, and tranquility, and reflected back the American dream of home ownership. We harnessed all that passion and, as a result, our viewers and our teams were together, on the same page, connected.

Unilever implements what it calls USLP—the Unilever Sustainable Living Plan. "USLP sets out our plan to decouple our growth from its environmental impact and increase our overall social impact," said its champion and CEO Paul Polman. The company's goals are to reduce the carbon imprint of its products by half, to improve the health of a billion people, and to double revenue, as measured from 2008 to 2020. By serving these ideals, Paul links business good with the common good. "Nobody asks the right questions," he said. "Why can't you attract the right people? Is it because you're not paying enough or because the purpose has disappeared out of your business model?"

The hope born out of a mission pushes ego to the back burner. Your people feel called to not just *do* more, but to *be* more. They gain strength and momentum. And they get a more expansive view of themselves. When we expand spiritually through a mission, Meister Eckhart's saying comes to mind: "God is greater than God." When we carry hope, the possibilities can't even be fathomed by our mortal minds.

# GENEROSITY OF SPIRIT

You will find lots of leaders who inspire their troops with exciting hope-filled messages. Generosity of spirit is harder. It takes all the willingness work you've done and adds trust building and pride dismantling, and, finally, a rich inner life, all so you can move out of your own way. The goal of generosity is to be able to lead unshackled from self-interest, which allows the values that guide our inner life to shine through. The poem from Rabindranath Tagore comes to mind:

> *I slept and dreamt that life was joy.*
> *I awoke and saw that life was service.*
> *I acted and behold, service was joy.*

Emotional stability comes when we embody a generous spirit, because we're not dependent on what people, places, and things can give us. Many qualities reflect generosity of spirit, but the three I've found most meaningful as a corporate leader are compassion, gratitude, and respect.

## COMPASSION

### A Relationship of Equals

Over the years, I've learned that compassion is not just a relationship of strong to weak, but between equals—people who carry each other's loads when needed. Father G calls this "kinship," our willingness to see ourselves in everyone else. Life happens to us all, and it can spill over at work; great leaders make room for the lives of their employees.

Sitting with another person in a moment of compassion is more than your employee expects of you, and the least that you can do for them. The work stuff is easy—you can justify being there when a colleague is having coworker issues or a team clash. Being present for personal struggles is always a judgment call. My rule of thumb was this: If someone rarely brings these things into work, and now they are, then it must matter. Don't mistake them coming to you as an interruption. The members of your workforce are as much a part of your mission as the shared purpose of the organization.

I've sat with employees who were struggling as a parent, or to become parents after years of trying, or dealing with a family loss that's heartbreaking beyond words. Look, I get it, we're running tight ships and not therapy sessions, but as you take on leadership roles, you grow the judgment to discern when compassion is the finest emotion you can offer someone. Often, if someone can just "say it," as we learned in chapter two, they'll walk out of your office restored and ready to begin their work anew. They'll be a better employee, and may well model acts of compassion to help others become emotionally fit too.

## The Relationship of Self-Care to Compassion

I now know that I need to take care of myself before I can show a morsel of compassion to someone else. That means I need to be well rested and in a general place of peace, whether that's via a share circle or the quiet of meditation. When I do these things, I can show up with my heart pliable, not brittle. For most of my career, I've been charged with running negotiations for distribution deals, which had me emotionally spent because they were always so contentious. It's no surprise I couldn't readily offer compassion after one of the rounds in the ring. Connecting those dots came late for me. But as I became more emotionally mature, I brought Eckhart's expansive God to help move me aside, so I could show up in support to another in need of it. That same God guided me into the rooms of recovery, a supreme act of self-care—although in the first many months it feels like you're putting yourself through hell.

## GRATITUDE

From the 1.6 million respondents to its 2016 annual survey of what makes companies the best places to work, Workplace Dynamics found that employees consistently rank "appreciation" as the second most important quality, following only "believing their organizations are headed in the right direction."[5] One thing HGTV CEO Ken Lowe taught me, maybe more than anything else, was to say a simple "thank you" every time I addressed a group. It never was hard for me to thank someone one-on-one, but frankly I had never considered how important it was when I was asked to speak or lead a meeting. By "naming" your gratitude, it's a little reminder that your team makes or breaks your success, and tells them you appreciate their efforts. Maybe, as future leaders, they'll model this behavior as well.

You met trust-builder Joyce Russell, president of Adecco Staffing, in chapter five, where she had a difficult, but appreciated, discussion with a staffer. Joyce has a philosophy she calls "cherry on top," which is to go the extra mile in expressing gratitude—something she learned from her parents.

"When I was a child, my parents always made an effort to turn the ordinary into something better—something often a little unexpected. I remember one vacation and we were driving to get there, staying at Holiday Inns along the way. But then one night we got to stay in a luxury hotel. Woo-hoo! What a cherry on top that was! They did little things that gave me a grateful heart," Joyce shared.

Then she told me a story I could totally relate to—a girl story. "My assistant was heading out at the lunch hour to get her hair colored. She told me she needed to get rid of her gray roots. I said, 'You know what? I'm the one who's given you that gray, so charge your service to my personal card.'"

Something a little unexpected. The cherry on top. Joyce is a glorious example of an EQ Fit leader who not only sees the world through a lens of gratitude, but also puts it into practice.

Author Melody Beattie says gratitude helps us makes sense of the past.[6] It's in the rearview mirror that we can see the lesson in full. In that moment, even a troubling experience has context and makes sense. Once I lost a promotion to a colleague, and I was devastated. Just three months later, Ken Lowe called me, pitching this little idea of his called Home and Garden Television. If I had gotten the promotion, I wouldn't have even entertained the call. Much later, the person I would have worked for was unceremoniously escorted out of the building after multiple counts of sexual harassment. I can't say how many times I've whispered *thank you* for not getting what I really wanted. We can even be grateful for our fears, because they help us survive. Say thank you, take some willingness actions, then let fear go.

## RESPECT

Sometimes the smallest things give us the biggest trouble. Every time late autumn came around, the HGTV senior team knew we had to have the Discussion: What would our holiday cards say? And how should we decorate the building for the holidays?

The wide-ranging perspectives of the founding team came in part from our religious diversity. We had two southern Baptists, two northern Catholics, a Mormon, a Jew, and an agnostic. What were the odds of such a mix in seven people? As one of the northern Catholics, I found this breadth of spiritual perspective a gift, one that could inform and broaden each of us when we had issues like the Discussion.

Most of us have a general sense of what's meant by "inclusion" and "diversity." But I think there's an even bigger idea that encompasses those practices, which I call respect. Having respect for your whole team helps you grow in emotional fitness and stretch into leadership roles. An EQ Fit leader values gender, ethnic, sexual-orientation, and religious inclusion in her workplace, because having a broad cross-section pushes you past narrow-minded and locked-down ways of thinking. Excellent leaders know that people who don't look like you or come from your background elevate the level of debate around the table. This is good business, too, especially when the majority of the American population will be people of color by 2045.

Paul Polman told me, "We work on this a lot to ensure we draw on the strength and contributions from everybody. I just gave an interview on what we do with people with disabilities, or what I call 'diffabilities.' We have many programs of inclusion for them. After all, 20 to 30 percent of the world's population is classified as having a disability. The programs attract talent, reflect the consumer base we serve, bring additional skills, and result in a more engaged workforce."

Respect invites tolerance and dismantles the barriers that exclude, so no one is left outside the circle. To be an inclusive leader means showing everyone respect, and in that way, we don't end up dismissing entire groups of people for no good reason.

I'm a big Detroit Lions fan (which is painful to admit). Our quarterback, Matthew Stafford, does something that makes me smile every time. When he's in the huddle, he takes a knee and looks *up* at his team. In that moment on the field, he can scan their faces and see who's tired, who's in pain, or who's so mad he's ready to strike. He takes it all in from a position of respect, of *homage*, as he calls the next play.

I've mentioned I'm big on visuals, and that's a compelling one for me. Your job as leader is to bring along your whole organization, to leave no one outside the huddle; to take a knee and pay homage to the diverse voices of your people. This is emotional fitness at its finest.

# MORAL COURAGE

## CONSISTENCY

Moral courage is doing the right thing even in the face of repercussions. It's staying true to who you are in challenging situations. You're morally courageous when you maintain a set of principles regardless of circumstance. That kind of consistency helps your people understand the ground rules of behavior and how they can be successful. Anyone wanting to advance will watch how you lead, so it's important to get this right.

When we learned that our Food Network star Paula Deen was treating her minority employees in disrespectful ways, we terminated her. (When, years later, Roseanne Barr was fired by ABC because of racist posts on social media, it gave me flashbacks.) As Ken Lowe made clear at the time, we couldn't claim to value inclusion if we kept Paula Deen on the air. Consistency matters.

Ellen Kullman, who ran a multi-line company at DuPont, offered me this example of how complicated it can be to maintain consistent principles. "It hit me—you're constantly asked to make decisions that benefit just some in the job," she explained. "So I tried to be as clear about our guiding principles and, most importantly, consistent with them." This included business strategy as well as values. When her team running the Corian products—those used on countertops and kitchen islands everywhere—expressed concern about not fitting into any of DuPont's three core strategies, she told their leader, "Look, you're good, you're differentiated, and you're making money. Your job is to convince your people you are in the strategy."

Ellen was modeling moral courage by reminding him to stand proud and do his job, which included expressing solidarity with the company's vision, instead of looking for the nits of difference—to think like and act like a leader for his team *and* the organization at large.

## BETTER THAN THEY WERE

A few years before 9/11, New York Police Department deputy commissioner **Maureen Casey** was part of a monumental project. The NYPD had uncovered a backlog of sixteen thousand unanalyzed rape kits. She told me, "The Medical Examiner's Office didn't have the capacity to handle the volume. The scope and scale of tackling this volume had

never been done, and I kept being told, 'It can't be done.' I kept pushing back, 'Wrong answer.'" She hired private forensic labs to get the
kits analyzed, and as a result of her leadership, they linked hundreds
of cases and identified thousands of perpetrators.

Then 9/11 happened. That morning, amid the panic and terror,
Maureen ran toward the Twin Towers and helped set up a command
post for responding police officers. Afterward, her background working with DNA became critical once again, and she led the effort to
collect samples from the families of those missing in order to identify
the remains of victims. This was heart-wrenching work, but Maureen
remained focused on results. Largely because of her work, the US han-
dling of mass disasters and fatalities has evolved to make DNA evidence a crucial part of the process.

Today Maureen is chief operating officer for the Institute for Veterans and Military Families (IVMF) at Syracuse University, where she
again leads by doing what's right. She stands up for veterans, support-
ing them in the transition to civilian life and offering skills like "trans-
lating" their military experience into expressions common to hiring
HR managers. Throughout her career, Maureen has taken on multiple
roles that required an unfaltering hand, and she has helped many,
many people because she's remained focused on the victims, families
of victims, and those in service to our country.

I asked Maureen if she was proudest of any one accomplishment,
one that might be considered her legacy. She replied, "No, I just want
to leave things a little better off than they were. That's it." Ah: that's
what moral courage looks like.

## ACTIONS ARE WHAT MATTER

It's nice to throw around fancy words like "We Principles," "core values," and "mission statements." As a leader, I always needed verbal and
visual templates like these until I had enough spiritual insight and

emotional maturity to lead from the heart. But what really matters to your people is *how you act*. Do you promote a scoundrel? Terminate someone everyone sees as a good egg and team player? Do you live with the same rules as everybody else, like taking a pay cut when times are tight or when layoffs are necessary? Do you turn mistakes into learning moments or a reason for discipline?

You can have all the pretty words in the book, but the hope you've instilled, generosity you've offered, and moral courage you've modeled goes out the window when you don't act with emotional fitness. That's why, at least for me, value templates matter. They remind me of what my ego wants me to forget.

It's also why actions matter. You can behave yourself into right motives by practicing enough, or as Father Richard Rohr says, live yourself into a new way of thinking.[7] One day you wake up and say, "This *feels* right." An alignment of right actions with right motives truly does fill a hole in your soul, bringing peace with it.

I'll close with another visual. One of my top five movies of all time is *The Elephant Man*. It's based on the true story of John Merrick, a severely deformed man, and his challenges to be accepted into society in the early 1900s. When Merrick's treatment is taken up by a surgeon named Frederick Treves, Merrick becomes more than just another case, and Dr. Treves invites him to stay in his home. There's a scene that's always spoken to me. It's the middle of the night, and Treves's wife realizes he's not in bed, so she wanders downstairs to find her husband behind his desk, crying. She asks him what's wrong, and he says, "I don't know if I'm doing all this for him or for me."

If you're still with me at this point, I'd like to call you friend. This scene gets to the heart of what matters, my friend: our actions. Sometimes it's hard to sort out our motives, even with all the words I've spilled on these pages to help. Are we practicing We Principles from the heart? Are we doing them for *others* or for *ourselves*? Most likely the answer is both, and that's OK. Remember, emotional fitness is a program of progress, not perfection. There's nobility in just trying.

# CHAPTER TEN

# WE PRINCIPLES & RECOVERY

## A Surprising Road to Emotional Fitness

*There is a crack in everything God has made.*

—RALPH WALDO EMERSON

I t's New Year's Day as I write this, and, not surprisingly, many of the headlines are focused on willpower and resolutions. One statistic jumps out at me: since 2000, there's been a 50 percent uptick in emergency room visits due to heavy drinking.[1] This catches my eye because early this New Year's morning I was stopped by a cop for speeding. He swaggered up to my car in the way they get trained to do in cop school. "Have you been partying all night?" he asked. I had a really good answer to this question. "Not anymore," I said. "I've been in recovery a few years now." He smiled, gave me a break, and just issued a warning. Well, how about that.

Along the way to growing in emotional fitness, I came to a jumping-off place where I couldn't live numbed-out anymore, and I couldn't imagine life without needing to be. In the journal I'd been writing during this time, two words captured how I felt: "Everything hurts." It was the loneliest place I'd ever been. As they say in the rooms of recovery, I was given a gift—the gift of desperation.

There was no five-alarm, cymbal-clanging wake-up call, just a feeling of tremendous emptiness. It was like I watched my two feet walk into my first recovery meeting. I describe that moment now as a moment of grace. I'd never faced any consequences—no DUIs, no jail, no lost jobs, no daytime binges. In fact, if you waded through chapter seven, you saw how successful the surface trappings of my life were. Before things ratcheted up, I was a workaholic, another version of this disease. Over time, I turned to substance abuse in the evening hours. My model of living was achievement equals acceptance and approval, those factors from chapter one that keep a lot of us suspended in emotional immaturity.

Such toxic behaviors have many names, all derivatives of "addiction," and the programs to help often end in "Anonymous." These addictions are all the ways we run away—with drugs, alcohol, work, sex, food, or crunch-until-you-drop fitness. Many of us call chasing these compulsions the "disease of more," because we want "more" things that are a slick right turn away from the real source of the trouble, which is buried deep. We dull the anguish of the emotions we don't want to feel, or the confusing history we don't want to face. We run toward chaos so we can run away from ourselves. A quiet room is the most terrifying of all. Thomas Keating, the monk who helped develop Centering Prayer meditation, said that addiction is the last resort of the psyche to avoid unbearable pain.[2]

My editors and close friends will tell you I struggled with including this part of my story, but I ultimately knew it had to be here because, unchecked, addiction keeps you frozen in emotional adolescence. Plus, diagnosis rates are on the rise, yet only about 10 percent of Americans who suffer from substance abuse get specialized treatment,[3] a hard data point to absorb when I've witnessed many (me just being one) who have found new, healthy ways to live. Addiction manifests in such painful ways that we don't want to understand it. When you're in the loneliest place you've ever been, numbing out is a survival skill. But perhaps the most important reason to talk about it is this: addiction is potentially deadly. Overdoses from our current opioid epidemic are clear evidence.

I've seen the triumph in someone's eyes after they've overcome the unimaginable: abandonment, parent addicts, sexual abuse, or domestic violence; kids who grew up in closets because it was the only safe place. Adversity lives in the rooms of recovery, yet people overcome it time and again because getting treatment teaches us to take responsibility for our behavior and begin to *live in the solution. Living in the solution* means turning away from self-destructive habits and toward life-affirming ones. This mind-set reflects enormous emotional fitness.

Those of you who have had brushes with substance abuse through family members or friends, or in your own life, might be eager to read on. But even if addiction has not touched your life directly, I'd urge you to keep reading. Emotional fitness means seeing the full humanity of the people with whom we work and the struggles they carry, sometimes into the office too. With empathy comes illumination, and a larger understanding of how to live one's own life.

## LARGER PERSPECTIVES

Recovery offers many perspectives we all could use, and We Principles weave their way through how those of us in recovery live.

### SELF-RESPECT IS ALWAYS THE STARTING POINT TO EMOTIONAL FITNESS

The process of willingness in Step One is about coming to peace, so you can feel good and be productive with your workmates. These positive emotions stem from foundational self-respect. Experience has taught me that most of us could use improvement here. Whether it's among coworkers or family, I find lack of self-worth is like an epidemic. It's as if we've forgotten that we're human.

Through the tools of recovery, we get "returned to ourselves," as Father G says. Not the facade, which is our presentation to the world, but who we were born to be. I needed a lot of work here, too, as I entered recovery confused and beaten down—beaten down by myself, mostly. I'd had C-suite jobs, presented to hundreds of shareholders, and sat on corporate boards, yet when I walked into a recovery meeting about a week in, and a woman stretched out a hand of welcome and said, "Hi, Susan," my heart clenched. She knew my name. I became someone.

Self-respect is nourished by people who believe in you. In *New Rules of the Game*, I wrote about the importance of building your work network; it's not just your supervisor who can help you advance. This is also true for recovery, except this network also helps you stay alive. But it's still wrenching to change up your whole life with new friends and new routines, filling huge yawns of time that were once busy with one form of escape or another. As I transitioned to this way of living, I tethered myself to the rooms of recovery like a life raft.

Six women became my anchors. They taught me that laughing and crying are connected at the hip, and we need both to move through life's hurdles. Most had been at this recovery thing for a while, and they seemed genuinely happy. They surrounded me with their spines of steel and fierce hearts, and kept saying they'd love me until I loved myself.

In *Small Victories*, Anne Lamott wrote about the moment she found her trusted girlfriends in recovery: "I told them about my most vile behavior, and they said, 'Me, too!' I told them about my crimes against the innocent, especially me. They said, 'Ditto. Yay. Welcome!' I couldn't seem to get them to reject me. . . . It turns out that welcome is solidarity. We're glad you're here, and we're with you. This whole project called you being alive, you finding joy? Well, we're in on that."[4]

My girlfriends spun a similarly tight circle of love and acceptance, and gave me their experience, hope, and light. They remain my closest friends today. We give one another the rare gift of unconditional love.

## OPEN TO THE UNLIKELY

When your old ways aren't getting the results you want, be open to new ones, even if they seem radical or strange. Sometimes our best tools, either in the moment or over time, come from unlikely places. I sure didn't expect a bunch of addicts and alcoholics to teach me how to live. This is where willingness and moral courage come in: the willingness to reach down deep and admit that this life isn't working; to think, *This isn't true to the potential that is me.* Then, moral courage urges you to take action, no matter how hard or radical, because you grasp that there's a better path.

We've looked at the importance of openness as we build work relationships, especially being receptive to people who don't look like you or come from your same background. Entering recovery requires openness too. Trust me, it was not part of my career—or life—plan. My friend Suzanne[5] wasn't too happy to be there either. She knew she had a drinking problem. But when she was forced into Alcoholics Anonymous by the courts, she couldn't believe it: "What a slap in the face. I even failed at being an alcoholic, so they're making me go to AA." Yeah, it's kind of the last stop.

Now I go to meetings happily, always feeling "a part of," and I leave feeling lighter. The person next to you might be living in their car, but on any given day they've got the most wisdom in the room. From Yale to jail, we come from all parts. There are no high-pressure sales pitches, only suggestions and a promise that *hope* lives here. We all want to get better and stay better, and to live in joy without numbing agents. People who relapse are welcomed back, not fired. To the person who says they can't stay clean and sober and they're going back out, we say, please don't, but if you do, please try not to die.

## A FRESH START EVERY DAY

Embarking on a trek like, say, *changing your whole life*, can be overwhelming, so we stick to the day we're in. A familiar slogan is "One day at a time." In early recovery, sometimes we count hours or even minutes when trying to avoid sliding back to escape. To imagine stopping *forever*, whether it's drugs, alcohol, food, gambling? That's too much to ask, even at our most desperate. Instead, we say, "Try not to drink or use today." The power of the message is its simplicity. There was a guy who relapsed after thirty-one years sober, and when someone asked him how that could be, he said, "I had enough years. I just didn't have enough days."

Starting fresh each day makes sense for a lot of reasons. There's promise in seeing each day as the start of something new, and the small triumphs from yesterday, or an hour ago, add up to more meaningful victories. Besides, life changes in an instant, and your weekly and monthly goals have to change with it. One morning you're at work on a normal day, and then you get the call that your sister's been in a car wreck and your deadlines become meaningless. Buddhism teaches that we're a part of this constantly changing landscape. If you don't believe me, write down everything that happens over the course of one day and see how much turned out the way you expected. It's like the Yiddish proverb "Man plans, and God laughs."

## LIVE FROM A SPIRITUAL CENTER

The destructive force of addiction is bigger than most people, me included. For someone who has crashed through roadblocks her whole life, realizing I couldn't beat this thing alone was extremely humbling. It was the first time I'd truly accepted the limits of my own willpower, and my only hope was to find something greater than addiction, a force bent on preserving, not destroying, my life. I found this in the rooms, and in the God I try to understand every day. Recovery is a spiritual program—not religious, but spiritual—which was another surprise. I had no interest in being preached to; I just wanted to kick these compulsions, and I figured the people there would show me how. Turns out I was shown a whole lot more.

How we define "spiritual" varies from person to person. For me, it's a connection to something beyond my own four walls. It's the nudges that move me to say yes when a friend needs a ride at night, even though I'm in my pajamas. It is the goodness of our shared hopes and triumphs, like when your niece tells you that after all these years of trying, she's finally pregnant, and your hearts break open together. It's the fierce kinship that binds you to others and gets you out of your own screwy head. Those moments say you're a part of something beyond your own humanity.

I was a few years into recovery when I was listening to Terry Gross's interview with Mary Karr, a favorite author of mine, on NPR's *Fresh Air*. Mary said that she'd been sober a bunch of years and that she prayed all the time, in need or in joy. She talked about her rich inner life and said if it weren't for that, she'd gladly murder someone in the subway, which made me laugh. When I repeated the story for one of my girlfriends, she said, "Susan, I'm convinced that if I didn't have recovery, God, and all of you, I could murder someone too." The pain we carry can spill over into real life, but when we keep picking up the tools of emotional fitness, our lives only get better. Opening up to spiritual insight is a key emotional fitness tool.

Many believe our very essence is God. "The brilliance of the true self is our soul, which is a unique manifestation of God. One God, zillions of souls, all unique manifestations. One ocean, many waves," Joe Zarantonello tells me. I don't know about all that, but I do know that the goodness I have I didn't make myself, like a soufflé or turkey tetrazzini. The best of me comes from somewhere else, like the recovery rooms where I can feel grace circling. Grace gives me the willingness to tell the truth, and to find the *generosity of spirit* so I can show up for family, friends, and coworkers as a better person than anyone, especially me, thought possible.

Our spiritual center is the place where our emotional balance and well-being reside. Our lives can be both secular and sacred all the time.

# GROWING AND PRACTICING EMOTIONAL FITNESS

When we're entering recovery, we're some of the most emotionally immature people you'd ever want to meet. We may have the trappings of adulthood, like a job, a family, a home. But we're still dependent on other people or things to provide what we've found lacking in ourselves. Or we're closed off, in retreat, like a child who didn't get her way. When we stay in that fog, we're not able to learn or to grow. And if alcohol is our drug of choice, we may not be able to remember either.

Then, slowly, with hard work, something remarkable happens. We get better.

We learn an entirely new set of life-affirming responses to the world. We jump off the roller coaster, full of thrills and terror, and choose a steady, unfaltering way. *We become emotionally fit.* The before and after pictures are like what you'd see in the *National Enquirer* about a pop star's weight loss, except they're real. This experience has taught me that emotional fitness is achievable for everyone, but, like recovery, it's not some onetime prize. You keep picking up the tools, and you keep growing. And you find that what's worth having—hope and gratitude and inner strength—stays and grows only when you give it away in service to others. It's a paradox I'll never understand, but one I try to live.

When our organizations contain emotionally fit people, they influence everyone around them. We can build communities where everyone drops their causes and opprobrium and just wants to shake your hand and welcome you, the new recruit. The We Principles of hope, generosity of spirit, and moral courage will be the everyday practices we live by.

When I talk to Joe about recovery from time to time, he reminds me that at the end of the day, we're all in recovery, seeking to recover our full humanity.

# WE PRINCIPLES
## Letting Your Inner Life Speak
## Through We Principles

### PRACTICE:
### We Principles Pop Quiz

Read the scenarios, each calling for emotional intelligence, and the responses guided by EQ Fitness. Decide whether each response is an example of hope, generosity, or moral courage. If it's generosity, is it an act of compassion, respect, or gratitude? In the case of generosity of spirit, there can be multiple right responses.

### SCENARIO 1

*You've learned to manage your temper at work, and you notice a colleague who's having similar issues.*

> *EQF response*: Take a quiet moment to speak one-on-one, privately, with your colleague, acknowledging that you've had the same tendencies and describing how you've learned to combat them.

> *Choose one*: [ ] Hope [ ] Generosity [ ] Moral Courage

*If generosity, it is an act of* [ ] compassion [ ] respect
[ ] gratitude

## SCENARIO 2

*You're a woman whose female boss keeps pressing you to adopt her tough, confrontational style with men. You've respectfully demurred, but she brings it up over and over.*

*EQF response*: Acknowledge her success at the company, but tell her, calmly but firmly, that you'd like to be evaluated on your results, not on the style in which you achieve them.

*Choose one*: [ ] Hope [ ] Generosity [ ] Moral Courage

*If generosity, it is an act of* [ ] compassion [ ] respect
[ ] gratitude

## SCENARIO 3

*You know a normally outgoing person in your team is upset, because they're avoiding eye contact.*

*EQF response*: Stick around after a meeting or at the end of the day and ask how they're doing.

*Choose one*: [ ] Hope [ ] Generosity [ ] Moral Courage

*If generosity, it is an act of* [ ] compassion [ ] respect
[ ] gratitude

## SCENARIO 4

*You work with a colleague who lives to get his name in the press. Your boss doesn't stop him, and it burns you.*

*EQF response*: Accept that this one's out of your control because he doesn't report to you.

*Choose one*: [ ] Hope [ ] Generosity [ ] Moral Courage

*If generosity, it is an act of* [ ] compassion [ ] respect
[ ] gratitude

## SCENARIO 5

*You're a coordinator who's doing more work for your boss than the coordinator in the cube next to you is doing for his boss. It's not fair!*

*EQF response*: Acknowledge that with the extra work, you're learning more than the guy next door, and maybe that will lead to more career options down the line.

*Choose one*: [ ] Hope [ ] Generosity [ ] Moral Courage

*If generosity, it is an act of* [ ] compassion [ ] respect
[ ] gratitude

## SCENARIO 6

*You are a charismatic leader, inspiring and persuading your team to follow in any direction you point.*

*EQF response*: Stay vigilant: don't get drunk with ego and power, and recognize their role in your success openly and often.

*Choose one*: [ ] Hope [ ] Generosity [ ] Moral Courage

*If generosity, it is an act of* [ ] compassion [ ] respect
[ ] gratitude

• • •

Answer key: 1. Generosity, compassion; 2. Moral Courage; 3. Generosity, compassion; 4. Moral Courage; 5. Hope; 6. Generosity, gratitude and respect

## PRACTICE:
### Gratitude

**THE JEWEL TREE**

Imagine sitting on a bluff over a beautiful and still crystal-clear lake. Slowly, an island emerges from the center of the water. On this island, a dazzling tree begins to grow and form. It's made of all the precious jewels of the world, blinking brilliantly. But as you look closer, you begin to see that the jewels are not jewels at all. They are all the teachers you've had the profound luck to encounter. They are your favorite grade school teachers, family members who've helped you mature, friends who love and guide you, and all the others who have spiritually enriched you. They have all shown you love and care, including beloved pets.

Make a list as you envision them, and begin each day imagining your jewel tree of teachers, thanking each of them for helping you to grow.

## PRACTICE:
### Compassion

Take a compassion class. Compassion Cultivation Training involves eight weekly two-hour classes in which you're guided through a series of meditations to develop an awareness of thoughts, emotions, and behaviors, so you can relate to the world in a more active way. Classes are offered on- and offline.

## PRACTICE:
### Turning Points

Our lives are like a river. If you've ever seen one from an airplane, you've noticed how it bends as it flows. If you've river-rafted, you know you can't see the bends in advance, and they can take you out. These are moments of feeling groundless. The river's in control, but you can be OK if you work *with* it instead of against it. Our lives are like that too; we can't predict all the bends—the groundless moments—but if we do our best to accept and meld with them, our lives are infinitely richer.

On a piece of paper, list six to eight turning points in your life. You could do a separate list for your career, or incorporate both career and life into one. You can use these turning points as moments of hardship or moments of grace. Now draw your own river, graphing the turning points as bends in its path. What "paddle" did you use in that moment? What wisdom has your river taught you?

## PRACTICE:
### Modeling Respect

If you are a supervisor meeting with someone from outside the organization, take the time to introduce each of your team members. Don't rush it. Include not just their name and the job they do, but also a bit on their work background and something they've done in your company that you're proud of.

# EPILOGUE
## Emotionally Fit

I n 2018, some friends and I traveled to Nashville to hear from This-tle Farms founder Becca Stevens, an Episcopal priest who has created a thriving community for women survivors of sex trafficking. We went because we're thinking of launching a local sister organization where we live.

We spent the morning learning how Becca built the organization, then listened to some of the survivors' experiences. Later, we toured the manufacturing facility she created, where the residents make lotions, soap, and other natural body and home products that they sell direct to consumers and through wholesale. I think Becca could easily run a billion-dollar company, and run it a whole lot better than many are run today. That's also true of Father G, another priest-entrepreneur who has launched a business from scratch that brings in millions of dollars every year for Homeboy Industries, and who stands in solidarity with his workforce. They would both tell you, in fact, that their workforce *is* their mission.

We don't hear much about leaders like Becca and Father G, or those others you've met in this book, like Joyce Russell from Adecco Group, who creatively shows gratitude to her people. Or Leroy Ball, who came to peace with his introverted nature and has used it to connect to others. We don't hear enough about people like Unilever's Paul Polman, whose threads of wisdom are woven throughout this book. The men and women profiled here are living, breathing testimony to the power of emotional fitness. They stand on the solid ground of knowing who they are and what they can offer back to the world. Amid their strengths and limitations, they've found a centered, stable place from which to live and lead. They exemplify the best of "fully human" leadership.

## "FULLY"

Sometimes I wish emotional fitness *just* dealt with emotions! My older, undeveloped version of emotional intelligence did; I knew not to bring crankiness into work, and that offering a hand or ear to someone strengthened that relationship and got things done. But I stuffed away emotions, and lived and worked like an automaton. Living fully human is just the opposite of shutting emotions down. It brings together and into light all three dimensions of ourselves: physical, emotional, and spiritual. Integrating our physicality completes us (see figure N).

We've done the self-awareness work that emotionally fit people do, so we can see and access all these facets of ourselves.

Another word for "full" is "whole." Getting to wholeness takes effort to grow and blend all parts of the self. Let's look at how this integration works. Take self-respect. While it falls under "Spiritual" in figure N, because it springs from knowing your life has intrinsic value and purpose beyond just you, it also plays into the emotions that spring from feeling confident. Self-respect means taking care of yourself physically too—we have only one body and hopefully a lot of years to live in it! You keep your brain fresh, not addled by compulsions for *more*—be it sugar, alcohol, or your fiftieth pair of shoes—so that it's ripe for learn-

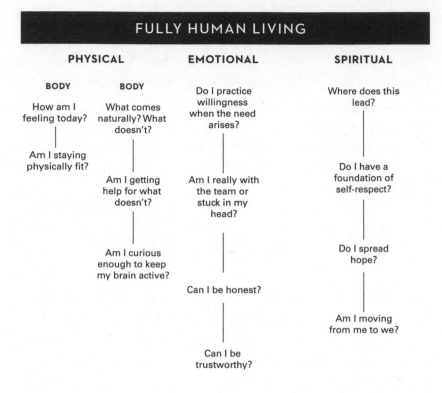

**FIGURE N:** Three Dimensions of Being Fully Human

ing. Body, soul, and emotions all participate in building and maintaining self-respect.

Fully human living stresses integrating inner and outer lives. The workplace uses your mental firepower, which manifests outwardly through projects well done or promotions received. But it can also be about finding greater meaning in your work, as does Paul Polman's team, which unites around the Unilever Sustainable Living Plan. Purpose strengthens your inner life and makes work not just an academic exercise, but one that connects you with a world beyond the four walls of your cube or office. Living "fully" human is breadth (outer life) and depth (inner), and it's ongoing. As we grow up and out, our lives become touch points to the lives of those around us. Given the divisiveness perpetuated by leadership every-where we turn today, living *fully* is a model for work and life that can't come soon enough.

Emotional fitness means checking in with and blending *all* your dimensions, whenever opportunities arise. There's a huge payoff when you do, because you can then move with ease in the world and feel *useful*, a life-affirming emotion that keeps us alert and growing. Use-fulness shifts us from the boxed-in world of ego to a more expansive place. Being useful might mean coming up with a novel process that makes work easier for you and others, or it might mean giving our vets tools to assimilate after military service, like Maureen Casey does. Usefulness through work is the force that has shaped Father G's kids and Becca's survivors, and it is what allows us to know that our life has purpose. Being useful keeps us living in the solution, a laudable prac-tice of emotionally fit people.

It's said that only a soul can hold paradox—two conflicting things that can both be true at once. Learning to honor—instead of battle—paradox is another gift of emotional fitness, and a frequent companion of anyone pausing long enough to ask questions. It opens us to won-ders and mysteries that our minds will never understand, but we're still nudged to explore. Honoring paradox moves us from being a head on a stick to becoming fully human. There's even paradox in being useful, because the more I give of myself, the more I have, especially self-worth.

We become open, too, to what Mother Teresa called the "ultimate" paradox: if you love until it hurts, there is no more hurt. Just love.

## "HUMAN"

In *Letters to a Young Poet*, Rainer Marie Rilke wrote that loving another is the most difficult task a human being has, that it is the work for which all other work is but preparation. Because we're human we get a colossal gift, the capacity to love. Love isn't a workplace emotion, but its cousin, kinship, has the potential to be. Kinship is our willingness to see ourselves in others. It arises when you stand on common ground with those in your workplace. Employees want to know of their leaders, and colleagues, "Are you standing with me?" Kinship stares down the emotional and physical distance our conditioning often imposes, and fosters strong teams and successful cultures.

As employees, kinship is expressed as respect and trust, and hopefully in many fun moments too! If you're a leader, it is expressed as solidarity, guidance, and getting people to believe in themselves. Kinship is also understanding that there's more at stake than the economic health of your company; that, in fact, the *emotional* health of your organization, like your people feeling safe at work, precedes any financial victory. And robust emotional health starts with tending to your own.

Along the road of career, I've learned that business isn't as clear-cut as "effective outcomes," "return on investment," or a column of numbers that add up right. Emotional fitness helped me to see achievement not as a huge, onetime event—*profit! promotion!*—but as all the little collective successes that my teams and I experienced, and those I was privileged enough to watch take shape in other parts of the organization.

On the other end of kinship is technology. I've written about its impact on emotional fitness throughout this book. As a society, we're bracing for what tech's most sophisticated iteration, artificial intelligence, will bring. The result we fear most is job displacement. But here's the thing—we can't automate our way to emotional well-being. Today, nine of the twelve fastest-growing jobs are variations of nursing, all of which require human connection.[1] Jobs demanding a human touch will be around as long as we populate the planet. A robot may simulate the rudimentary behaviors of emotional intelligence, like "reading" and "responding" to facial expressions, but no machine can simulate We Principles, which are grounded in human experience and understanding. Let's never forget the takeaway from Apple CEO Tim Cook's commencement speech at MIT: technology is capable of doing great things, but it doesn't want to do great things, because it doesn't want to do anything.[2] Machines will never recognize the cry of the human heart.

* * *

We all write the stories of our own lives. At times they can be dramas, comedies, romances, or tragedies, but we have the power to edit the plotlines. Once in a while, when I pick up my first book, *New Rules of the Game*, I can see perspectives I've gained even since then when it comes to emotional intelligence. I've edited that plotline through vigilant practice of emotional fitness, a deeper and more abiding form of emotional intelligence. Each morning brings new opportunity to use the tools in this book.

When I wake up, I ask for two simple things: to try not to judge people, especially myself, and to find gratitude. Not to "feel" gratitude, but to *find* it—it's an action—and there it appears, in the tribe of people I run with, family, friends, and workmates. And in those groundless moments, or when those pesky unproductive emotions rear up, I have solutions and tools. Now you do too.

OK, one final movie reference. Picture this: It's a scene from the Peter Weir–directed *Witness*, one of my all-time favorites. The "witness" is six-year-old Samuel, an Amish boy who sees a murder take place as he's hiding in a bathroom stall. Harrison Ford is the detective investigating the crime, and when he realizes the danger Samuel is in, he takes him and his mom back to their home in Amish country, where they can hide out until Ford can crack the case. But the bad guys finally locate them and come for Samuel.

Being trapped in their home as the criminals close in, Samuel's grandfather maniacally signals to Samuel to ring this loud, clanging bell—a signal—as the scene pans to their hillside. From everywhere, over the green hills surrounding their small farm, come neighbors and friends and family, all running to support this family in trouble.

An astonishing horizon of people, as far as the eye can see, running toward you.

# Test Your Emotional Fitness

Emotional fitness is a steadiness of mind and heart reached by practicing three areas: self-awareness, openness to trust, and self-transcendence. Take this quiz periodically to measure your emotional fitness as you begin, and continue, your EQF practice.

Rate your answers according to the following scale:

1 = Strongly Disagree
2 = Disagree
3 = Neutral
4 = Agree
5 = Strongly Agree

**SELF-AWARENESS**

_____ I can name what's bothering me when I feel off.

_____ Feeling unsafe is not an issue in my life.

_____ I am an excellent friend to myself.

_____ I have solutions for getting emotionally unstuck, so I can move forward.

_____ I know quickly when I need help with something.

_____ I have someone I can tell all my secrets to.

_____ I know what I'm good at, and what I'm not.

_____ I would describe myself as content.

_____ I have healthy ways to release unproductive emotions.

_____ I'm comfortable in a quiet room, with no music,
noise, or people.

_____ I'm rarely self-critical.

_____ What people see on the outside matches how I
feel on the inside.

_____ I'd describe my upbringing as a happy one.

_____ Total points for this section.

*Up to 39 points*: You are in the beginning stages of becoming self-aware. Consider practices that could help you, such as meditation, journaling, or opening up to someone you trust, such as a work or life coach.

*40 to 51 points*: You have a good grounding in self-awareness and use resources actively to gain more self-knowledge when needed. Be conscious of coupling your self-knowledge with practices of self-worth, because one is not of much value without the other. If you tend toward being reserved, you can do things such as saying to yourself, "My voice is worth listening to" before a meeting, and making sure to speak up in the room.

*52 to 65 points*: You carry yourself comfortably and confidently. You know your talents and maximize them, and your limitations and acknowledge them. Team up with a friend so you're accountable to each other for sharing stories of dawning self-knowledge, and why it is of value.

**OPENNESS TO TRUST**

_____ I am worthy of receiving others' trust.

_____ I'm willing to put myself out there and take a first
step in building a relationship.

_____ I practice respectfully telling the truth, even if
uncomfortable.

_____ I ask for help when I need it.

_____ When I'm with others, I practice pausing before
reacting with impulse.

_____ I maintain the relationships I have today by reaching out for face-to-face time, not just communicating through texts or emails.

_____ I feel a sense of belonging in my workplace.

_____ I believe those with whom I share confidences will hold them.

_____ Total points for this section.

*Up to 24 points*: You have the courage to acknowledge that trust is challenging. It would help to identify "allies," those you know well enough to risk entering into a trustful relationship. Don't be afraid to tell them that trust doesn't come easily, so they can understand you a little better.

*25 to 31 points*: You're willing to take emotional risks to build relationships of trust, and you see the promise in connecting with people in a real way. Don't become impatient; trust takes time!

*32 to 40 points*: You have an open, comfortable, and authentic way about you, and seek to develop wholehearted relationships with others. It's likely people gravitate to you, so be aware that you can model what trust building looks like to those who do.

**SELF-TRANSCENDENCE**

_____ I feel my work has a greater meaning than just getting a paycheck.

_____ On most days, I feel grateful.

_____ My life is productive and useful to others.

_____ I'm comfortable with spiritual things I may never fully understand.

_____ I feel there's promise in each person's life.

_____ I try to make decisions with both head and heart.

_____ I'm open to mystery and wonder.

_____ I'm aware of when pride gets the better of me and have ways to tame it.

————— I have beliefs or principles that move me beyond self-serving behaviors.

————— Total points for this section.

*Under 27 points:* You prefer only what your brain can understand and tend to live in your head. Engage in some right-brained practices, like meditation, journaling, yoga, or reflective walks, to begin opening to a larger world.

*28 to 35 points:* You're comfortable knowing that not everything is an equation that's solvable and are observant and responsive to others' needs. When in a group setting and moments of stress arise, thinking "we, not me" will be helpful to facilitate workplace or family unity.

*36 to 45 points:* You show up for life trying to make a difference, even if it's a small one. You're imbued with hope and grateful on most days. You wear life loosely and well! Never forget that laughter is a wonderful connector and tension reliever.

## COMBINE THE TOTAL POINTS FROM EACH SECTION TO FIND YOUR CURRENT EMOTIONAL FITNESS PROFILE.

### A NEW AND BRAVE EXPLORER *(UP TO 90 POINTS)*

You're ready to start on the path of emotional fitness, and brave to keep accepting the willingness work to know your emotions and temperament better. You may, however, be strong in one of the three given areas, which is great, and which will focus you to pick up tools in the other areas. To a certain extent we're *all* novices at emotional fitness, because these practices are called for throughout life!

## KEEN AND BALANCED PRACTITIONER
## (91 TO 115 POINTS)

Bravo, you're well on the path to emotional fitness! You have some practices already in place to do self-discovery, build trust, and move aside self-interest, when appropriate, for better group outcomes. Be sure to look at the results of each of the three parts so you can know if there's work needed to grow in a particular area.

## A STEADY MASTER (116 POINTS AND HIGHER)

Life is continuously revealing itself to you, and it's a full and rich picture. You tend to the physical, emotional, and spiritual parts of you regularly, recognizing they all work together to form the broadest emotional fitness lens. Please consider mentoring others in your best practices, actively through a mentee relationship if asked, or simply by modeling your own emotional fitness. To be sure, we need more emotional fitness masters!

• • •

You can find printable versions of the quiz for retesting at www.susan packard.com/eqf_test.

# Resources

## PART ONE

### BOOKS

- *Simple Abundance* **by Sarah Ban Breathnach.** A classic best-seller that includes inspiring daily readings for women to help them fight through fears and limiting behaviors and embrace authentic living.
- *Tattoos on the Heart* **by Gregory Boyle.** The founder of Homeboy Industries tells the stories of how his brave and fragile kids, who made it out of Los Angeles gang culture, have transformed their lives through his intervention program.
- *Breathe* **by Belisa Vranich.** Written by a clinical psychologist, this book shows you how breathing consciously is a practical and effective (and inexpensive!) way to manage your emotional and physical health.
- *The Power of Now* **by Eckhart Tolle.** One man's journey to understand the value and beauty of being present.
- *Hardwiring Happiness* **by Rick Hanson.** Written by a neuro-psychologist, this book explains how our thoughts can change the makeup of our brains, and how we can override our natural tendencies toward pessimism.
- *How God Changes Your Brain* **by Andrew Newberg, MD.** A look at the science behind why meditative practice is so effective, including an insightful section on how we can teach our brains to learn compassion through regular meditation.

- *The Practice* by **Barb Schmidt.** A short, simple, elegant book about mindful practices.
- *Gift from the Sea* by **Anne Morrow Lindbergh.** A bold and courageous author writes about how she was called to leave behind her husband and children every summer for two weeks to refresh and restart her life. Her book invites reflection just the way mindful practice does.
- *Open Mind, Open Heart* by **Thomas Keating.** Father Keating explains Centering Prayer and answers many questions that arise when we practice.
- *What Color Is Your Parachute?* by **Richard N. Bolles.** Covers just about everything for finding a good job that matches your personality and passion.
- *Designing Your Life* by **Bill Burnett and Dave Evans.** Applies principles of design thinking to your life and work.
- *The Defining Decade* by **Meg Jay.** For job-searching help in your twenties.
- *Crossing the Unknown Sea* by **David Whyte.** For inspiration about making work and life choices
- *Let Your Life Speak* by **Parker Palmer.** For inspiration about making work and life choices.
- *The Positive Enneagram* by **Susan Rhodes.** Helps focus on the positive insight the instrument can provide, not just the areas of improvement.

## ARTICLES & LINKS

- **"Why Learning Resilience Is Good for Your Health,"** Laura Landro, *Wall Street Journal*, February 16, 2016, www.wsj .com/articles/why-resilience-is-good-for-your-health-and -career-1455560111.
- **"Meditation for Travelers on the Go,"** Stephanie Rosenbloom, *New York Times*, January 29, 2017, nyti.ms/2kn30ZV.

- "Why You Should Thank Your Aging Brain," *Harvard Women's Health Watch*, March 2015, www.health.harvard.edu/mind-and-mood/why-you-should-thank-your-aging-brain.

- "What Keeps Us from Showing Self-Compassion?," Kristin Neff, PhD, *Psychotherapy Networker*, September–October 2015, reprinted in *Utne Reader*, September 2016, www.utne.com/mind-and-body/what-keeps-us-from-showing-self-compassion-zm0z16uzsel.

- "How to Practice Mindfulness Throughout Your Work Day," Rasmus Hougaard and Jacqueline Carter, *Harvard Business Review*, March 4, 2016, hbr.org/2016/03/how-to-practice-mindfulness-throughout-your-work-day.

- "Why You Should Make Time for Self-Reflection (Even If You Hate Doing It)," Jennifer Porter, *Harvard Business Review*, March 21, 2017, hbr.org/2017/03/why-you-should-make-time-for-self-reflection-even-if-you-hate-doing-it.

- "Mindfulness in the Age of Complexity," interview with Ellen Langer, *Harvard Business Review*, March 2014, hbr.org/2014/03/mindfulness-in-the-age-of-complexity.

- "What's Your Influencing Style?," Chris Musselwhite and Tammie Plouffe, *Harvard Business Review*, January 13, 2012, hbr.org/2012/01/whats-your-influencing-style.

- "A Scorecard to Help You Compare Two Jobs," Allison Rimm, *Harvard Business Review*, April 27, 2017, hbr.org/2017/04/a-scorecard-to-help-you-compare-two-jobs.

- "No Passion? Don't Panic," Angela Duckworth, *New York Times*, June 5, 2016, nyti.ms/2lztCVn.

- Find your temperament type at www.enneagramspectrum.com.

WATCH

- "**My Stroke of Insight**," Jill Bolte Taylor, TED Talk, www .ted.com/talks/jill_bolte_taylor_s_powerful_stroke_of _insight.
- *Overview*, Planetary Collective, weareplanetary.com /overview-short-film.

DOWNLOAD

*Apps to help you meditate.*

Let's face it—it can be hard starting anything on willpower alone. Check out these apps that help keep track of your practice: Calm, Simple Habit, Pause, Buddhify, SOS Method, and Insight Timer. I like Insight Timer the most because even the free version allows you to meditate, and when you finish, to communicate with others who are meditating at the same time.

## PART TWO

BOOKS

- *The Power of Followership* by **Dr. Robert E. Kelley.** Kelley explores the central role that followers play in every organizational success, and also how leadership and followership can shift many times in the course of a day.
- *Crucial Conversations* by **Kerry Patterson, Joseph Grenny, Ron McMillan, and Al Switzer.** The authors use real-life, high-stakes examples of how to carefully craft language to solve problems, transform anger, and create safe environments for airing organizational issues.
- *The CEO Next Door* by **Elena L. Botelho and Kim R. Powell, with Tahl Raz.** One of the four most powerful traits for successful leadership is being "relentlessly reliable," according to

the authors. This means those CEOs most effective in producing results feel a strong personal accountability to their people.

## ARTICLES & LINKS

- "Not Leadership Material? The World Needs Followers," Susan Cain, *New York Times*, March 24, 2017, www.nytimes .com/2017/03/24/opinion/sunday/not-leadership-material -good-the-world-needs-followers.html.
- "To Defuse an Argument, Think About the Future," Alex Huynh, *Harvard Business Review*, January 23, 2017, hbr .org/2017/01/to-defuse-an-argument-think-about-the-future.
- "How to Handle a Colleague Who's a Jerk When the Boss Isn't Around," Amy Jen Su, *Harvard Business Review*, November 22, 2016, /hbr.org/2016/11/how-to-handle-a-colleague -whos-a-jerk-when-the-boss-isnt-around.
- "Leaders, Here's Why You Should Be More like Tina Fey," Kim Getty, *Fortune*, October 24, 2015, fortune.com/2015 /10/24/tina-fey-leadership-lesson/.
- "Help Us Learn How to Listen," Abby Olcese, *Utne Reader*, Fall 2016, www.utne.com/mind-and-body/helping-us-learn -how-to-listen-zm0z16fzsel.
- "When Leaders Are Hired for Talent but Fired for Not Fitting In," Tomas Chamorro-Premuzic and Clarke Murphy, *Harvard Business Review*, June 14, 2017, https://hbr.org /2017/06/when-leaders-are-hired-for-talent-but-fired-for-not -fitting-in.
- "How to Make an Awesome Remote Team," Kirsten Helvey, *Fortune*, May 1, 2017, fortune.com/2017/05/01/leadership -career-advice-working-remotely-team-telecommute-home -flex-schedule/.
- "Want Your Employees to Trust You? Show You Trust Them," Holly Henderson Brower, *Harvard Business Review*,

April 5, 2017, hbr.org/2017/07/want-your-employees-to
-trust-you-show-you-trust-them.

- **"Some Things Never Change,"** Susan Packard, susanpackard
.com, March 19, 2017, susanpackard.com/some-things
-never-change/.

## WATCH

- **Surprising and funny "Trustfalls" on Youtube**, www
.huffingtonpost.ca/2013/01/04/i-trust-you-video-trust-falls
-strangers_n_2412211.html.
- **"Anatomy of Trust,"** Brené Brown, brenebrown.com/videos
/anatomy-trust-video.
- **"Evan,"** Sandy Hook Promise, www.youtube.com/watch?v=
bNAFBxRBkV0.

## PART THREE

### BOOKS

- *Return on Character* by **Fred Kiel.** This book is fabulous because it offers hard data showing how having strong character
leads to better business results.
- *Lead from the Heart* by **Mark Crowley.** Crowley shares medical and social science to prove that it's the heart, not intellect,
that drives employee engagement.
- *Leaders Eat Last* by **Simon Sinek.** Sinek uses simple prose
and compelling storytelling to demonstrate how leaders who
put employees first are rewarded with loyalty.
- *The Heart Aroused* by **David Whyte.** If you're like me, this will
be a transformational read. Whyte is a renowned poet who
teaches corporate leaders (and everyone else) to bring more
heart and humanity into our places of work, and our lives.

- *The Road to Character* by David Brooks. Brooks focuses on the deeper values that should guide our lives and highlights stories of others who model those values, with transcendent results.
- *Blackout* by Sarah Hepola. An honest, funny memoir about one woman's reluctant journey into sobriety.

### ARTICLES & LINKS

- "Bringing Global Teams Together," Claire Glackin, *Executive Grapevine*, March 9, 2017, www.executivegrapevine.com /content/article/insight-2017–03–08-bringing-global-teams -together.
- "If Humble People Make the Best Leaders, Why Do We Fall for Charismatic Narcissists?" Margarita Mayo, *Harvard Business Review*, April 7, 2017, hbr.org/2017/04/if-humble -people-make-the-best-leaders-why-do-we-fall-for-charismatic -narcissists.
- "The Best Companies Know How to Balance Strategy and Purpose," Laurent Chevreux, Jose Lopez, and Xavier Mesnard, *Harvard Business Review*, November 2, 2017, hbr.org/2017 /11/the-best-companies-know-how-to-balance-strategy -and-purpose.
- "How to Be the Best Deputy: When Second Best Is Best," Sue Shellenbarger, *Wall Street Journal*, April 19, 2017, www.wsj .com/articles/how-to-be-the-best-deputy-when-second-best -is-best-1492529374.
- "The Men Who Mentor Women," Anna Marie Valerio and Katina Sawyer, *Harvard Business Review*, December 6, 2016, hbr.org/2016/12/the-men-who-mentor-women.
- "Four Radical Leadership Practices That Will Dramatically Increase Engagement," Ron Carucci, *Forbes*, March 1, 2016, www.forbes.com/sites/roncarucci/2016/03/01/four-radical

-leadership-practices-that-will-dramatically-increase
-engagement/.

- **"Empathy Is Actually a Choice,"** Daryl Cameron, Michael
  Inzlicht, and William A. Cunningham, *New York Times*, July
  12, 2015, www.nytimes.com/2015/07/12/opinion/sunday
  /empathy-is-actually-a-choice.html.

## ·NOTES·

### INTRODUCTION

1    Benedict Carey, "Suicide Rate Climbed 25 Percent Even as Prevention Efforts Grew," *New York Times*, June 8, 2018, A17.

2    Lydia Dishman, "These Are the 4 Emotional-Intelligence Job Skills You'll Need in the Future," *Fast Company*, August 30, 2007, www.fastcompany.com /40458569/these-are-the-4-emotional-intelligence-job-skills-youll-need-in-the -future.

3    Rianna Fulham, "7 Signs You're Working with a Psychopath," *Executive Grapevine*, December 7, 2017, www.executivegrapevine.com/content/article/news-2017–12 –07–7-signs-youre-working-with-a-psychopath.

4    Tomas Chamorro-Premuzic, "Why Bad Guys Win at Work," *Harvard Business Review,* November 2, 2017, hbr.org/2015/11/why-bad-guys-win-at-work.

5    Arthur Brooks, "Rising to Your Level of Misery at Work," *New York Times*, September 6, 2015, SR9.

6    Delivered at the Massachusetts Institute of Technology on June 9, 2017.

7    Julie Holland, "Medicating Women's Feelings," *New York Times*, March 1, 2015, SR6.

8    Melvin Konner, "A Better World, Run by Women," *Wall Street Journal*, March 6, 2015, www.wsj.com/articles/a-better-world-run-by-women-1425657910.

### CHAPTER ONE: What Holds You Back from Trust?

1    Maulana Jalaluddin Rumi was a thirteenth-century Persian poet, who more than 800 years later remains a perennial bestseller in the US. With Rilke and Neruda, he is among the few foreign poets whose translated work has become so popular with Americans that he is a go-to credit on quotations and memes that may or may not belong to him. This is one of them. The attribution may be apocryphal, but the wisdom sound. I hope it inspires you.

2    M. Scott Peck describes this patient story in his 1978 bestselling book *The Road Less Traveled*.

3    Father Greg Boyle, interview by Krista Tippett, *On Being*, Krista Tippett Public Productions, April 2, 2015, onbeing.org/programs/greg-boyle-the-calling-of -delight-gangs-service-and-kinship/.

4    Kate Murphy, "Yes, It's Your Parents' Fault," *New York Times*, January 7, 2017, www.nytimes.com/2017/01/07/opinion/sunday/yes-its-your-parents-fault .html.

5    M. Scott Peck, *The Road Less Traveled* (New York: Touchstone, 1978), 47–48.

6    Anna Quindlen, *Being Perfect* (New York: Random House, 2009), 15.

7    Statistic prepared by the Anxiety and Depression Association of America, adaa.org /about-adaa/press-room/facts-statistics.

8    Parker J. Palmer, "Heartbreak, Violence, and Hope for New Life," *On Being*, April 15, 2015, onbeing.org/blog/heartbreak-violence-and-hope-for-new-life/.

9    Laura Hilgers, "Let's Open Up About Addiction and Recovery," *New York Times*, November 5, 2017, SR3.

10   Ibid.

11   Ibid.

12   Hannah Arendt, *Totalitarianism: Part Three of The Origins of Totalitarianism* (New York: Harvest Books, 1968), 176.

13   Nicole Brodeur, "Amy Schumer: 'People have such a low threshold for women being sexual and selfish and human'," *Seattle Times*, July 10, 2015, www.seattle times.com/entertainment/movies/amy-schumer-people-have-such-a-low-threshold -for-women-being-sexual-and-selfish-and-human/.

14   Thomas Merton, *Conjectures of a Guilty Bystander* (New York: Crown, 2009), 155.

**CHAPTER TWO: The Daring to Succeed**

1    Pema Chödrön, *When Things Fall Apart* (Boston: Shambhala, 2002), 102.

2    Father Greg Boyle, interview by Krista Tippett, *On Being*, Krista Tippett Public Productions, April 2, 2015, onbeing.org/programs/greg-boyle-the-calling-of-delight -gangs-service-and-kinship/.

3   Name changed to protect privacy.

4   Parker J. Palmer, *A Hidden Wholeness: The Journey Toward an Undivided Life* (New York: Wiley, 2009), 26.

5   Ibid.

6   Tracey O'Shaughnessy, "Ministers Lend an Ear to Those Dealing with Hardships," AP, May 29, 2017.

7   Lisa Feldman Barrett, "The Benefits of Despair," *New York Times,* June 5, 2016, SR10.

8   Benedict Carey, "Mind Experiment," *New York Times,* July 25, 2017, D1.

9   Chödrön, *When Things Fall Apart,* 84.

10  Brené Brown, *The Gifts of Imperfection: Let Go of Who You Think You Are Supposed to Be and Embrace Who You Are* (Center City: Hazelden, 2010).

CHAPTER THREE: Why Peace of Mind Matters

1   Rumi, "A Great Wagon," *The Essential Rumi, translated by Coleman Barks* (New York: HarperCollins, 1995): 36.

2   Rachel Emma Silverman, "Workplace Distractions: Here's Why You Won't Finish This Article," *Wall Street Journal,* December 11, 2012, www.wsj.com/articles/SB100 01424127887339204578173252223022388.

3   Ibid.

4   Phileena Heuertz, "Contemplative Activism: Doing Good Better," *Contemplative Outreach* 32 (December 2015): 12.

5   Father Richard Rohr, interview by Krista Tippett, *On Being,* Krista Tippett Public Productions, April 13, 2017, onbeing.org/programs/richard-rohr-living-in-deep -time-apr2017/.

6   Drake Baer, "Why You Need to Unplug Every 90 Minutes," *Fast Company,* June 19, 2013, www.fastcompany.com/3013188/why-you-need-to-unplug-every-90 -minutes.

7   *National College Health Assessment Fall 2016,* American College Health Association, www.acha-ncha.org/docs/NCHA-II_FALL_2016_REFERENCE_GROUP _EXECUTIVE_SUMMARY.pdf.

8     Jessica Bennett, "Learning to Fail," *New York Times*, June 24, 2017, ST1.

9     Suzanne Craig Robertson, "Just Breathe: How Mindfulness & Meditation Can Ease Stress in Your Life and Law Practice," *Tennessee Bar Association* 52 (September 2016), www.tba.org/journal/just-breathe-how-mindfulness-meditation-can-ease -stress-in-your-life-and-law-practice.

10    Julie Corliss, "Mindfulness Meditation May Ease Anxiety, Mental Stress," *Harvard Health Publishing*, January 2014, www.health.harvard.edu/blog/mindfulness -meditation-may-ease-anxiety-mental-stress-201401086967.

11    Alexia Elejadre-Ruiz, "High Rates of Alcohol Abuse, Depression Among U.S. Attorneys, Study Says," *Chicago Tribune*, February 3, 2016, www.chicago tribune.com/business/ct-lawyers-problem-drinkers-0204-biz-20160203-story .html.

12    George Johnson, "The Brain Versus the Mind," *New York Times*, July 5, 2016, D3.

13    Gretchen Reynolds, "Yoga May Be Good for the Brain," *New York Times*, June 1, 2016, D6.

14    James Doty, interview by Krista Tippett, *On Being*, Krista Tippett Public Productions, February 11, 2016, onbeing.org/programs/james-doty-the-magic -shop-of-the-brain/.

15    Andrew Newberg, MD, *How God Changes Your Brain: Breakthrough Findings from a Leading Neuroscientist* (New York: Ballantine Books, 2009): 18–19.

16    Jon Kabat-Zinn, interview by Krista Tippett, *On Being*, Krista Tippett Public Productions, January 27, 2011, onbeing.org/programs/jon-kabat-zinn-opening -lives/.

17    Sometimes attributed to Bi-Lo Stores founder Frank Outlaw; many versions and precursors date back to the 1850s.

18    Thomas Keating, *Manifesting God* (New York: Lantern Books, 2005), x.

19    Thomas Keating, *Invitation to Love: The Way of Christian Contemplation, 20th Anniversary Edition*, (London: New York, 2011), 105.

20    Richard Rohr, *Breathing Underwater: Spirituality and the Twelve Steps* (Cincinnati: St. Anthony Messenger Press, 2011), 99.

21    Thomas Merton, *Conjectures of a Guilty Bystander* (New York: Image, 1968), 73.

## CHAPTER FOUR: Good Job Fit

1  I wrote about this in a piece for *Refinery29* called "Why I Turned Down the Chance to Be CEO," July 27, 2015, www.refinery29.com/susan-packard-work-life-balance.

2  Susan Rhodes, *The Positive Enneagram* (Seattle: Geranium Press, 2009).

3  Bill Taylor, "4 Kinds of Workplaces, and How to Know Which Is Best for You," *Harvard Business Review*, April 10, 2017, hbr.org/2017/04/4-kinds-of-workplaces -and-how-to-know-which-is-best-for-you.

4  Erik Oster, "Majority of Consumers Want Brands to Take a Stand on Social and Political Issues, According to New Study," *Adweek*, January 12, 2018, www .adweek.com/brand-marketing/majority-of-consumers-want-brands-to-take-a -stand-on-social-and-political-issues-according-to-new-study.

5  Erin Meyer, "Being the Boss in Brussels, Boston, and Beijing," *Harvard Business Review*, July–August 2017, hbr.org/2017/07/being-the-boss-in-brussels-boston -and-beijing.

6  Leigh Ann Henion, "A Job That Nourishes the Soul, If Not the Wallet," *New York Times*, January 3, 2016, www.nytimes.com/2016/01/03/jobs/a-job-that-nourishes -the-soul-if-not-the-wallet.html.

7  John Koblin, "In a Surprise, CBS's Long-Serving Head of Entertainment Programs Is Stepping Down," *New York Times*, September 16, 2015, B3.

8  David Whyte, *Crossing the Unknown Sea: Work as a Pilgrimage of Identity* (New York: Riverhead, 2001), 75.

9  Ibid., 121.

## PART TWO: Trust

1  Ernest Hemingway, *Selected Letters 1917–1961*, Carlos Baker, ed. (New York: Scribner, 1981), 805.

2  Adam Bryant, "How to Be the Big Boss," *New York Times*, October 29, 2017, BU1.

## CHAPTER FIVE: Trust in Action

1  Daniel Cave, "Men or Women: Who Opens Up More at Work?" *HR Grapevine*, March 15, 2017, www.hrgrapevine.com/content/article/news-2017–03–15-men-or -women-who-opens-up-more-at-work.

2  Monica Lewinsky, "Jay-Z, Prince Harry, Brad Pitt, and the New Frontiers of Male Vulnerability," *Vanity Fair*, July 2017, www.vanityfair.com/style/2017/07/jay-z-prince -harry-brad-pitt-male-vulnerability.

3    David Whyte, *Crossing the Unknown Sea: Work as a Pilgrimage of Identity* (New York: Riverhead, 2001), 43–44.

4    Chris Fussell, "Make Your Team Less Hierarchical," *Harvard Business Review*, July 15, 2015, hbr.org/2015/07/make-your-team-less-hierarchical.

5    Susan Cain, "Followers Wanted," *New York Times*, March 26, 2017, SR1.

6    Julie Creswell and Tiffany Hsu, "The Whisper Network Raises Its Voice," *New York Times*, November 5, 2017, BU1.

## CHAPTER SIX: Becoming Chief Trust Ambassadors

1    Uber Newsroom, March 1, 2017, www.uber.com/newsroom/a-profound-apology.

2    Mike Snider, "Uber, Lyft End Forced Arbitration for Sexual Assault Claims by Passengers or Employees," *USA Today*, May 15, 2018, www.usatoday.com/story /tech/news/2018/05/15/uber-ends-arbitration-sex-assault-claims-passengers -employees/610616002.

3    Emma Seppela and Kim Cameron, "Proof That Positive Work Cultures Are More Productive," *Harvard Business Review*, December 1, 2015, hbr.org/2015/12/proof -that-positive-work-cultures-are-more-productive.

4    John Watson, *The Homely Virtues* (London: Hodder & Stanton, 1903), 168–169.

5    Jonathan Soble, "After a Suicide, Soul-Searching in Japan," *New York Times*, December 29, 2016, B1.

6    Claire Cain Miller, "The Best Jobs Require Social Skills," *New York Times*, October 18, 2015, SR4.

7    Daisuke Wakabayashi, "At Google, Backing Values While Also Fostering Debate," *New York Times*, August 12, 2017, B1.

8    Daisuke Wakabayashi, "Google's Female Workers Receive Lower Wages, Data Suggests," *New York Times*, September 9, 2017, B3.

## CHAPTER SEVEN: My Career Story

1    Ernest Kurtz and Katherine Ketcham quote Vincent, from his article "Education and Baseball" in *America* 164:13 (April 6, 1991), in the introduction to their book *The Spirituality of Imperfection* (New York: Bantam, 1992).

## PART THREE: Embracing "We" Principles

1   Rumi, "A Great Wagon", *The Essential Rumi, translated by Coleman Barks* (New York: HarperCollins, 1995): 3.

2   M. Scott Peck, *The Road Less Traveled* (New York: Touchstone, 1978), 301.

## CHAPTER EIGHT: Managing Pride & Ego

1   Bertrand Russell, "The Triumph of Stupidity," *Mortals and Others, Volume II: American Essays 1931–1935*, (London: Routledge, 1998), 28.

2   Nathan Bomey and Marco della Cava, "Sexual Harassment Went Unchecked for Decades as Payouts Silenced Accusers," *USA Today*, December 1, 2017, www.usa today.com/story/money/business/2017/12/01/sexual-harassment-went-unchecked -decades-payouts-silenced-accusers/881070001/.

3   Elana L. Botelho and Karen Powell, *The CEO Next Door: The Four Behaviors That Transform Ordinary People into World-Class Leaders* (New York: Currency, 2018).

4   "Measuring the Return on Character," *Harvard Business Review*, April 2015, hbr .org/2015/04/measuring-the-return-on-character.

5   Travis Bradberry and Jean Greaves, *Emotional Intelligence 2.0* (San Diego: TalentSmart, 2009), 235.

6   Rianna Fulham, "7 Signs You're Working with a Psychopath," *Executive Grapevine*, December 7, 2017, www.executivegrapevine.com/content/article/news-2017–12 –07–7-signs-youre-working-with-a-psychopath.

7   Tomas Chamorro-Premuzic, "Why Bad Guys Win at Work," *Harvard Business Review,* November 2, 2017, hbr.org/2015/11/why-bad-guys-win-at-work.

8   Thomas Merton, *No Man Is an Island* (New York: Mariner Books, 2002), 121.

9   Matthew Hutton, "When Power Doesn't Corrupt," *New York Times*, May 21, 2017. BU11.

10   Rabbi Rami Shapiro, *Recovery—The Sacred Art: The Twelve Steps as Spiritual Practice* (Woodstock: SkyLight Paths), 55.

11   Sarah Ban Breathnach, *Simple Abundance: A Daybook of Comfort and Joy* (New York: Grand Central Publishing, 2009).

12   Watch it at the TEDx YouTube Channel, www.youtube.com/watch?v=EPjYx2 edKK0.

13  Kevin Roose, "Best Buy's Secrets for Thriving in the Amazon Age," *New York Times*, September 19, 2017, B1.


## CHAPTER NINE: We Principles in Action

1   Name changed to protect privacy.

2   Father Greg Boyle, interview by Krista Tippett, *On Being*, Krista Tippett Public Productions, April 2, 2015, onbeing.org/programs/greg-boyle-the-calling-of -delight-gangs-service and kinship.

3   From Wiesel's Nobel Peace Prize lecture, "Hope, Despair and Memory," delivered December 11, 1986, www.nobelprize.org/nobel_prizes/peace/laureates/1986 /wiesel-lecture.html.

4   Lewis Garrad and Tomas Chamorro-Premuzic, "How to Make Work More Meaningful for Your Team," *Harvard Business Review*, August 9, 2017, hbr.org /2017/08/how-to-make-work-more-meaningful-for-your-team.

5   Steve Trosky, "Top Workplaces Know Appreciation Matters," *USA Today Network— Tennessee*, March 17, 2017, www.knoxnews.com/story/money/business/2017/03 /17/top-workplaces-know-appreciation-matters/99202934.

6   As discussed throughout her 1990 book, *The Language of Letting Go* (Harper & Row).

7   One of the eight core principles of Rohr's Center for Action and Contemplation is "We do not think ourselves into new ways of living, we live ourselves into new ways of thinking," https://cac.org/about-cac/missionvision/.


## CHAPTER TEN: We Principles & Recovery

1   Gabrielle Glaser, "America, It's Time to Talk About Your Drinking," *New York Times*, December 31, 2017, SR4.

2   Thomas Keating, *Divine Therapy and Addiction: Centering Prayer and the Twelve Steps* (Brooklyn: Lantern Books, 2011), 86.

3   Editorial Board, "An Opioid Crisis Foretold," *New York Times*, April 22, 2018, SR10.

4   Anne Lamott, *Small Victories* (New York: Riverhead, 2014), 22.

5   Name changed to protect privacy.

## EPILOGUE: Emotionally Fit

1    Binyamin Appelbaum, Introduction, "The Jobs Americans Do," *New York Times Sunday Magazine*, February 26, 2017, MM36.

2    Delivered at the Massachusetts Institute of Technology on June 9, 2017.

## · ACKNOWLEDGMENTS ·

In no particular order, I'd like to thank: Arriana Yiallourides, my young Cypriot friend, who kindly translated the Cavafy poem, the first thing the reader sees. We needed to get this right, because it lays out the reader's journey, and with Arriana's help I feel we did. Another crucial "A" I want to thank is Antonella Iannarino, who was my guiding light, my life preserver, and my comic reliever, knowing just when I needed which of the three. She's a brilliant editor, creator of lovely images, and strategic thinker. Antonella, words can't describe your value to me on this project. Thanks as always to Joy Tutela, my agent and friend, who keeps pushing me to write in ways I hadn't thought capable. And to Nina Shield, my Penguin editor, who was incredibly responsive to my questions and manuscript, with good humor even when I wanted "just one more" word or phrase to be changed.

Thanks to the mighty team around me all the time, Joyce Ortiz, coordinator and all-around organized genius—you keep me sane! To Joseph Cartwright, social media whiz, and to Kimberly Maki, who is helping me to give voice to this book.

Thanks to my longtime friend Ed Spray, who looked at the manuscript from a male perspective, and pointed out all the areas I needed to rethink. I couldn't have offered gender balance without you.

Thanks to Father Greg Boyle, "Father G," a daily inspiration to me on how one leads with emotional fitness. I shamelessly cribbed many of his lines from his writings because I couldn't make my points any better than he already had. And to Father Tom Ward, who critiqued my descriptions on Centering Prayer. Of course to Joe Zarantonello, my spiritual teacher whose insight comes shining through this whole book.

Thank you Angela Teague and Dena Pinsker—you helped me through writing the hardest part of the book, the part that had to be written, if I was to stay true to the promise of emotional fitness.

Thanks for all who sat with me or hung on the line with me to be interviewed—Paul Polman, Jarl Mohn, Ellen Kullman, Leroy Ball, Jim Ethier, Sara Rose, Jerry Freij, Anisa Telwar, Greg Jordan, Diana Reid, Mary Ellen Brewington, Joyce Russell, Angela Teague, Brenda Moyers, Erin Wolf, Jim Emerick, Lisa Parker, and all the Carnegie Mellon University faculty, especially Dr. Kelley and Dr. Anita Woolley. A special thanks, too, to Leanne Meyer, the faculty member and friend at CMU who allowed me access to the faculty. Beth Marcello of PNC was a huge help with that too.

Finally, thanks to my dear husband, Bill, who allowed me to take over just about every flat surface in our house to get this book written.